FUNDAMENTALISM
in
American Religion
1880 - 1950

A forty-five-volume facsimile series
reproducing often extremely rare material
documenting the development of one of the
major religious movements of our time

■ *Edited by*
Joel A. Carpenter
Billy Graham Center, Wheaton College
■ *Advisory Editors*
Donald W. Dayton,
Northern Baptist Theological Seminary
George M. Marsden,
Duke University
Mark A. Noll,
Wheaton College
Grant Wacker,
University of North Carolina

A GARLAND SERIES

■ Two Reformers of Fundamentalism Harold John Ockenga and Carl F. H. Henry

Edited with an introduction by
Joel A. Carpenter

Garland Publishing, Inc.
New York & London 1988

For a list of the titles in this series, see the final pages of this volume. The facsimile of *Park Street Prophet* has been made from a copy in the Billy Graham Center of Wheaton College; that of *The Uneasy Conscience of Modern Fundamentalism* is from a copy in the Moody Bible Institute.

Introduction copyright © 1988 by Joel A. Carpenter
All rights reserved.

The Uneasy Conscience of Modern Fundamentalism copyright 1947 by Wm. B. Eerdmans Publishing Company.
Reprinted by permission of the publisher.

Library of Congress Cataloging in Publication Data

Two reformers of fundamentalism : Harold John Ockenga and Carl F.H. Henry/edited with an introduction by Joel A. Carpenter.
    p. cm. — (Fundamentalism in American religion, 1880-1950)
Bibliography: p.
Contents: Park Street Prophet/Harold Lindsell — The uneasy conscience of modern fundamentalism/Carl F.H. Henry
ISBN 0-8240-5047-9 (alk. paper)
    1. Ockenga, Harold John, 1905- . 2. Congregational churches—United States—Clergy—Biography. 3. Evangelicalism—United States—History. 4. National Association of Evangelicals.
5. Fundamentalism. 6. Church and social problems. I. Carpenter, Joel A. II. Lindsell, Harold, 1913- , Park Street prophet. 1988.
III. Henry, Carl Ferdinand Howard, 1913- , The uneasy conscience of modern fundamentalism. 1988. IV. Series.
BX7260.O3T86 1988
277.3'082—dc19

                                                                                  88-21198

Design by Valerie Mergentime
Printed on acid-free, 250-year-life paper.
Manufactured in the United States of America

CONTENTS

■ *Introduction*

■ *Park Street Prophet*
The Life of Harold John Ockenga
Harold Lindsell

■ *The Uneasy Conscience of Modern Fundamentalism*
Carl F. H. Henry

INTRODUCTION

During the late 1940s and early 1950s, conservative evangelical Christianity showed signs of reemerging from the hinterlands of American culture. Billy Graham's revival crusades in particular were restoring evangelicals' visibility, and boosting their morale and sense of efficacy as well. His widespread acceptance encouraged them to reconsider their alienated stance against the main currents of American life. Less visible than stadium crusades and golf dates with national officials but equally important as part of the postwar evangelical resurgence was the development of an intellectual reform movement within fundamentalism.

A group of young fundamentalist theologians led this movement. Calling for a "new evangelicalism," they sought, through their own leadership and scholarly production, to cure the fundamentalist movement of its sectarian insularity and contentiousness, its disdain for learning and culture, and its lack of social responsibility. By achieving the "united evangelical action" of a broad coalition of conservative Protestants, these reformers of fundamentalism and their allies from other evangelical traditions hoped to prompt a great religious awakening in America. Thus the air was charged with revival expectation as they led in the formation of the National Association of Evangelicals in 1942–1943, and eagerly lent their support to the new surge of evangelism, which by 1949 and 1950 was being spearheaded by Billy Graham.[1]

Ashamed of fundamentalism's anti-intellectual stereotype, the new evangelicals also hoped to create outstanding theological literature, which would constitute a "vigorous apologetic" for historic Protestant orthodoxy against all opposing theologies and ideologies. Emanating from this theological center, they hoped, would be a "new Reformation" in the broader cultural realm, in which an evangelical Christian perspective would come to bear on all of life. In particular, they yearned to improve conservative evangelicals' recent record in the realm of social ethics. The two short books republished herein portray the early excitement, visionary aspirations, and assumptions of strategic importance that characterized the "neo-evangelical" movement.[2]

Harold Lindsell's *Park Street Prophet: A Life of Harold John*

Ockenga (Wheaton, Ill. Van Kampen Press, 1951) sings the praises of one of the most important leaders of the new evangelicalism. At the time this book was written, Ockenga (1905–1985) was only forty-five years old, but was already at the pinnacle of leadership in fundamentalist circles as pastor of the historic Park Street Church in Boston and founding president of both the National Association of Evangelicals (1943), and Fuller Theological Seminary (1947). His biographer, Harold Lindsell (1913–), was also his employee, serving as registrar and professor of church history and missions at Fuller Seminary.

It is hard at first to understand why Ockenga would have consented to this biography, since the author's relationship to his subject readily prompts the impression that the book's purpose was personal promotion. A clue to the book's larger purpose, however, comes from its preface, which was written by another Fuller professor, Wilbur M. Smith. Smith enthused that a new and brighter day was dawning for conservative Protestant thought, and he commended the book as "an important contribution" because it recorded fresh information on this new conservative movement (p. 7). So it seems that a major purpose for this biography was to publicize the new evangelicalism.

A continuing note in the rhetoric of the new evangelicals was that new times and new challenges demanded new leadership. In this biography, the author lays out a prototype for the guiding hands and heads that the movement needed. Lindsell takes pains to show that Ockenga had solid credentials in character, training, and connections to take up the prophet's mantle. Ockenga was of a solid middle-class stock, and he displayed his intellect, initiative, and leadership qualities early in life. He was educated at Taylor University, a midwestern, conservative Methodist school. His training for the ministry came from the scholarly pinnacle of fundamentalism in the 1920s, Princeton Theological Seminary, and from Princeton-in-exile, J. Gresham Machen's new Westminster Theological Seminary. Professor Machen and his band of militant conservatives had left Princeton in 1929 in a dispute over the seminary's reorganization, which was intended to change the school from a thoroughly conservative, Calvinist institution to a theologically more inclusive one. Machen's group founded Westminster Seminary in Philadelphia that same year, and enrolled a group of devoted followers from Princeton that included Harold Ockenga.[3]

Ockenga quickly attracted the friendship and sponsorship of both Machen and of Clarence Macartney, pastor of the First Presbyterian Church of Pittsburgh, who was for a time Machen's most powerful denominational ally in the conservative cause.[4] After a brief sojourn with two Methodist pastorates in New

Jersey shore towns, Ockenga accepted a call to be one of Macartney's assistant pastors, beginning at that post early in 1931. Machen preached at the young man's ordination. Before the year was out, Ockenga was installed as a pastor of a congregation in suburban Pittsburgh, with Machen and Macartney participating in his installation ceremony. As Ockenga proceeded to revitalize the dormant congregation, he also began graduate study in philosophy at the University of Pittsburgh,[5] where he met his future wife, Audrey Williamson. In 1936, at age 31, Ockenga succeeded the aged fundamentalist champion of Boston, A. Z. Conrad, as pastor of the distinguished Park Street Congregational Church. Conrad had hand-picked Ockenga, on the advice of Machen, Macartney, and Harold P. Sloan, who was a conservative Methodist leader from New Jersey. Clearly (as the author seems careful to show), the young pastor was well-thought-of by important fundamentalist leaders and thus well-sponsored; he moved rapidly to a position of influence and prestige.

Lindsell's account of Ockenga's first decade at Park Street emphasizes the pastor's intellectual gifts and productivity by describing his devotion to study, sermon preparation, and publishing. He also recounts Ockenga's leadership as a board member of a variety of evangelical and educational institutions. In an apparent effort to convince the reader of this young pastor's stature, the author gives detailed accounts of several tempting calls from some of the nation's leading conservative Presbyterian congregations, each of which Ockenga turned down. Lindsell also reports Ockenga's organizational initiatives, as the pastor developed a variety of new ventures at Park Street Church. As a professor of missions, the author obviously relishes the record of the annual missions conference which Ockenga instituted in 1940. In ten years' time, the program prompted a seven-fold increase in the congregation's annual missions budget.

The last four chapters of this brief biography sound the major themes of the neo-evangelical movement, and demonstrate Ockenga's central role in each of its first three projects: the National Association of Evangelicals, Fuller Theological Seminary, and the revival excitement stirred by Billy Graham's early meetings. Suffice it to say that on the first project, Ockenga worked with J. Elwin Wright of the New England Fellowship to promote pan-evangelical unity nationwide, and as a result Ockenga was named the first president of the National Association of Evangelicals in 1943.

On the second project, Fuller Theological Seminary, Ockenga was approached by Charles E. Fuller, the radio preacher of a nationally famous program, the Old Fashioned Revival Hour, to help in the creation of an evangelistic and missionary training school. Ockenga urged Fuller to found a graduate theological seminary instead, and to recruit the very finest scholars that fundamentalism had to offer for its faculty. Fuller Theological Seminary opened in the fall of 1947 with Ockenga as its president *in absentia.*

Finally, Lindsell describes the yearning Ockenga felt for another great revival—in his own congregation, in New England, and in America. Despite many blessings accruing to the church and the region from a variety of preachers and programs, the great, soul-and-society-stirring wave of religious interest and commitment for which evangelicals longed had not come. But 1950 proved to be the *annus mirabilis* for Ockenga, for Park Street Church, and for greater New England. Ockenga was the organizational leader, while, as Lindsell put it, God's chosen man for the "hour of revival" was Billy Graham (p. 145). The author gives an account of the exciting days of this campaign, and how the Spirit of God seemed to be moving beyond all human accounting or expectation. This chapter on revival brings the biography to a close and the revival thus becomes the crest of the young pastor's career.

Lindsell ends *Park Street Prophet* with a look to the future. He sounds once again all the themes of the new evangelical agenda: the postwar crisis of civilization, the opportunities for a revitalized evangelicalism to fend off the tides of unbelief ("with the destiny of men and nations hanging in the balance" [p. 170]), the need for "evangelical humanitarianism," the need for a "twentieth century apologetic second to none" (p. 169), and the need for evangelical cooperation. Lindsell concludes that "truly into the kingdom for such a time as this" did God send Harold John Ockenga. This youthful leader has a bright future despite the enemies that "have risen to smite him" (p. 174).

It is perhaps a bit easier for readers to digest such expressions if they remember that Lindsell's reverential treatment is probably being bestowed on the new evangelical ideal as much as on the movement's chief executive officer. And the dark note about enemies reflects another continuing theme. Throughout the last third of the book, Lindsell pauses to argue with critics who are never clearly identified, and whose concerns are never given full expression. These opponents are in fact separatist fundamentalists, most notably Carl McIntire, whose American Council of Christian Churches was a rival to the National Association of Evangelicals. The "new evangelical" reformers of fundamentalism were forced to pursue their mission in the face of constant sniper fire from these militants on fundamentalism's right wing. Indeed, the new evangelicals' reform agenda put them in a tension-fraught and relatively unstable no man's land in American Protestant Christianity, as several recent studies have shown.[6] Nevertheless, Ockenga remained an important leader until the very last year of his life. A judicious, fulsome account of his career, character, and times would be an immensely valuable contribution to our understanding of the entire career of post-1925 fundamentalism and neo-evangelicalism.

If *Park Street Prophet* was an early promotional piece and apologetic for the neo-evangelical movement, *The Uneasy Conscience of Modern Fundamentalism* (Grand Rapids: Eerdmans, 1947) was its manifesto. Carl F. H. Henry (1913–) was a young Baptist theologian who was near to the completion of his doctorate at Boston University when he published this book and joined Ockenga's faculty at Fuller Seminary. Henry became the leading theologian of the new evangelicalism, for which his six-volume *God, Revelation and Authority* (Waco, Tex.: Word, 1976–1983) is the fullest theological statement. *The Uneasy Conscience*, however, is a brief tract that urges fundamentalists to lay aside their besetting sins and press forward to meet the challenges of the postwar world.

The year before *The Uneasy Conscience* appeared, Henry published a larger and intellectually more ambitious work, *Remaking the Modern Mind* (Grand Rapids: Eerdmans, 1946), in which he argued that the humanistic philosophical premises of western culture were bringing on its collapse. This crisis was providing a historic opportunity, he believed, for evangelical Christians to help shape civilization according to a Christian world and life view. Henry thus was calling for evangelicals to see culture-building as part of their mission to the world, and not just personal evangelism.

The Uneasy Conscience contrasted this mandate with fundamentalism's social record. In a withering attack on the movement's lack of social responsibility, Henry claimed that fundamentalists had focused so narrowly upon issues of ecclesiastical separation and personal morality that they had made the Gospel appear irrelevant. A chaotic world was desperately searching for a new order, but fundamentalists, he charged, were fiddling over whether or not to play with Rook cards while the nations were playing with fire (p. 20).

Henry called instead for what Harold Ockenga, in an introduction to this book, described as "a progressive fundamentalism with a social message."[7] Evangelical Christianity had been on the front lines of social reform movements in the past, Henry argued, but in the present day, fundamentalism had divorced the gospel of redemption from a passion to right the world's wrongs, and had abandoned the field of social reform to the secularists. Henry stressed that fundamentalists needed to recover two basic truths: that Christianity opposes all evil, both personal and social; and that it offers redemption and regeneration as the only sufficient solution to the world's problems (p. 45). He argued that evangelism is the necessary first task of the church, but that improvement of society should follow. If fundamentalist evangelicals would recover this social ethic and follow through on it, Henry predicted that the world would witness "a reformation," led by a "divinely-empowered Christian community" (p. 89).

Historian George Marsden is right to remind us that Henry's call for evangelical social and political engagement "was little more than that—a call." Henry's continued insistence that personal redemption and regeneration were the only sources from which lasting social reform could spring was not followed by a careful or compelling explanation of how these spiritual operations translated into social reform. The new evangelicals were always more adept at asserting their social principle—often as a criticism of secular reformers—than at putting it into operation. The movement continued to devote much greater energy to its other priorities, evangelism and theological education.[8]

Because of this reflexive hesitation about social action, Henry's *Uneasy Conscience* remained an accurate indictment of conservative evangelicalism for another twenty-five years. By the early 1970s, however, another generation of evangelicals responded to the book's social mandate. Both Henry and his son Paul, a political science professor at Calvin College, signed the Chicago Declaration of 1973, a call to social action and in effect the charter for a new advocacy group, Evangelicals for Social Action.[9] But when given the opportunity in 1987 to reflect upon these themes during the fortieth anniversary of the *Uneasy Conscience*'s publication, Henry devoted greater attention to the theological themes he had sounded in *Remaking the Modern Mind*.[10] In his memoirs, *Confessions of a Theologian: An Autobiography* (Waco, Tex.: Word, 1986), Henry expressed his dissatisfaction, for the most part, with the outlook and actions of these evangelical social activists.

Henry has remained, nonetheless, a consistent advocate of a principled evangelical political presence. Rather taken aback by the rise of the Moral Majority's politicized fundamentalism, Henry criticized these folk for their unreflective activism and their simple equation of ultra-right policy positions with biblical norms.[11] His preferred political company has been with conservative intellectuals, as his board membership with the Ethics and Public Policy Center in Washington, D. C., suggests. The *Uneasy Conscience* continues to transcend ideological points of view, however, in its call for an evangelical social and political mission. This brief tract is both the product of an important juncture in the history of modern evangelicalism, and a timely challenge to contemporary Christians.

Both *Park Street Prophet* and *The Uneasy Conscience*, then, are important early expressions of a grand (some might say grandiose) vision for a world-engaging, world-shaping evangelical Christianity. They show also the enormous ambitions and energies that the new evangelicals poured into their work, and thus help us understand the resulting resurgence of evangelical Christianity. These documents mark an important juncture in the history of American fundamentalism, and in American religious and cultural history more generally. This was a moment when, unbeknownst to the religious and cultural powers, a vital new force was being generated that would change the equations of social and religious power in the decades to come.

The new evangelicals' deep-seated yearing to transcend their marginalized, sectarian inheritance, their thirst for intellectual respect, for social respectability, and for meaningful cultural participation come through very clearly in these works. So do their often triumphal presumptions about their centrality to history's—or God's—course in the late twentieth century. This movement's leaders would experience their share of frustration and disillusionment, as Carl Henry's memoirs, George Marsden's *Reforming Fundamentalism*, and Rudolph Nelson's *The Making and Unmaking of an Evangelical Mind* make clear. With an overreaching vision comes disappointment, sometimes even despair; but without vision, movements perish. As these two books show, the new evangelicalism had plenty of hopes and dreams. Perhaps these documents can give perspective to leaders of present-day movements, religious and otherwise, on the value and the dangers of world-encompassing aspirations. And perhaps they can provide some insight, by implication, about how to accept with grace both the achievements and the inevitable failures that come when human beings seek to do God's work on earth.

Joel A. Carpenter
Institute for the Study of American Evangelicals
Wheaton College

NOTES

1. On the National Association of Evangelicals and the yearning for revival, see *Evangelical Action! A Report of the Organization of the National Association of Evangelicals for United Action* (Boston: Fellowship Press, 1942); and Joel Carpenter, "The Fundamentalist Leaven and the Rise of an Evangelical United Front," in *The Evangelical Tradition in America*, ed. Leonard I. Sweet (Macon, Ga.: Mercer University Press, 1984), 257–88.

2. Two fine recent treatments of the new evangelical movement are George M. Marsden, *Reforming Fundamentalism: Fuller Seminary and the New Evangelicalism* (Grand Rapids: Eerdmans, 1987); and Rudolph Nelson, *The Making and Unmaking of an Evangelical Mind: The Case of Edward Carnell* (New York: Cambridge University Press, 1987).

3. On Machen, the fundamentalist-modernist controversy in the Presbyterian Church, and the formation of Westminster Theological Seminary, see Edwin H. Rian, *The Presbyterian Conflict* (Grand Rapids: Eerdmans, 1940), a thorough, though partisan (fundamentalist) account of these issues and events; as is Lefferts A. Loetscher, *The Broadening Church* (Philadelphia: Westminster Press, 1957), from the moderate/liberal perspective. Other helpful studies are Ned B. Stonehouse, *J. Gresham Machen: A Biographical Memoir* (Grand Rapids: Eerdmans, 1954); C. Allyn Russell, "J. Gresham Machen, Scholarly Fundamentalist," in Russell, *Voices of American Fundamentalism: Seven Biographical Studies* (Philadelphia: Westminster Press, 1976), 134–61; and Darryl Hart, "*Doctor Fundamentalis*: An Intellectual Biography of J. Gresham Machen" (Ph. D. dissertation, The John Hopkins University, 1988). On the importance of the Machen legacy to Fuller Seminary and the intellectual development of the new evangelicalism, see Marsden, *Reforming Fundamentalism*, 22–25, 27–28, 32–42, 162, 189–190, 249.

4. Machen's and Macartney's partnership in the fundamentalist controversy and their eventual estrangement over the question of separating from the Presbyterian Church are discussed in detail throughout Stonehouse, *J. Gresham Machen*, and Rian, *The Presbyterian Conflict*. One very important question that Lindsell's account does not explain about Ockenga's early career is why Ockenga sided with Macartney and not with Machen.

5. Ockenga received the Ph.D. in 1939 for a dissertation titled "Poverty as a Theoretical and Practical Problem of Government in the Writings of Jeremy Bentham and the Marxian Alternative."

6. To understand the substance and significance of these controversies within the fundamentalist tradition, the reader should consult some recent studies, notably Marsden, *Reforming Fundamentalism*; Nelson, *The Making and Unmaking of an Evangelical Mind*; and Mark A. Noll, *Between Faith and Criticism: Evangelicals, Scholarship, and the Bible in America* (San Francisco: Harper & Row, 1986). Butler Farley Porter, Jr., "Billy Graham and the End of Evangelical Unity" (Ph. D. dissertation, University of Florida, 1976), traces the issues and personal dynamics involved in the major split between the new evangelicals and the separatist fundamentalists.

7. George Marsden correctly cautions the reader *not* to interpret this statement to mean "fundamentalism with a progressive social message" (*Reforming Fundamentalism*, 81). Neo-evangelicals remained cautious about social activism and were conservative in their social and political views (*Ibid.*, 156–57).

8. Marsden, *Reforming Fundamentalism*, 82. For detailed examinations of the new evangelicals' social and political expressions, see Robert Booth Fowler, *A New Engagement: Evangelical Political Thought, 1966–1976* (Grand Rapids: Eerdmans, 1982); and Dennis P. Hollinger, *Individualism and Social Ethics: An Evangelical Syncretism* (Lanham, Md.: University Press of America, 1983).

9. See *The Chicago Declaration*, ed. Ronald J. Sider (Carol Stream, Ill.: Creation House, 1974), especially Sider's introduction on pp. 11–42, Carl Henry's reflections on pp. 127–31, and Paul Henry's reflections on pp. 137–39. Paul Henry later served for six years in the Michigan state legislature and was elected to the House of Representatives from Michigan's fifth district in 1984. Carl Henry's wish that a "statesman with the convictions of Paul" would arise who "would echo the great evangelical affirmations throughout world politics" (*Uneasy Conscience*, 70), takes on a suggestive new dimension in light of Paul Henry's rising political career.

10. Carl F. H. Henry, "The Uneasy Conscience Revisited: Current Theological, Ethical and Social Concerns," *Theology, News and Notes* 34 (December 1987): 3–9.

11. Carl F. H. Henry, "The Fundamentalist Phenomenon: The Ricochet of Silver Bullets," *Christianity Today* 25 (September 4, 1981): 30–31.

Park Street

Church

and Its

Pastor

Harold John

Ockenga

Park Street Prophet
A Life of Harold John Ockenga

by

HAROLD LINDSELL
Author of *Abundantly Above, The Thing Appointed,
A Christian Philosophy of Missions*

Van Kampen Press
Wheaton, Illinois

Copyright 1951, by
Van Kampen Press
Wheaton, Illinois

Printed in the United States of America

To

The membership of the Park Street Church and the Faculty of the Fuller Theological Seminary to whom this servant of God has been an inspiration and through whose life and ministry the cause of the Lord Jesus Christ has been advanced.

AD MAIOREM DEI GLORIAM

Preface

About twenty years ago, I was sitting in the shade of a large oak tree at a Bible conference in Pennsylvania, conversing with one of the outstanding Bible teachers of his generation, now in heaven. I asked him why we did not have in America at that time another such group of men as appeared then on the title page of the Scofield Reference Bible, all of whom are now deceased. His reply was that God had raised up this particular group of men to bear a final testimony at the end of this age to the Western World, and that we need not expect another such group before the Lord's return. In this my friend was definitely wrong; I thought so then, but knew I could also be mistaken. Conservatism was then at a low ebb, and nearly every important ecclesiastical body or institution was dominated by liberalism, and certainly ruled by men of liberal convictions.

But twenty years have seen a great change. Today there is a wonderful upsurge of conservative thought, and a new generation of conservative leaders, most of whom are still comparatively young. One of the most outstanding of these men who has led the army of Bible-honoring Christians to victory after victory, and has restored confidence in the hearts of multitudes who were growing weak in the battle, is the one who life appears in these pages—Dr. Harold John Ockenga.

There is a great page in Alexander Whyte's chapter on Elisha which is almost a prophecy of this very thing. You will remember that it was immediately after Elijah's depression—when God encouraged him by reminding him there were seven thousand yet in Israel who had not bowed the knee to Baal—in fact, in the very same chapter (I Kings 19:19-21) that Elijah for the first time met Elisha and cast his mantle of succession upon him. This is what Alexander Whyte says:

All the time that Elijah was repining the meditating death under the juniper tree, God was preparing the young ploughman of Abel-Meholah to wear Elijah's mantle, and to carry forward Elijah's work. And when we are prognosticating the headlessness and the collapse of the church when this man and that man shall have fallen asleep, all the time God has His hidden servants, quite well known to Him, and quite ready to take up this man's and that man's great office when they shall demit it. There may be to be seen following the spring plough in Strathmore or in the Lothians at this moment some young man who shall be as well known and as great in a few years in Scoltand as Elisha was in Israel. There are certainly at school, at college, in the shop, in the office, on the hills, in the mine, young men who, five and twenty years after this, shall be as great preachers, as great writers, as great discoverers as any of those who are now in such fame, and far better suited for the time to come. Elisha was not Elijah. But he was the gift of the living God to the living Israel of his day. And I would have you all keep your dejected hearts in perfect peace, sure of this, that God will look after both the church and the world far better than the most anxious-minded and censorious-minded of His people.

And so, even as my friend twenty years ago was bemoaning the sad condition of the Church throughout the world, God was preparing a few men, among whom Dr. Ockenga takes a leading place, for the great work He knew would be done in the next generation.

Dr. Ockenga displays a remarkable combination of gifts. He is a powerful preacher, a keen thinker, willing to wrestle with the greater problems of theology, and at the same time he has a great evangelistic passion. Probably the meatiest sermons preached in New England from week to week by any one man are heard from the Park Street Church pulpit in Boston, and at the same time, without any doubt, the largest budget of any church in New England, and possibly on the North Atlantic coast, for missionary enterprises is that given every year by the members of this famous congregation. Behind these gifts of Dr. Ockenga, however, are three fundamental factors without which the gifts themselves would only be partly effective, or perhaps rusting in burial. First of all, Dr. Ockenga is a hard worker. I happen to know that his day of labor often runs for sixteen consecutive hours. Sometimes he stays in his study all night, catching a few hours of sleep on a couch. All of his messages, many of which are an hour long, are delivered without notes. They show a mastery of the subject about which he is speaking and are presented with relentless logic. This means hard work. It is not simply preparing messages, and delivering them, but he also carries what Paul called the labor of the church, the shepherding of thousands of souls.

Secondly—and I do not mean by this, second to hard work, but second only in my enumeration—is his constant recognition of the work of the Holy Spirit. For years now I have heard my friend speak in one part of the country and another on this much-neglected subject, and as he speaks, one recognizes before he has listened many minutes that the one who is unfolding some aspect of the work of the Holy Spirit is speaking out of personal experience. To these two factors a third must be added. With these gifts and an acknowledgment of the work of the Holy Spirit, constantly seeking enduement from Him, there must be a life of personal victory over every besetting sin, and this our friend unceasingly claims from God. The life of such a servant of Christ I feel sure will prove a blessing to thousands of others who seek also to serve and honor the same Lord.

Many pages in this volume convey information regarding the great movements of conservatism in this country that have never appeared in print before, and consequently this book will take its place as an important contribution to the permanent records of conservative Christianity in North America.

Wilbur M. Smith
San Marino, California

Contents

Preface	5
Birth and Early Years	11
The Formative Years	17
What God Hath Joined Together	39
The Park Street Church—An Open Door	47
As A Man Sows	71
Fields White Unto Harvest	97
The National Association of Evangelicals— A Widening Horizon of Conservative Cooperation	109
Fountainhead of the Church— A Vision in Theological Education	127
Revival Comes!	141
The Future—As Bright as the Promises of God	165

Chapter

> Lives of great men all remind us
> We can make our lives sublime,
> And, departing, leave behind us
> Footprints on the sands of time,
>
> Footprints, that perhaps another,
> Sailing o'er life's solemn main,
> A forlorn and shipwrecked brother,
> Seeing, shall take heart again.
>
> A Psalm of Life
> —*Henry Wadsworth Longfellow*

> "For this child I prayed; and the Lord hath given me my petition which I asked of him: Therefore also I have lent him to the Lord; as long as he liveth he shall be lent to the Lord."
> —*I Samuel* 1:27,28

One

BIRTH AND EARLY YEARS

JULY 6, 1905, Chicago's streets baked beneath a sweltering sun. Those who could arrange such pleasures thronged to the beaches and to the countrysides. But Herman Ockenga and his wife Angie remained in their apartment on the city's west side, for they had an appointment with destiny.

That night their only son was born. They named him Harold John.

"He's a fine lad," the nurse said. Then, examining the infant's head, she added, "Lots of brain in that skull. And look at the shape of his head. See that bit of a bump there. And that one there." She turned to the young mother. "Mrs. Ockenga, your son will some day be a brilliant man. He'll be very famous."

Whether or not the nurse had an interest in phrenology, or was merely giving her usual O.B. chatter to proud parents is not known. Regardless, her prediction rang true.

Today that boy is Dr. Harold J. Ockenga, one of the finest preachers and staunchest defenders of the faith this country has ever known—or the whole world, for that matter.

Like so many great men, young Harold John Ockenga had a troublous childhood. His frail body, often beset with illness, kept him from playing as other children did. It was not that he minded, for the boy was a dreamer. He would sit for hours pondering problems far beyond his years, and at the age of seven—his mother recalls—he distinctly showed many of the characteristics which today so vividly label him the man he is.

With foresight and initiative, he built box kites, and sold them to boys in the neighborhood. He had a monopoly on the market, since his were the only kites of this variety which could be kept successfully and consistently air-borne.

Leadership, too, marked these early years. Maybe the Ockenga boy couldn't lay a three-base hit into left field, but he could stand at first or third and tell a team-mate when to lead off and when to steal and seldom be wrong in his judgment.

And then there was that famous Ockenga polish. By nature he was cast in the die of a gentleman, a prodigy in the art of good taste. If he had any failings along this line, it was his delight in teasing the four sisters who made up the remainder of the family. That was seldom, however, more than mutually-shared fun.

But intelligence, leadership and poise were not left to grow untended. The boy had a Godly mother, and the father—though not a Christian—also helped make those formative years count for a good deal.

Angie Ockenga, the mother, was a Methodist, but since the nearest Methodist church was not close enough for her to take the children, she took them to the Austin Presbyterian Church. Harold remembers accompanying his mother to prayer meetings as a lad. He and his sisters attended Sunday school regularly.

The Ockenga family knew neither riches nor poverty. Middle class in economic status, they enjoyed the privileges common to that class. They owned their own home, almost never knew what it was to be without an automobile, and did not lack for the essentials of life. While the family income was not large, both mother and father practiced thrift. Herman Ockenga engaged in remunerative labor outside his regular work with the Chicago "L"; at one time he owned a grocery store while on sick leave from his regular position.

Despite the lack of formal education, Herman Ockenga, the father, was a well-read man, conversant with the issues current in his day. Among his friends in the neighborhood were a judge and several lawyers. He could hold his own with them on almost any subject.

Above all, his wife meant much to him. Unfortunately, however, those early years were marred by his unwillingness to come to Christ for salvation. This prevented the two from having a family altar and kept the home from being tightly knit together around the church and the things of the Lord. In fact, when his son announced—early in life—that he had chosen Christ to man the helm of his life, the father spoke straightforward disapproval.

But Angie Ockenga, the mother, did not falter. She kept the children active in the church. She read to them—from the Book and from other books which molded their spiritual thinking. She was a tender, loving, sacrificing woman, one who held high before her young the glories of purity and honesty. She inspired their confidence, and they generously rewarded her with obedience and devotion.

As an infant, Harold Ockenga was baptized in the Austin Presbyterian Church. He grew up in the Sunday school of that and the Olivet Methodist Church. When eleven years of age, he was received into the membership of the Olivet Church, but the connection with the church was nominal and surely not based upon salvation received through the new birth in Christ.

A story lies back of his membership in the church. His Sunday-school teacher, a Christian fireman, had a concern for his boys which did not end with the Sunday-school lesson. He took them camping and on outings, and on one occasion took as many of the boys in his class as he could gather and took them to an old-fashioned Methodist camp ground at Des Plaines.

When some of the boys responded to the invitation one night, Harold responded with them. They went weeping to the altar and later joined the church. But in the light of his experience in later youth it is doubtful that Harold was truly born again at this time.

In grammar school, young Ockenga gave new evidence of the nurse's prediction that he would be a brilliant man. His studies gave him no trouble whatever and at Tilton Grammar School he learned the basic disciplines—reading, writing and arithmetic. Normal in every sense, he played the games common in his childhood. The great American game of baseball challenged him, especially after a tonsillectomy routed him onto the road of health. In the summer he became proficient on roller skates and in the winter on ice skates. In both methods of transportation, neighborhood boys used hockey sticks to play their games, winter and summer. He became a proficient swimmer, and served with the Boy Scouts several summers as a camp lifeguard.

Harold inherited energy and ambition from his parents, and turned toward the production of income when most other boys turn away from it. When nine years old, he got a Saturday job delivering orders for a grocery store, working from 8:00 in the morning to 9:00 or 10:00 at night. For this varied service he received one dollar compensation each Sunday!

At thirteen, young Harold got another position. The family had moved to Austin, so he changed to a store located nearer home. Now he took up work after school and on Saturdays as a butcher, earning the munificent sum of ten dollars a week for his labors. He retained this position for two years when another advance came his way, employment after school and on Saturdays with the Chicago elevated, calling trains in the Loop. The job paid from eighteen to twenty-two dollars a week,—not bad for a young boy of fifteen.

High school was a snap. He finished in three and a half years the four-year course of study. This he did in addition to outside work. All during high school he made the honor roll and was exempted from final examinations.

In high school, he sparked the group of young people in whose company he traveled. Independent of mind and aggressive, he provided stimulating leadership in the days following the first World War when American youth floundered in a state of transition. Intelligent, ingenious, and far from timid, he made an imprint on the "gang" he led. He joined the Theta Kappa Delta fraternity, and became its president. Having no conviction in those days about the modern dance he was active in this and other activities common to the social life of his school. As president of the "frat," he sparked a dance in the LaSalle Hotel in Chicago. He could do the then popular but now extinct King Tut-ankh-amen shuffle without blundering a flick of the toe.

He never fell into deep sin, however, and most certainly never ran afoul of the law. He kept good company and his relations with the opposite sex were happy and carefree. His mother always marvelled at his choice of girls for the social life of his youth. He never failed to pick the finest of the lot.

To his mother, one prophetic statement Harold made in his youth stands out. When nine years old he told her that he was going to be a preacher and see the world. Succeeding events did not make either the first or the second declaration appear true. When in high school the ambition to see the world remained with him, but the desire to become a minister of the gospel of the Lord Jesus had evaporated. The declaration as a nine-year-old had no meaning whatever to the lad who had made his own way through life so far and who by the sweat of his own brow had earned enough money to help at home and to build up a substantial bank account.

The seeds of a future greatness grew on. Had the grace of God never touched this life in regeneration, America would by now undoubtedly have added to its stream of life a great man—even though a pagan. The seeds were there. The question was the direction the life took. Many men begin the same way and start with similar gifts. The directions they take and the objectives they seek to attain are all important.

> One ship goes East, another West,
> By the self-same winds that blow:
> 'Tis the set of the sail and not the gale
> That determines the way they go.

How was the sail of this life to be set? In what direction would the rudder steer? Toward which harbors would it head for anchorage? By what stars' reckoning would the craft prow into the night? Which way would the winds and storms drive it?

Chapter

> "The word is nigh thee, even in thy mouth, and in thy heart: that is, the word of faith, which we preach; That if thou shalt confess with thy mouth the Lord Jesus, and shalt believe in thine heart that God hath raised him from the dead, thou shalt be saved. For with the heart man believeth unto righteousness; and with the mouth confession is made unto salvation."
> — *Romans* 10: 8-10

> "Also I heard the voice of the Lord, saying, Whom shall I send, and who will go for us? Then said I, Here am I; send me."
> —*Isaiah* 6:8

Two

THE FORMATIVE YEARS

FROM HIS EARLIEST days, Harold Ockenga dreamed of going to college, for to him a college education was essential to the proper blueprints of a life. He had, in fact, two objectives which spawned in his adolescent years. One was to go to college, the other was to travel. Travel came during college days and later, but the choice of a college and the time spent there were determining factors in his later development.

At seventeen, young Ockenga had his eye fixed on high material goals. He desperately wished to attend the University of Chicago which had made such an enviable name for itself in the field of higher education. So with that university in mind, he set his sights.

He sent his high school transcript to the University for appraisal and was entertained by the Alpha Tau Omega fraternity. He had every reason in the world to feel confident. His grades were eminently satisfactory; his background guaranteed him a suitable fraternity. The future looked secure.

But this otherwise happy picture was dulled by a recurring problem which he could not shake off. Though he didn't realize it, the Holy Spirit was working in his life. During the closing days of his sixteenth year and during the seventeenth year, an inner restlessness dogged his trail. Life did not seem to have a consistent pattern to it, and instead of finding satisfaction with what he had and obviously could hope to have, he found only confusion.

This thing called life. What did it mean? How could a young chap make it all add up? He wanted to know who he was and where he was going. He needed a firm and fixed foundation.

His keen mind set out to find the answers, and like other young men, he did not try to find the answer to his problems by seeking the counsel of older and more experienced people than himself.

Thus it was that the University of Chicago and a law career gripped his soul and motivated his life. He envisioned himself as a famous trial lawyer pleading before the bar of justice and winning renown in a profession in which the famed exploits of criminal lawyers like Clarence Darrow filled the Chicago papers.

Searching an answer to the purpose and goal of life, he immersed himself in church work. He began to attend the services of the Methodist church. He went to class meetings. In those meetings spiritual experiences were exchanged and testimonies given. The leader was an elderly, gray-haired man of seventy-five; most of the people attending the class meetings were elderly. A young man could hardly expect to be edified and moved in an environment where there were few if any of his own age.

Yet before the regular Sunday-school session, he attended these class meetings, and God alone knows to what extent they furrowed the ground for later spiritual experiences.

He gave close attention to all teaching and preaching of the Word of God, and came to admire deeply the local pastor, Dr. Ladd-Thomas.

One would suspect that a young man attending three services in the morning—class meeting, Sunday school and worship—would have had enough. In his seriousness, however, young Harold went even further. He assisted at the Junior Epworth League in the afternoon, then went to a study group at five in the later afternoon, followed by the Young Peoples' Society and the evening service. He thus made it a habit in this critical time of his life to attend six or seven services every Sunday. Like Saul of Tarsus he was given over to religious exercises and sought to profit by the multitude of services without regard to their correctness or his personal relationship to God.

So much religious life, however, did not bring on great piety, and when the round of religious activities ended, he did not hesitate to go out to a dance in some home. A close examination of his life does not show that it was tinted with scarlet sin. At no time did he fall into the deeper pits into which young men often sink. He did not get into immorality; he was never arrested; he did not drink and in all his life only three occasions have witnessed any forms of beer, wine or liquor touching his lips. He was typical of the crowd of his day—careless about spiritual things, but as moral as the average and as worthy of commendation as anyone—but without Christ.

At this stage in his life God did what He has done again and again in the lives of people who have been marked by Him for distinguished service. He sent into the life of young Harold Ockenga a Christian who provided light. An interested Christian led Dwight L. Moody to Christ in the rear of a shoe store. A preacher, unknown by name to this hour, led Charles H. Spurgeon to Jesus Christ. And an earnest Christian woman led Harold John Ockenga to find in Christ the answer to his quest.

She was Mrs. Alice Pfafman. She asked Harold to attend an older boys' conference at Galesburg, Illinois, during Christmas vacation and young Ockenga went for the good time he anticipated. He got this and more. At one of the services a man, whose name has been forgotten but whose message was soaked with the dew of heavenly blessing, preached a sermon that touched this seeking heart.

The text came from I Chronicles 11:19. ". . . shall I drink the blood of these men that have put their lives in jeopardy?" And from this text the preacher exalted the blood of Jesus Christ, spilled out as a substitutionary offering for the sins of men on the Cross of Calvary. For the first time in Harold's life, the Holy Spirit drove home what Christ had done. He did not immediately accept Christ. He simply possessed the facts and gave intellectual assent to them.

That afternoon, however, he went to his knees in his hotel,

driven by the Holy Spirit. There he personally appropriated the work of Jesus Christ and received Him as his Saviour. He arose from his knees a new creation in Christ. Old things were passed away. Behold all things were become new! But this conversion experience had more to it than that. On his knees he settled another matter. "Lord," he prayed, "If You will satisfy my heart, I will preach the gospel."

God took his words at face value, and he rose to his feet a different person. All of his problems were not solved then. Only eternity will do that. But in place of an empty, vacant longing, the thrilling experience of the new birth was his. He could truly sing: "You ask me how I know He lives? He lives within my heart!"

Harold returned home that afternoon and on the same evening, at a New Year's Eve service at the church where he had spent so much time on Sundays, he rose to his feet to give a testimony. He told the people how he had become a Christian, how God had given him the gift of everlasting life.

No doubt the words fell idly on many ears that night. He was still only the Ockenga boy, one among the crowd of local young chaps.

He did not tell the people that he had covenanted with God to preach the gospel if God would satisfy his heart. Cautiously, he thought to hold that back for a while.

Shortly after his conversion, the church ran a calling campaign. Harold plunged into the enterprise with such fervor that fifteen people were led into the church. A visiting preacher, observing the work of this bright young man in action and impressed with what he had done, asked him a significant question: "Isn't the Lord calling you to be a preacher?"

The inquiry of the visiting pastor rooted all the more deeply his own hidden conviction about this matter: God calling him to the ministry of His Son!

Into his heart surged unhappiness and restlessness. This was a different species of restlessness than he had experienced

The Formative Years

before salvation, a restlessness rising out of his lack of willingness to follow Christ all the way. Not that he was unsure of his salvation. Not that he doubted what he had done on his knees in the hotel room.

Harold John knew he ought to be a preacher but he did not want to tell anyone. He had it figured out in his own mind that he would take four years of work at the University of Chicago and then go to some seminary instead of law school. In this way, he reasoned, no one would know the difference. He rationalized and sold himself on the argument.

Again God used Mrs. Pfafman as an instrument for the accomplishment of the divine purpose. Her continuing interest was to count for eternity. One day she collared him and said bluntly, "I think the Lord is calling you to be a minister." These words also burned deeply into the heart of young Ockenga, insisting that he had to settle the issue. Further equivocation was impossible. It had to be a clear-cut proposition one way or the other.

Ockenga did not capitulate without a struggle. For several days the issue raged within the secret battlements of his heart. At last the Holy Spirit gained a definite victory. Harold John surrendered.

He went to see Mrs. Pfafman, and told her that God was calling him to the Christian ministry. So thrilled was she that the thought entered her mind to communicate with Harold John's mother by telephone. She called Mrs. Ockenga and repeated the wonderful news, for in those days it was considered a high and splendid occasion when a young man dedicated his life to God for full-time service. To the great surprise of both Mrs. Pfafman and Ockenga the mother's response to the news was, "Thank God. I dedicated him to the ministry before he was born."

So another mother's prayers and hopes were justified. Another Hannah had waited patiently for the birth of a Samuel given to God before the child had seen the light of day.

Mrs. Pfafman did not leave the young minister-to-be at this point. She counselled with him further to make sure he had the help he needed to keep him moving toward the newly announced objective. Law school and the University of Chicago were forgotten. Mrs. Pfafman urged him to go to Taylor University, a Methodist institution. She made an agreement with him that if he went to Taylor for the spring term and returned home dissatisfied, she would gladly pay all of his expenses for the period he was away. Young Harold went to Taylor on this basis.

One semester in residence there did something to his life. He returned home convinced that this was the place for him to complete his collegiate work. He sought out his home church and gave his public testimony. This time it was not only to speak in terms of his personal salvation but also to witness concerning the sloughing off of certain elements previously prominent in his life. He turned in his "frat" pin and resigned the presidency. Smoking had never been a question and card playing was foreign to him. It was not that Ockenga then or now considers Christianity to be a negative faith but that God was speaking to him about the hindrances to the most effective running of the Christian race. The Lord began to fill his life with so many positive things he had to do that the elements inconsistent with a sacrificial life faded out of the picture. Lower things were laid on the altar for higher ones.

Harold Ockenga remained at Taylor University from 1923 to 1927, graduating with the bachelor of arts degree. These years cannot be covered by a simple statement like this, for important happenings transpired in this period that molded his life and changed his pathway. It is not amiss to speak of these years as formative years in a real sense. He was still a Methodist; he was still a young man with vestigial remnants of the old life; he still had not found the complete pattern for his future. But at least two of life's most important decisions had been made— the choice of Jesus Christ as his Saviour and the choice of a life work.

The Formative Years

As a student, Harold fulfilled the prophecy of his nurse and made his scholastic mark in college. His academic average was 94 per cent through four years at college. Having an unusual memory, he grasped facts and retained them easily. His logical mind catalogued these facts and synthesized them into usable patterns of thought. On the basis of his superior work he tried for a Rhodes Scholarship preceding graduation. This effort came to nought, but his academic attainments at least put him in line for this competitive prize.

Ockenga worked his way through college, although he had saved eight hundred dollars before he matriculated in '23. Not above doing menial work, he turned his hand to whatever job offered the prospect of income. He washed dishes, waited on tables, rolled tennis courts. In his senior year he was physical education instructor, replacing a man who had been stricken by an attack of appendicitis.

Ockenga, despite his slender frame, could have carved a few niches for himself in the realm of athletics, but his major interests in other fields of endeavor prevented him from spending too much time in this one. He engaged in intramural sports, playing tennis, basketball, and softball. To this day he plays an excellent game of tennis or softball and is a fine archer and marksman. As a Red Cross life-saving examiner he had complete charge of the waterfront at a Boy Scout camp for several summers. Each summer a thousand boys swam under his care, and not one single fatality occurred.

College also saw Harold develop forensic skill. He earned a debate key and made the varsity squad most of the time he was in school. But again the pressure of the other things prevented him from devoting full time to this activity exclusively. The usefulness of debate to his future life is unquestionable, however. He learned to organize his material, employ the techniques of logic, and think quickly and accurately on his feet. He learned to display poise, to face audiences as well as opponents.

Aside from preaching, debate benefitted him as much as any extracurricular activity in which he engaged while in college.

The Christian college campus replaces fraternities with literary societies. Harold John joined the Thalonian Literary Society in addition to his membership in the Eulogonian Debating Society. The one met on Friday evenings in a more social atmosphere, the latter met on Saturdays. The literary society, like debate, helped train and develop his latent natural talents.

In these college years, Harold enjoyed the association of many girls on the campus but nothing serious came from these friendships. Generally, he remained aloof from serious attachments, not by deliberate choice so much as by reason of that lack of response that comes to young hearts when they fall in love. He also found companionship and fellowship with campus men and counted those hours well-invested when "bull sessions" covering the disputed phases of theology, ethics, and morals gave deeper insight into the opinions, backgrounds, and spirituality of his college mates.

He lived off-campus the first two years, on-campus for the last two. For two years he had an older man for his roommate and together they sought the deeper things of the spiritual life. It was apparent that the members of the college faculty were devoted to the cause of Christ and their lives made an impact on Ockenga through the classroom. They helped him greatly by their Christian view of education and by their personal consecration to Christ.

It was in connection with his roommate and their search together for spiritual verities that he recalls appreciable progress. They spent an hour each morning before breakfast reading the Bible and praying. This meant rising at 5:00 A.M., for breakfast was at 6:30.

The student body had its public prayer meeting on Thursday evenings at Taylor. Harold John attended them regularly and also had the privilege of helping administer them part of the time.

THE FORMATIVE YEARS

College provided numerous opportunities for other kinds of spiritual outreach, too. Ockenga engaged himself in the work of the Holiness League, headed a gospel team, and for two years had major responsibility in sending out students on deputation work. At times as many as one hundred and twenty-five students went out for a weekend, preaching, testifying, holding meetings of one kind or another. This involvement in spiritual activities curtailed his other commitments. He preferred spiritual rather than secular leadership, sacrificing debate and sports for things spiritual.

Harold Ockenga loved to preach. With this desire burning in his heart, doors opened all over the Middle West. Including summer gospel team work, he spoke more than four hundred times while in college. This was no minor accomplishment in an age when ministers rarely preach more than one hundred times a year. God attended his preaching with power so far as results can be observed. Time and again fifty to seventy-five people came to the altar for consecration or for salvation. The speaker may have lacked polish and oratorical brilliance, but what he lacked in finesse, the Holy Spirit made up in a fiery passion for the souls of men.

While Harold was yet in college, God gloriously saved his father. Harold had testified to his father about Jesus Christ and the need for personal acceptance of Him, but never made any visible progress.

In Harold's second year of college, however, his father suffered a heart attack. The attending physician held out small hope for his recovery, and the young son was summoned home. Imagine his happiness upon discovering that his father had accepted Christ as his Saviour and that he was soundly converted.

Up to the moment of his conversion, Mr. Ockenga waged a militant warfare against his son's entrance into the Christian ministry. He would not contribute a penny to this end, and plainly said so. After his conversion, however, his heart softened toward the divine call of God and his attitude changed perceptibly. Later in his Christian experience, this father often said that had he his own life to live over again he would devote it to the Christian ministry.

In his Junior year of college Harold Ockenga came to a conclusion about eradication of sin in the life of the Christian. The college taught the doctrine of holiness in such a way that the Christian could reach a plane of life in which sinless perfection was the order of the day. Puzzling and pondering this doctrine peculiar to most forms of Methodism Ockenga became convinced after his own study of the Bible that eradication was not actually taught in the Word. Further study convinced him that the doctrine commonly known as eternal security is taught in he Word, although he thinks of it in terms of the keeping power of God. Shifting to eternal security did not nor has it ever meant in his thinking that a man can live as he pleases and remain in a state of grace. The regenerate life must match one's profession and if the profession is discountenanced by the life of the so-called believer then the serious question arises whether the individual has ever been saved. But once a man is saved, Ockenga believes he will have fruit in his life and will be kept safe by the power of the living God unto the day of final redemption.

The greatest spiritual experience in his college life came in connection with his gospel team work. Here it was that God dealt with him about the matter of surrender, for he discovered in his own life those remnants of the old man mentioned before. He saw his life far from all the Bible revealed it ought to be, as the Holy Spirit pointed out defects he had allowed to remain unremedied: deep-rooted pride, a sense of unconcern about the feelings and rights of other people, the human equations of life and the unconscious items and reactions one does not often think about but which alienate others and hinder one's testimony for the Lord.

Like all men of great gifts, the same type of besetting sins served to prevent him from being at his spiritual best. Nowhere are such defects more easily evidenced than in the closeness of gospel team work when men live with each other day by day. Then it is that little things crop up; then sins covered by isolation are clearly revealed in community relationships.

Ockenga was not alone in his imperfections but he was alone in the sense that God moved in to deal with him. God wanted him to get away from self, crucifying the old man and burying him to rise no more as a spectre haunting his life and wrecking its usefulness.

God again worked through human instrumentalities.

One of the team members tactfully spoke to Harold Ockenga about these defects. "Ockie," he said, "there is something wrong with either you or me." And Harold was willing to concede that perhaps the fault lay with himself, rather than with his colleague.

Together the two found their way to a nearby field. Climbing over a fence, they went to a haystack sheltered by a yellow apple tree. On their knees before God, they let the Holy Spirit speak to them about their sins, humbly praying to the One who makes things right.

Neither of the young men was filled with the wisdom of years. Both did what they thought was best. Harold had some peace of mind after this unexpected encounter with his co-laborer. He felt that the matter was settled and that he was on the right track toward a good testimony in life and precept with these sins eliminated.

With no small feeling of surprise and shock to Ockenga, a second member of the team came to him and spoke in almost identical terms about his sins. There was no collusion; no getting together to put a fellow worker on the spot. It was spontaneous, rising out of hearts filled with an anxiety to know and to do the will of God. When Ockenga heard the phrase, "There must be something wrong with either you or me," the second time, he was decidedly taken aback, crushed in spirit, wounded deeply.

"What shall I do?" he inquired of the brother in Christ.

The reply came back to him as swiftly as the question. "Go out and pray all night." The advice was typical of Methodist practice and theory about such matters. Praying through to the bitter end was not unusual and such prayer generally accomplished its objective.

Harold Ockenga did not think he should pray through the night, but he did rise up early in the morning to fight it out. On his knees, he sought to find peace of heart and to experience the finality of self crucified with Christ. He prayed and prayed but no peace came. At last his desperation brought him to a moment of reckless abandon. He meant to do business with God and these sins of pride and all else had to go. The prayer he prayed now demonstrated his determination to get right with the Lord.

"Lord," he cried out, "if You don't do something for me, I'm not going to preach about something that I do not have in my own life!" This was the penitent's plea. Whatever he lacked, that he wanted. Whatever it was he needed to make his preaching powerful in his own life as well as by the spoken word was the urgent desire and wish of his young heart. This petition to God he prayed during the middle of the week. And the following Sunday was pivotal in the spiritual life of God's chosen vessel.

On Sunday the sermon preached by one of the team members was based on a text taken from Acts 1:8. The sermon was not powerful oratorically, nor in the gifts of homiletical excellency possessed by the speaker, but God used it as a sword to pierce Ockenga's own heart. When the invitation was given, nothing happened. No one came forward to make things right with God. The closing hymn was sung, the invitation generously extended, but still nothing happened. The speaker promised that following the singing of the next verse, unless there was a definite response, he would close the service with the benediction.

The Formative Years

Then it was that God's Spirit strove with Harold Ockenga.

As though a voice from heaven spoke to him, he heard: "If you want the blessing you seek, *this is the time* to get it." He did want the blessing he felt he lacked, but he did not have the will or the courage to go down to the altar, to go forward before his teammates and the people to whom his team was supposed to be ministering.

The audience commenced the stanza of the hymn that was to conclude the service if no one came forward, and the Holy Spirit's voice spoke softly but insistently to him.

The battle went on.

The hymn came to a close and for a moment it looked as though the benediction would complete the service and end the opportunity. Then it was that courage came to leaden feet and humbled spirit found its voice. Ockenga, interrupting his comrade, began, in broken speech, to tell the people what lay on his heart. He spoke of his conversion, of his call to the Christian ministry, of the blessing which God had so freely bestowed upon their efforts. Then he spoke of the need of his own heart and of his determination to quit preaching if the Lord did not do something for him. Deliberately, he told the people, who listened spellbound to this unexpected turn of affairs, "I am going to the altar and ask Him to do something for me."

The meeting broke wide open. Harold Ockenga went down to that altar in penitential tears to meet with God in the great renunciation of self. He went there to see self die unto Him, and to find that which saints of all ages have had to find, the mystery of identification in the death of Christ in that "I live, yet not I, but Christ liveth in me."

Once again the Word of the living God was fulfilled, "Reckon ye yourselves to be dead indeed unto sin, but alive unto God through Jesus Christ our Lord." There at that altar, in that tiny church, God broke through and touched his soul in a moment which would follow him throughout the remainder of his life.

Something in Harold Ockenga died that night. It was not reduced; it was crucified. It was not hidden; it was brought forth to be slain. The self life was dealt with just as his sins had been dealt with in salvation. The course of his life changed and from that time onward his one thought was to have the will of God for his life pre-eminent in every decision. He now could say in simple sincerity, "Not my will but Thy will be done."

The full fruit of the night's decision did not appear immediately. Ockenga went back to college to complete his preparation looking toward the ministry. He graduated from Taylor University with a major in English and history and with a minor in philosophy. Faced with a choice of seminary for further training he decided the Lord wanted him to go to Princeton Theological Seminary in New Jersey. Although still a Methodist with plans to enter the ministry of that denomination, he selected Princeton largely because of its formidable array of academic leadership. Men of God like Wilson, Machen, Armstrong, and Allis were challenges to scholarship as well as outstanding defenders of the faith once for all delivered unto the saints. By his standards, Princeton provided the finest opportunity for obtaining a balanced conservative theological training to fit him for a Bible ministry.

From 1927 through 1929, he studied at Princeton Seminary. His grades were highly acceptable and in his second year he received the Archibald Alexander New Testament prize. During the first summer while a Princeton student, he undertook a nationwide gospel-team tour with Bill T. Blackstone, now a missionary in China, and Bill Martin, now professor of Semitics at Oxford.

The group traveled fourteen thousand miles as the Princeton Evangelistic Team. God honored the work of these young men, and gave them fruit. The experience taught them valuable lessons not available in college or seminary curricula.

During Ockenga's student days at Princeton, the Presbyterian Church's ecclesiastical struggle which had existed internally erupted into the open. The reorganization of the Seminary at Princeton took place, inevitably precipitating the creation of the Westminster Theological Seminary. Machen provided the leadership for the protesting group, and under his dynamic leadership, a train of events was sets in motion which led eventually to further trouble in the church.

Ockenga took no active part in the fray. He was still a Methodist, still anticipated service in that communion. However, he left Princeton for Westiminster to finish his theological training under the men whose reputation had been responsible for his going to Princeton.

The decision to go to Westminster proved one of the most fateful in his whole experience. Had he not gone, the tenor of his life would have been altered considerably, for his whole future hung on that decision—although he was totally unaware of it when he faced the issue.

Had he not gone to Westminster, he would never have come into contact with Dr. Clarence Edward Macartney. Had Dr. Macartney not taken men from the Westminster Seminary into the work of his church, Ockenga would never have gone to the First Church of Pittsburgh. His connections with the First Church led him later to Point Breeze and Point Breeze and his contacts with Dr. Macartney and Dr. Machen opened the door to his work at Park Street in Boston.

No young man could have known the full implications of such a choice, but God was working behind the scenes, preparing the way.

From his studies at Princeton and Westminster, Harold Ockenga became a Calvinist, though more so as a student than is true today after many years in the work of the pastorate. However, his theological training steeped him in the Reformed tradition from which he has not departed in the main since student days. In his final year at Westminster, Ockenga decided to enter the Presbyterian ministry.

He did not enter that fold immediately, however.

In the spring of 1929, Harold Ockenga pastored a Methodist church in Avalon, New Jersey. He was ordained a deacon in that fellowship in the spring of 1930. His ministry in Avalon lasted a year, at the end of which time he moved to the Chelsea Methodist Episcopal Church in Atlantic City, New Jersey. While at this church Dr. Macartney invited him to accept an assistantship in the First Presbyterian Church of Pittsburgh. Ockenga refused the call.

Again at the close of the summer in 1930, Dr. Macartney came along with another opening. Fervent prayer was made unto the God of heaven for guidance. Confirmation came of the divine leading and with this in mind Harold Ockenga decided to accept the offer to work.

For years Dr. Macartney had been an honored servant in the Presbyterian Church. He was considered, then and now, one of the leading evangelicals in that denomination. In the struggle in the 1920's over the question of the Auburn Affirmation, the leadership of Dr. Macartney shone forth as a beacon light in the midst of perilous storms. Reaffirming the five essentials of the Christian faith, he was swept into the office of Moderator of the General Assembly in 1924. Pastor at that time of the Arch Street Church of Philadelphia, Macartney at 42 was the youngest moderator of the General Assembly. Going to the First Church of Pittsburgh after his pastorate at Arch Street this new charge stood the tests of time and represented one of the great forces for Christ in America. With a membership close to three thousand, an annual budget of one quarter of a million dollars and ten thousand people attending the various services of the church every week, it was a beehive of evangelical activity.

Dr. Macartney himself was greatly beloved by his people. A bachelor, stern with himself in personal life, devout and surrendered to the will of God, he was a force for good in his

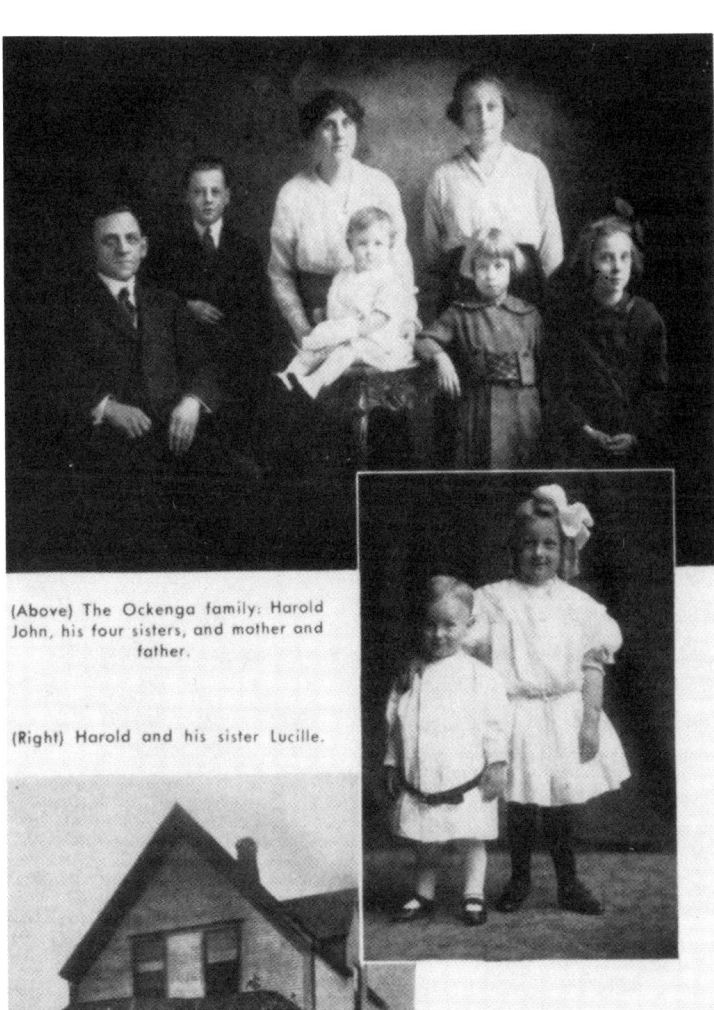

(Above) The Ockenga family: Harold John, his four sisters, and mother and father.

(Right) Harold and his sister Lucille.

(Left) The family home in Chicago where Harold Ockenga was born.

(Top) Debate champions at Taylor University. Ockenga at right. (Left center) Harold John as a waiter during college days. (Right center) as a basketball player for Taylor. (Bottom) The Princeton gospel team with Harold Ockenga at left.

community. Gifted as an administrator, filled with a saving sense of humor, influential as an author, revered as a topical, biographical, and historical preacher, he wielded an immense influence in the life of young Ockenga. And in accepting the call, for one year Ockenga was privileged to have close association with this man and with his church.

<u>Dr. Macartney did his own preaching. His assistants labored in other fields.</u> Harold John supervised the work of young people, and taught a class for Sunday-school teachers, designed to aid them in their own teaching on the Lord's Day. He conducted the boys' club and engaged in visitation work, which usually consisted in making <u>approximately fifty pastoral calls each week</u>. In seven months' time, he called on almost the entire congregation listed on the rolls of the church and upon his recommendation and that of the other assistant pastor, some three hundred were dropped from the church rolls. He was instrumental in initiating a men's club which grew until it had a membership of better than two thousand with a weekly attendance of six hundred.

The work of the young people quadrupled and became a strong factor in the life of the congregation during the year Ockenga served at the First Church.

While assistant pastor in the First Presbyterian Church, the Presbytery of Pittsburgh ordained Harold Ockenga to the gospel ministry. Previously, the Philadelphia Presbytery licensed him and now the Pittsburgh Presbytery proceeded with his formal ordination. This transpired in January of 1931 at which Dr. Macartney gave the charge to the candidate and Dr. J. Gresham Machen of Westminster preached the ordination sermon. During his connections with the First Presbyterian Church, the Independent Board for Presbyterian Foreign Missions was not an issue. This came later.

Energetic and untiring in his efforts, the young pastor decided to further his education. This he did by enrolling in the University of Pittsburgh to pursue graduate work in the field of philosophy. As a part-time student it took him several years to acquire the master of arts degree and still longer to receive the doctorate in philosophy.

Again the providential leading of the Lord opened a new door for this coming leader. One day he called upon some folk living in the home of an elder connected with the Point Breeze Presbyterian Church in Pittsburgh. This elder took a liking to the splendid looking minister from the First Church and recommended him as a candidate to the chairman of the pastoral committee of his congregation. Shortly thereafter, Ockenga received an invitation to preach there.

This invitation came to him not as a candidate, however, but as a supply preacher while they looked for a new pastor. But, the minutes of the church Session, written five years later, reveal the working out of God's will from the human side. "When Harold John Ockenga, on Sunday, March 15, 1931, preached in the Point Breeze pulpit as supply, the committee members then seeking a pastor for the congregation were bombarded with the question from members of the church who heard him, 'Why don't you call this young man?' The members of the committee were asking themselves the same question. The hope that the search for a minister had come to an end, that that search had revealed in our midst the very one who combined all of the qualities we were seeking for, was a unanimous one.... History, only too recent and too short, will reveal that these hopes were realized and that they were in no measure to see disappointment."

So the records indicate that the church extended a call to this young preacher whose message indelibly affected them and whom they thought the Lord had led into their midst.

God led young Ockenga to accept the call to the Point Breeze Church. The membership on the rolls was thirteen hundred. It was a wealthy and influential parish.

This outward facade was deceiving, however. The first Sunday he preached in the church, twenty-five people attended.

One could hardly call that impressive. The prayer meeting was nonexistent. In terms of opportunity, it was a rich field. One would not have to do much to improve the situation providing discouragement did not lay hold of a man before he persevered.

On May 8, 1931, he was installed in the church. This time Dr. C. E. Macartney preached the sermon and Dr. J. Gresham Machen gave the charge to the pastor. <u>Dr. Machen</u> spoke stirringly and with feeling about the problems and opposition Harold Ockenga could expect to face. <u>His sage counsel was for the new pastor to be a man of one Book; to know its mysteries; to search out its glories; to present its claims.</u>

He acknowledged that Ockenga had already "put ambition aside deliberately to stand without hope of preferment of what this world can give" in going to Westminster for his last year when Machen left Princton.

And that a cost attached itself to this decision, later events in his life and work fully testify.

For five and a half years, Harold John Ockenga labored at Point Breeze. During this period of time, changes occurred. The attendance at the services were pushed to higher figures. Before he left the church to go to Park Street, about three hundred and fifty people came regularly to the morning worship services. The evening services normally brought about two hundred and fifty. The non-existent prayer meeting went up to an average of seventy, which never satisfied the pastor but which represented considerable improvement over none.

Throughout the pastorate, the minister's heart was burdened for increasing the prayer meeting attendance and for a spiritual deepening in the lives of the people. The young people's work flourished. It, too, had been dead, but before he left the church, the normal attendance was in the neighborhood of one hundred. The Sunday school climbed from two hundred to between three hundred and fifty and four hundred.

Depression days gripped America from 1931 to 1936. Churches suffered along with all segments of American life. Yet in the midst of the deepest depression America has known, the Point Breeze Church under Ockenga's leadership managed to pay off a mortgage of seventeen hundred dollars and also to renovate the church building.

Every church has "dead wood" on its roll, the Point Breeze Church being no exception to the general rule. In his first three years as pastor, six hundred members were dropped from the records. That left approximately seven hundred. Counting the additions to the church while Ockenga was there, the membership rose to about nine hundred and fifty—a substantial tribute to the effectiveness of the ministry of a man so few years out of seminary.

What help Ockenga had in the church during his stay there was in the form of student assistants. He did all his own preaching and consolidated the work of the church through the administrative gifts God had given him. Parish activities took most of his time but still the pastor continued his work toward a doctorate at the University of Pittsburgh. Before he left Pittsburgh he had taken all of the normal examinations and had completed his residence work; all that was left was the dissertation and final defense of his thesis.

1930 to 1936 were formative years in Ockenga's life, distinct from the preceding academic years. In this Pittsburgh interlude the vision which God laid upon his heart became a reality. The effectual call of God to the Christian ministry had been met and he was in the ministry. Many young men begin, but somewhere along the way lose out, never to reach the goal.

Harold John Ockenga had been gloriously saved out of his sins and was significantly called to his life work. He embarked upon his course of training and at the end of that period found a place of service. Men laid hands upon him and recognized the call of God for his life. He was on his way! But God had not yet sent into his life the woman of His choice.

However God had a perfect will in this as in all things. It was chiefly a question of timing. Normal in every regard, this young prophet of God expected a home of his own and looked forward to rearing children. But he was not anxious to force the issue, being content to wait before God for assurance in this important choice.

Chapter

"Rachel, like Rebekah, met her lover at a desert well. It was love at first sight. It remained love, beautifully, to the end."
— *Frank S. Mead*

" . . . Rachel was beautiful and well favored. And Jacob loved Rachel . . . "
— *Genesis* 29: 17,18

Three

WHAT GOD HATH JOINED TOGETHER

INTO THE LIFE of Harold John Ockenga God brought a woman who would have a vital role to play and whose influence and impact on him would exceed that of all women except perhaps his mother.

Heretofore Ockenga had not spent much time in the company of the opposite sex. His interest in them was casual and on a friendly basis only.

Time fled by until he was almost thirty. His years had been filled with arduous labor; and perhaps the influence of the sainted bachelor Dr. Macartney inclined him to look with favor on a life of celibacy.

One day, however, the inevitable transpired. He chanced to go to the Hotel Webster in Pittsburgh to have supper. He sat idly in the restaurant waiting for service. While waiting he scrutinized the streams of people going in and out.

Into the line of Harold Ockenga's vision came the figure of a young lady in white. And with the first glance something happened in his heart that shook the previously impregnable citadel. He did not know the young lady; they had never met before. He did not have the faintest idea where she might be from but he wished he did. It was like the casual passing of ships at sea in the night. For all he knew he would never see this girl again. And he knew nothing about her! After all, one cannot hope to meet again all the people who pass before his eyes. In this instance, however God had a plan; and when God works, things do happen mysteriously and providentially. He said in ejaculatory prayer: "Lord, give me that girl and I'll marry her." Later he commented, "He did, and I did."

One August afternoon Ockenga walked into the library of the University of Pittsburgh and sat down to study and read. He looked across the table and to his amazement and unspeakable joy saw the same young lady he had seen in the restaurant of the hotel. It was so fortuitous that he could not let his golden opportunity pass by. A university campus and library provide good opportunities for informal conversation and passing the time of day. So he struck up a conversation across the table.

On that August afternoon of 1934 they walked out of the library together. The preacher had his automobile parked near the campus and suggested that he take her home. To this suggestion she gave cordial assent. By this time they had learned each other's names and then and later he was able to elicit additional information about her. He learned that she was Audrey Laura Williamson. She lived in Pittsburgh and was studying at the University, looking toward teaching as a life work. She had been born in Lee, Massachusetts.

Miss Williamson's mother came from Virginia, of English-German ancestry. Her father came from West Virginia and was of Scotch descent. The family was Christian, both mother and father being Methodists.

To say that Harold Ockenga developed an interest in attractive Audrey Williamson is to put it mildly. Rather, he fell head over heels in love with her from the first moment in her company. His love was not simply a matter of infatuation. It was conditioned upon the inward assurance that this was the girl of God's choice for his life.

Perhaps he may have exhibited a strange theological inconsistency for a Calvinist. But apparently many a Calvinist, theologically, has slipped into Arminianism when in love. At any rate he did not sit back to let God work apart from human effort. Subconsciously he reacted, as he later admitted,—as a synergist (meaning that there must be the co-operative work of divine grace and human responsibility and effort).

Harold let no grass grow under his feet. Instead he wore a rut to Audrey's door. In ten days time he had fourteen dates with Audrey Williamson. He was losing no time in prosecuting his cause with her. In the language of the collegian he was "rushing" her.

Audrey's heart was not quickly pierced by this insistence, although she instinctively felt an attraction for this splendid young graduate student. She enjoyed his company, and his ardent seeking of her company was exhilerating. This gracious, charming, affable girl and her distinguished looking escort made an attractive picture.

And the young man was not to be denied. "No" had no meaning for him. The objective was clear; all that remained to be done was to secure a favorable verdict from the girl. This Harold John set his heart on accomplishing and left no stone unturned to secure from her a "Yes."

Summer school ended in August and before the beginning of the new school year Audrey left for a vacation in Canada. She went to Limberlost. Harold pried from her the location of the summer resort and then proceeded to follow her there. They had a glorious vacation at this resort and a turning point in their lives was reached. They indulged in the sports this vacationland offered, hiking, swimming, riding, and rowing. Together they talked and walked and dined. But beneath the exterior covering of vacation and recreation was Harold Ockenga's one undeviating purpose: to win Audrey Williamson.

Before they left the Limberlost life was bound in pledge to life. That mysterious human relationship was agreed upon, that estate of which the Bible speaks in holy terms and makes analogous to the Church of Christ and the Lord Jesus.

Audrey did not receive an engagement ring from her husband-to-be for some months. They waited for that until two months before their marriage—just one year after they had met in the library of the university. These were glorious months,

months of anticipation and expectation, months of preparation and planning. Audrey's parents were delighted that their daughter had pledged her troth to this minister of the gospel. They fully appreciated him.

The Pittsburgh papers gave much publicity to the engagement and marriage. One article, humorously entitled "Cupid Snares Pastor," told the story of their approaching wedding. Another stated, "Wedding bells will soon ring for one of East Liberty's youngest and most popular ministers and his attractive bride-to-be." Still another wrote that the minister would wed "a pretty teacher of the Wightman school at an August wedding ceremony."

At long last, the time of the wedding approached. The couple agreed to be married in the Point Breeze Church, with Dr. Holley, pastor of Audrey's church, performing the marriage ceremony.

At the appointed hour the church was crowded with an expectant throng of people. The Point Breeze Church looked forward with great joy to having their pastor married. They redecorated the manse into which the bride was to come. They prepared everything for them and showered them with gifts. Detailed arrangements were made at the Schenley Hotel for a special wedding breakfast for fifty people most intimately related to the bride and groom. Six new Chryslers awaited the wedding party for transportation to and from the church and site of the breakfast. All was ready.

In a real sense it was Audreys' day. Audrey was the chief center of attraction. The groom himself wanted it that way, for to him she was the main figure. His cup was filled to the brim. God had saved him; God had called him to His service; God had given him the gift of Audrey Williamson to be his wife.

Swiftly the ceremony was over. They returned up the

aisle that Audrey had come down with her father. She was now Audrey Williamson Ockenga.

For several days the newlyweds stayed at Eaglesmere in Pennsylvania and then they turned toward New York City and the German liner *Bremen*. Boarding this, they headed for Europe to spend the major portion of their honeymoon.

For six wonderful weeks together they toured England, Scotland, the Netherlands, Germany, Switzerland, and France. The Alps in Switzerland; the lakes of Scotland; the fascinating cities of London and Paris; the Rhine—these were all theirs to enjoy and remember.

The manifold blessings of God did not cease when the Ockengas married. They came back in 1935 to the work of the church in Pittsburgh. Twelve months later they embarked upon their journey to Boston and the Park Street Church.

And the years began to spin by with evident tokens of divine favor in the gift of children. First Audrey Starr, named after her mother, came. A picture-book baby, she grew up a sweet and lovely child, serious in demeanor, obedient. Later Aldryth Sabra came. Quite different from her sister, she was never lost in a crowd. Open, affectionate, inquiring and aggressive Aldryth wormed her way into everything—including the hearts of people.

Again God answered prayer. Into the home came a third child, a son, sturdy and strong, Harold John Ockenga, Jr.

A charming informality characterizes the Ockenga home in Boston and in New Hampshire. There is no pretense, no desire to impress. Visitors to their home are common and welcome. And the Ockengas gladly share with them what they have to offer. Mutual love and affection dominate their home and lives.

Harold Ockenga has strong convictions about the place of a pastor's wife in the ministry. He thinks a woman belongs in the home and does not look with favor on a pastor's wife holding office in any of the church organizations. In a metropolitan pulpit where the home of the pastor is far removed and separated from the center of church activity this conception is more possible than in a community where the church and the parsonage are close together.

Their living in Belmont, a suburban town, leaves the center of gravity for the work of the church in Boston. This makes it far easier for Mrs. Ockenga to occupy herself more with her family and less with the work of the church than if she lived next door to it.

Dr. Ockenga defers to his wife's opinion and values it highly. But he is the head of the family. Mrs. Ockenga has such confidence and trust in her husband as the leader of the home, and she so believes in the Biblical view of the man as the head of the house, that no difficulty arises. Loved universally by the members of the Park Street Church and by all those who know her and come in contact with her, Audrey Ockenga is certainly the Lord's provision for this prophet of God. Affable, sincere, sweet and winsome, there is nothing false about her. No shams to mar; no affectations to impress people—just a gracious and sweet simplicity which makes people wonder whether this man knows fully how excellent the blessing of God has been in the gift of this woman.

The Point Breeze Presbyterian Church voiced through its Session what is the universal consensus of those who know Mrs. Ockenga. She "has endeared herself to all of us. Quietly, modestly, she has won us all . . ."

Chapter

> But he was beloved of his God: also, he had a good heart of his own or else he could never have done it.
> — *John Bunyan*

> "By faith Abraham, when he was called to go out into a place which he should after receive for an inheritance, obeyed . . ."
> — *Hebrews* 11: 8

Four

THE PARK STREET CHURCH — AN OPEN DOOR

THOSE WHOM OUR God uses He first prepares. Harold Ockenga never dreamed that God was preparing him for a significant ministry in New England, a ministry that in turn would influence all America and lead to further opportunities for even wider service.

In the summer of 1934, A. Z. Conrad of the Park Street Congregational Church (which has since changed its name to the Park Street Church) invited Harold Ockenga to preach in that Church during his vacation. Dr. Conrad began his ministry in Park Street in 1905, and under his leadership the church moved forward and had been blessed by revivals in 1906, 1909, and in 1920.

Realizing that his ministry was soon to end because of his advanced age, Dr. Conrad sought for a man to replace him. In his effort to find the right one for this most strategic opportunity, Dr. Conrad counseled with other Christian leaders. Through the strange working of the Lord's will he was led to seek the advice of three men: Dr. Clarence Edward Macartney of the First Presbyterian Church of Pittsburgh where Harold Ockenga had served, Dr. J. Gresham Machen, the president of Westminster Theological Seminary from which institution Harold Ockenga received his divinity degree, and Dr. Harold Paul Sloan, a leading Methodist conservative connected with the League of Faith.

While we have no way of finding out the reaction of Dr. Conrad to the replies of these men then, it is important to note that all of them suggested the same person to fill the Park Street pulpit: Harold John Ockenga. Their recommendations came independently. It appeared providential indeed that God should so reveal what might be His will.

At the time of this occurrence the facts were unknown to Ockenga and a year and a half went by before further word came from Park Street.

He was invited to preach there the Sunday after Easter. During this visit a long conversation with Dr. Conrad ensued during which time the great Park Street leader revealed that these three men had suggested his name for the pulpit. Dr. Conrad seriously urged the young man to join him at Park Street as co-pastor with the understanding that they would share the pulpit.

Feeling no compelling guidance from the Holy Spirit that this was the will of God for his life, however, Harold Ockenga refused the offer. He shut the door and so far as he knew when he made this decision the door was to remain shut.

Just one week after Ockenga's trip to Boston, Dr. Conrad was stricken with cancer and never preached from the Park Street pulpit again. At the age of eighty-one he was taken home to be with the Lord. But before Dr. Conrad's death, again in the providence of God, the Park Street pulpit was to become an open door for Harold Ockenga.

Boston is, of course, one of the oldest communities in America. Much of the history of our nation has revolved around this city and general area, and springing out of its soil have come generations of hardy men and women whose contributions to American life remain incalculable. Indeed, Boston is an historic city and no man can traverse its narrow, winding streets without seeing evidences on every side that recall to mind the glorious past of our people.

The very location of the Park Street Church brings back fond memories of trying days. It is situated on the ground

Audrey Ockenga and The Three Ockenga Children: Starr, Aldryth, Harold John Jr.

Harold Ockenga as a Young Minister

THE PARK STREET CHURCH

where the town granary used to be. On this site the sails for the frigate *"Constitution"* of Revolutionary War fame, were sewed together. In the crypt of the church itself, brimstone (sulphur, for discharging powder) was stored during the War of 1812, and from the storing of sulphur in the church building has come a name still used today: "Brimstone Corner."

Beside the church is a burial ground which shelters the mortal remains of men who fought and died for liberty and democracy. As one walks along Tremont Street, one of the busiest in all Boston, he is but a step off this main artery to the graveyard. In it can be found the stones erected to the memory of men like Samuel Otis, John Hancock, the parents of Benjamin Franklin, and the Adams' family.

Across from the church on the Park Street side is the Boston Common, a beautiful little park with its green grass and shady trees offering refuge for city dwellers during the hot summer months. Excellently located with regard to the church, it has been a fertile source for finding congregations when Harold Ockenga got a vision of reaching the unchurched masses with the gospel. All that was needed was a loud speaker and a man of courage whose voice could reach the crowded Common on a Sunday evening after the regular church service.

Up the hill off Park Street is the State House and the legislative halls of Massachusetts. Not far removed from Park Street is the famed Tremont Temple from whose pulpit great men of God of Baptist persuasion have preached the unsearchable riches of the Lord Jesus Christ. A short walk down the narrow streets of this city leads the visitor to the wharves—wharves at which sailing vessels used to be tied, ships that had visited every country in the world, returning with rich cargoes. The fortunes of many Boston "Brahmins" were built in the waters of this harbor where their ships anchored at these wharves. The famous triangular trade that worked in rum, and sugar, and slaves is part of the history of Boston. Solid, respectable,

God-fearing, church-attending merchants sat in their pews on the Sabbath and sold human flesh for the plantations of the South the rest of the week.

Rising out of this commerce and trade came a tightly knit class of aristocrats whose homes on Beacon Street one finds unchanged to this day. A society with its own mores, hedged in by its own conventions, and ruled by its own codes grew and flourished in this fertile commercial soil. The sons and daughters of this aristocracy walked within the confines of the area enclosed by convention and the sure exclusion from society, that was the lot of those who failed to keep the code. From birth, the sons were marked for Harvard just as the king's men before the American Revolution had emblazoned the mark of the monarch on the tall trees of the forest to tell all that they were reserved for the navy of the far-flung British empire.

To be sure, one cannot understand New England without understanding Harvard College. It is the oldest seat of higher learning in the United States, although in South America and Mexico the Spanish began institutions prior to 1636, when Harvard was founded. The roots of this institution are deeply woven in the flesh and bones of a religious faith. The Puritan and Pilgrim forebears who left the Old World for conscience' sake and liberty and whose blessed names have been inextricably mingled with the story of this nation were men and women of culture and foresight. Known to them was the unmistakeable lesson of history that their faith must be perpetuated through a succession of learned divines.

Its Biblical standard and crest remains the same: *Lux et veritas*—light and truth—although the college has long since departed from the faith of its fathers. Those whose lives in early days garnished its hallowed hallways would, no doubt, be the first to condemn this departure. Nevertheless, this ancient institution continues to mold the thoughts of men and condition the environment of a people It transmits a culture, and lends to this land of enchantment a prestige which time has enhanced, and which, humanly speaking, is an imperishable facet of our heritage.

Alongside Harvard, New England boasts other schools of note: Boston University, of Methodist birth; Radcliffe, sister to Harvard; the Massachusetts Institute of Technology; Simmons; Wheaton, a college for girls; Wellesley; and others that dot the academic landscape. It is a land with an intellectual climate, and the man whose voice will be heard is the man who can speak the language of its people and who can minister to them out of a similar academic background.

If Boston and New England reflect the academic environment of its schools, the area also is one of transition. The sacred cod may be a symbol of the state, and the sailing vessel the sign of its fortune, but into the picture have come the factory and the mill. No longer can one appropriately use this well-known ditty:

> And this is good old Boston,
> The home of the bean and the cod,
> Where the Lowells talk to the Cabots
> And the Cabots talk only to God.

With the bean and the cod are now the factory and the mill. An enterprising people began to manufacture shoes and milled woolens and cotton, but the labor involved in the process had to be cheap and manageable.

From the hungry countries of Europe in the nineteenth century came the supply of labor. Many of the laborers were those who could make the trip to Atlantic coastal cities and that was all. So the whole eastern seaboard was dotted with multitudes of people from Germany, Ireland, Scandanavia, Italy and Poland.

Boston got its share—mostly Irish and all Roman Catholic. Today Boston is politically dominated by a Democratic Roman

Catholic group, and liberally interspersed with centuries-old English street names are to be found squares with Irish names of recent vintage.

So far have the landmarks of the fathers been removed from this ancient city that Boston entertains the reputation of being the only city that recently has had a mayor re-elected by the people despite the fact that he was twice convicted of felony.

The Park Street Church for more than a hundred years has been the salt of the earth to Boston. During that period one steady unbroken stream of God's prophets has faithfully proclaimed Jesus Christ and Him crucified. From its pulpits men like Moody and Sankey preached and sang their way into the hearts of thousands. Revival after revival struck the church with purifying fire, and under the leadership and preaching of men like Charles G. Finney conviction of sin came and the Spirit of God worked in mighty power and unction.

This church was born out of spiritual stress and Unitarian apostasy in New England. From 1800 on, a tremendous movement away from the trinitarian evangelical faith characterized the religious scene in the area. In a short period of eight years, from 1800 to 1808, the powerful "Unitarian Landslide" occurred in which fifteen out of seventeen Boston churches departed from the trinitarian evangelical faith of their fathers to espouse the unitarian rationalism of the hour.

It appeared as though not one witness remained. But as in Israel God had reserved for Himself some who had not bowed the knee to Baal, so in Boston some of God's choicest elect did not turn aside from the trinitarian and evangelical faith of their fathers. In the Old South Church, which did not depart from the true faith in that dark hour, came the insistent plea for the establishment of a week-night service for prayer. When this plea was ignored, a group of men and a group of women, both of which had been meeting weekly for prayer,

THE PARK STREET CHURCH

determined that a standard should be raised and a new church formed to carry on the Puritan teaching and tradition. This determination and hopeful resolve was effectually strengthened following revival meetings under Dr. Henry Kollock of Savannah, Georgia.

On February 27, 1809, a small group of Christians met in the home of William Thurston. Acting as a council of Christians, the Park Street Congregational Church was formed with a charter membership of twenty-six brave souls.

Undaunted by obstacles, the group that formed this new witness for Christ marched forward in the construction of a meeting house. At the corners of Tremont and Park Streets they erected a structure to the glory of God and for the preaching of the trinitarian gospel of His beloved Son.

In less than a year the building stood ready for dedication. On June 10, 1810, the ceremony of dedication took place. Not only was there built on that site a church of the living God, a ground and pillar of the faith, but these people of vision also created a structure that is still considered to be one of the finest historical and patriotic shrines in all America. The steeple rises 217 feet from the pavement and is a Peter Banner adaptation of the Christopher Wren spire. From that moment of dedication to this very hour, the spire has constantly and consistently pointed men to the heavens where they will find the Creator and Sustainer of the universe who giveth light to all men in Jesus Christ. Today this spire further testifies to God; each night it is illuminated with such light that people miles away from it can the stately arm pointing heavenward, proclaiming that here is a place where Christ is magnified.

Ever since the erection of the Park Street edifice, one has been able to feel the pulse beat of American religious life in the pulse beat of this church. From its doors and out of its heart has come an endless succession of men and movements that have been a potent influence in the religious life of America.

In 1815 the American Education Society was formed at Park Street. The same year saw the founding of the Handel and

In 1824 the Prison Discipline Society was formed; in 1826 the *Puritan Recorder,* one of the first religious newspapers, was begun by Nathaniel Willis of the church. In 1817 one of the first Sunday schools in the nation began within the sacred confines of this progressive organization.

These early forward movements in turn brought immense spiritual blessing to the church. In 1817 this blessing was widely manifested when a monthly concert of prayer began. Out of this concert of prayer came the first missionary revival in the history of the fellowship. Springing forth from the overwhelming power of God's Holy Spirit, missonary-inspired people formed the Near East Mission and in October, 1819, established the Sandwich Islands Church, which was the foundation of the flourishing Hawaiian Islands churches of today.

In 1824 the Prison Discipline Society was formed; in 1826 the American Temperance Society came into being; in 1829 William Lloyd Garrison gave his first public address against slavery in Boston in the Park Street Church, with John Greenleaf Whittier, the American poet, in the audience. In 1821 Mr. Ray Palmer came into the fellowship of the church and later was called of God into the ministry as a consequence of his attendance on the divine services. Palmer wrote "My Faith Looks Up to Thee" and other hymns.

On July 4, 1832, in celebration of the American Revolution, "My Country 'Tis of Thee" was first sung by the Sunday school in Park Street Church—first played by the famed organist of the church, Lowell Mason, whose imprint on American hymnody can never be erased from the pages of American musical life. From this experience came the designation of the church as "The Home of America."

Charles Sumner, who was later caned and so badly injured that he never recovered when Preston Brooks attacked him in thte Senate chamber of the United States, delivered his tremendous address, "The War System of the Nations" before the second annual convention of the American Peace Society in the church. In 1859 the church was remodeled and the roof raised. Until 1889 the fortunes of the church waxed stronger and stronger, before a period of real testing came.

From the years of its founding until the year 1889, the church enjoyed one spiritual awakening after another. Revival on revival came to quicken the life of the people and aid the forward movement of the work. In 1823, 1826, 1831, 1857, and 1858 there were Spirit-led revivals. A highly important one came under the dynamic and soul-searching preaching of Charles G. Finney. And in 1876 Moody and Sankey came to the church with similar results.

From 1809 to 1889 the Park Street Church was well situated with respect to the residential life of the city. But from 1889 to 1902 changes took place in the residential life of the community. This portion of Boston was rapidly commercialized and people began taking up their residences in the suburbs of Boston. This change in the residential area brought low the fortunes of the church. Many of the members moved into adjoining areas and took up their work in other churches. Families with children moved away from the congestion and the Sunday school suffered.

So low did the tide run that in December of 1902 it seemed the church must close its doors and sell out to commercial interests. The Park Street Associates Trust, a syndicate, wanted to purchase the site for a million and quarter dollars. Public concern was manifested and appeals were directed to the State to prevent the sale. The enterprise was abandoned and the church was saved for the moment.

In 1905 Dr. A. Z. Conrad came as pastor and in his lengthy ministry of thirty-one years the church was revived and its ministry changed to meet the changing conditions. During this period it became a metropolitan and New England institution.

Throughout the period preceding the coming of Dr. Conrad, the church was blessed with a succession of noteworthy ministers. In the first half century of its life, there were six, and among them is the name of Edward Beecher. A brother of the noted Henry Ward Beecher, Edward was a powerful preacher, a man of God in his own right.

The membership of the church for the first fifty-year period up to 1859 clearly reveals the manifest blessing of God on the work. During this time almost two thousand members were received into the fellowship, and when time came for the semi-centennial celebration the membership stood at eight hundred and forty-seven. Curiously enough, and yet consistent with the same situation among the churches today, there were two women members to every male communicant.

At the time of the semi-centennial, Dr. A. L. Stone pastored the flock, and he remained in that capacity until 1866. This included the Civil War period during which eighty men from Park Street volunteered for the armed forces, including the pastor who became a chaplain. Following his ministry, five more of the Lord's servants ministered to the congregation before Dr. Conrad assumed the pastorate.

By November, 1905, when Arcturus Zodiac Conrad became minister, the situation had deteriorated seriously. Under his leadership things improved and again the Spirit of the living God came in mighty power. Revival broke out in 1906 within a year of his arrival and again in 1909 and 1920. In the first year of Dr. Conrad's pastorate the financial problems of the church resulted in certain internal changes. The basement was remodeled for commercial purposes and the entire church was redecorated. The commercial portion was to bring in considerable money over the years and partially solve the financial problem. In 1923 the services of the church were broadcast over the radio and after the initiation, this project has been sustained continuously to this hour in an effort to reach people for Christ, who are not in the fellowship of the church and who would not otherwise be reached.

Once again the Spirit of God visited in revival power in 1928 under the leadership of Dr. Biederwolf. Then the depression of 1929 hit America, affecting the Park Street Church as it did other churches. This was accentuated, by the criticism, on the part of some, rising out of Dr. Conrad's second marriage, which intensified the problem.

When Dr. Conrad died there were fifteen hundred members, of which number many were not active. When the church began, Boston was a city of less than fifty thousand, but when Dr. Conrad passed on, it was the ninth largest city in America with a metropolitan area population of more than two million and a city population of three-fourth of a million.

In 1936 Boston was the community, and Park Street the church, which were to open their doors of opportunity to the young prophet from the Middle West. Prior to the decease of Dr. Conrad, and at his request, the pulpit committee began its investigation of candidates for the co-pastorate. Dr. Conrad was now permanently invalided.

On his vacation during the summer of 1936 Harold Ockenga again filled the Park Street pulpit for two Sundays. Nothing was said concerning the pastorate and he was not there as a candidate. He was only a summer supply.

From New England that summer Dr. Ockenga went on his own vacation and upon his return to Point Breeze in Pittsburgh in the middle of September he discovered that the Park Street pulpit committee had been trying in vain to reach him. When they did reach him they had only one question to ask him. In effect it was this: "Will you accept a call from the church if it is extended?"

God had been working in his heart, and he was not prepared to say "no" categorically. He informed the committee that he would seriously consider such a call if it were unanimous. With this partial promise, and with an indication of Dr. Ockenga's interest in the call, the committee went to the church. But the church was not approached in the congregational meeting with the name of Harold Ockenga alone. Other names were included in the balloting, and among them were well-known men of God.

When the votes were counted the finger of God seemed to point in the direction of Harold Ockenga. Despite the fact that there were other names in the balloting, the final vote stood clearly in favor of this young man, with only three votes in the meeting going to all the other candidates. This demonstrated a remarkable unanimity on the part of this people, and on the strength of the vote a definite call was extended to this man of the people's choice.

When the call came to the minister of the Point Breeze Church only one question stood out. "Is it the will of God for my life? Is this the place God wants me to be?" Dr. Ockenga fervently prayed to God for guidance, and took occasion to counsel with Dr. Clarence Edward Macartney, who had been like a father to him in the ministry. On the strength of this counsel and rising out of the Spirit's leading obtained on his knees in the closet, Harold John Ockenga prepared to make the change.

The Point Breeze Church, notified of the decision, retaliated with immediate reaction. Not desiring to lose the man who had been with them from 1931 to 1936, the congregation tried to persuade him to change his mind. But the die was cast and once the assent had gone through to the Park Street Church,

Harold John Ockenga remained irrevocably committed to the decision he believed to be of God.

On Sunday, October 18, 1936, the Point Breeze Church calendar said in part, "When we learned that Mr. Ockenga had received a call to a large and important church in Boston, we at once envisioned the loss that in all probability it meant to us. Life is progress, and progress must be upward. The larger the field, the greater the opportunities to do good and serve the Master. Men who are capable of filling the large places in the scheme of things are not numerous, and we believe Mr. Ockenga to be one of these. Knowing these facts, we believe we anticipated his acceptance of the call before he himself decided to accept it. Hence, while we deeply regret his going and keenly feel our loss, there is not so much of the element of disappointment in the sense of meeting the unexpected as of sadness at facing what we feared would come sooner or later."

So Boston, the city of class distinction and of culture, was to be his citadel; and the pulpit of Park Street, that venerable and historic church, the place from which his voice would ring in clarion call to America and in other ways unto the uttermost parts of the earth.

Thus it was that in the thirty-first year of his life, Harold Ockenga and his wife began their journey to Boston and New England. His hopes were high as he went. The field itself presented a tremendous challenge; the Park Street pulpit was nationally known for its Puritan theology, its local autonomy, its excellent witness for Christ. To a young man God had opened a wide door for service.

Actually the wideness of the door that God opened was still hidden from view. Had Dr. Ockenga known at the time what the future had in store for him; had he known the heartaches that were to be his, the virulent and undercover attacks that would be made against his character; had he known that God would call him to labor in the national and international limelight under conditions demanding much grace and Christian character; had he known these and other things, perhaps he might have hesitated more than he did at this call.

But onward he went in the assurance that Abraham's God was his God, and that it is better to follow the call of God, whatever the cost, than to do anything else.

At the time the family moved into the Boston area no one dreamed how long this young man would remain. The years rushed by rapidly and with the passage of the years the roots set in a new soil lengthened. It was not going to be a ministry of a few years but a labor of many years, and the tiny shoot of a new ministry became in time a green bay tree under the branches of which many pilgrims found rest of soul and made their peace with God.

This ministry can be delineated by certain outstanding activities. Certain accomplishments characterize what God was calling this young man to do, with the aid of the people of the Park Street church. He did not remain here because no other doors of opportunity opened. From time to time open doors beckoned him, and over and over again the finger of a mighty God continued to point to the steeple of Park Street so that each door was shut by choice in the assurance that it was the will of God for him to stay in Boston.

Harold Ockenga had been at Park Street less than a year when the Westminster Presbyterian Church of Bloomfield, New Jersey, put out a "feeler" in his direction. Without the slightest hesitation, the door to this church was shut by the new Park Street pastor. Within that same year another opportunity came to him from Washington, D.C. The great New York Avenue Presbyterian Church in the nation's capital was pastorless. It was a church in which he had preached a half dozen times and which knew of him and of his ministry. It was also the church that later called Dr. Peter Marshall, recently deceased, who left a lasting impression on the Capital by his chaplain's prayers in the halls of our Congress.

One evening before prayer meeting, a long distance telephone call came through from Washington. The question was asked him whether he was interested in this pastorate and whether he would consider a possible call to this church. In that fall of 1937, having ministered less than a year to Park Street Church and with the knowledge that he had not had time to make his ministry count for Christ, he declined quickly without giving the matter a second thought. For him the will of God was Boston.

In 1940, after four solid years of work in Boston, the insistent call to leave came again. This time it was far-off Seattle. The First Presbyterian Church was seeking a pastor. Dr. Mark A. Matthews, under whose leadership a score of other churches were founded in the Seattle area, had gone to his reward. Dr. Matthews had been a leading conservative with strong premillennial convictions, and the church sought for a man of like stamp to replace him. At the time, the church was the largest in the U. S. A. Presbyterian denomination and operated more than twenty branch churches.

On November 19, 1940, James H. Berge, M.D., wrote Dr. Ockenga, asking him to visit Seattle. The purpose of the visit was to give the church an opportunity to look over Ockenga and for him to look them over. No commitments were made. It was purely an exploratory move.

Of interest and significance is a letter which Harold Ockenga received from Dr. Stewart P. MacLennan just before the Seattle communication from Dr. Berge. Dr. MacLennan resigned the pastorate of the First Presbyterian Church of Hollywood, California, to become vice-president of Cathedral Pictures. His former church was also looking for a pastor. In his letter to Ockenga he stated that he knew of no other man in America that he would prefer to see pastor the First Church of Hollywood. He said that he had recommended Ockenga's name to the church and that his own letter was not official but simply one of inquiry since one member of the pastoral committee asked him to sound out Ockenga regarding his interest in the pulpit.

When Ockenga got this letter, the Seattle church was expecting Dr. Louis Evans to give them an affirmative answer to their call extended to him to become their pastor. Meanwhile, the elder Dr. Evans supplied the Hollywood church and recommended his son as a possible pastor. When Louis Evans found the Hollywood door opening he declined the Seattle offer and eventually went to Hollywood.

Before looking to Harold Ockenga, Seattle checked over the credentials of Peter Marshall who had been trained in a Southern Presbyterian seminary and was rising rapidly to a place of note among the Presbyterians of both North and South. Dr. Marshall was a post-millennialist and this eschatological view predisposed the Seattle church against him because Dr. Matthews had carefully and fully expounded and convinced his people on the pre-millennial viewpoint.

The Park Street Church granted permission to their pastor to make the trip to Seattle. The time schedule was arranged to permit him to minister to the Seattle church the last Sunday in December and the first Sunday in January. At the time Harold Ockenga wired his acceptance of the invitation to visit with the people of this church, he knew the pitfalls that awaited him. Dr. Matthews pastored this church from 1902 to 1940. For thirty-eight years he ruled the church and the whole Northwest so far as Presbyterianism operated in that region. But Ockenga did not fear to make the visit, his name having been highly recommended to the church by Dr. Will Houghton of the Moody Bible Institute and Dr. Clarence Edward Macartney of the First Presbyterian Church of Pittsburgh.

In writing to Dr. Ockenga, Will Houghton revealed a belief that the far west was the frontier of America where a young man could do mighty things. He said that to him New England had its future behind it. "It is living in the memory of other days." The intimation was clear. He thought Ockenga would do well to go west. But he could not know the impact that Ockenga yet was to make on New England nor could he suspect to what heights God was going to lift the Park Street Church in missionary interest and giving.

The First Presbyterian Church of Seattle heard Ockenga for two Sundays. What he said and how he acted pleased them. They were thrilled by his scholarly messages and overjoyed that a comparatively young man appeared to have the abilities required for the handling of this large organization.

During the visit one incident marred an otherwise perfect stay. Certain members of the Seattle Presbytery came to the chairman of the committee and to other members of the church accusing Dr. Ockenga of things they felt would disqualify him for that pulpit. They charged that he did not co-operate with the denomination because he did not support the mission board and the seminaries. This blow came despite the easily demonstrable fact that five of his men were studying at Princeton and that whenever he served in Presbyterian churches the benevolent monies went to the support of the denominational work.

The leadership of the First Church was concerned about the charge and wanted to keep everything open and aboveboard. Its committee, composed of strong Presbyterian men of charity and insight, agreed that Dr. Ockenga should meet with them at the Rainier Club. The three accusers received invitations also to attend.

When the meeting convened Dr. Berge reminded the three gentlemen from the Seattle Presbytery that they had talked behind the back of Harold Ockenga and he invited them now to have their say publicly before him so that their charges could be heard openly and either refuted or admitted.

In this public meeting the three accusers had nothing to say, so Dr. Berge summarized the charges and gave the accused an opportunity to reply. Dr. Ockenga responded with the evidence that quickly refuted the fallacious mis-statements of fact, to the general satisfaction of the committee members from the First Presbyterian Church. Then it was that he faced his accusers and demanded of them where they obtained the information. In reply the evasive answer was, "It came from the East." It was hearsay spread by malicious defamers and repeated by uninformed men who never bothered to check the rumors.

On January 7 a telegram was dispatched to Harold Ockenga. It read as follows: "Just finished session meeting in which you were considered as pastor. Am pleased to inform you that all in attendance voted in your favor." And it was signed by Hugh Armstrong, the moderator.

Seventy members of the session out of a total membership of one hundred and one attended the meeting and voted for Ockenga as pastor. Further correspondence indicated to Dr. Ockenga that one member of the session reminded his brethren that on previous occasions they had voted "Yes" for candidates but had done so with their tongues in their cheeks. He stated that no man ought to vote for Ockenga unless he cordially assented to his coming without mental reservation. And on that basis the vote was unanimous. On January 24 Dr. Berge telegraphed Ockenga. "Macartney is right. You are the man we have chosen."

In his conversations with the leadership of the church Dr. Ockenga gave them assurances that he would not let his name come before the congregation unless he would accept the call. Previously Louis Evans had indicated to them that he would be inclined favorably to a call if it came. On the strength of this a congregational meeting was called and after the affirmative vote was made known to Louis Evans he declined the offer of the pastorate. Between the initial phases and the time of the final call, the Hollywood situation opened to Louis Evans and he preferred going there to Seattle. A little sensitive to the declination of Louis Evans, the Seattle church did not want a repetition of this by Dr. Ockenga. Upon leaving the far west Harold Ockenga gave the committee his word that in three weeks time they could expect an answer from him—one way or the other.

Humanly speaking, the Seattle offer was the biggest opportunity Harold Ockenga ever expected to have. On January 6 the offer of the church was concretely put on paper. His beginning salary in 1940 was to be $8500.00 a year with annual increases of $700 until his salary reached $12,000. They offered him ten week's vacation, his moving expenses, and agreed to renovate the church and do other repair work up to $30,000. The church was the largest in the United States in the Presbyterian denomination. It looked like a unique and unparalleled opportunity.

During the three weeks that Harold Ockenga pondered the invitation he received scores of letters and telegrams from Seattle. All of them were cordial. All of them expressed the hope that he would come. Individuals, organizations and families sent him enthusiastic endorsements.

In correspondence with his friend Dr. Macartney, he received advice to the effect that he should rule out the emotional element. With remarkable farsightedness Dr. Macartney told him that either in Boston or in Seattle he would have splendid opportunities.

Financial considerations appealed to a man with a family and heavy commitments—but the Shekinah of God seemed to hover over New England. Much prayer was made to God for guidance; every angle of the matter was turned over in heart and mind.

At the end of three weeks God had given no positive evidence that it was His will to make the change. Ockenga had no peace in his heart leading him to say "Yes" to the call.

So on January 25, 1941, he dispatched a telegram declining the Seattle church. He did it regretfully but for lack of divine guidance and in answer to his promise to let them know in three weeks' time.

The receipt of the declination of January 25 did not conclude the matter. The committee was not satisfied that he had shut the door completely. Back they came a second time. On February 5 he received a telegram which read: "Session met last evening. Our people hopeful. Having faith you're coming." On February 6 he got a wire: "Officers and congregation are anxious to call you. I am sure there will be no trouble with committee of Presbytery. Great need here for strong, fearless leadership. Congregation wants and expects it. We are praying that Seattle may be your Macedonia." On February 14 came still another wire: "Presbytery favorable. Answer at once. Can call Congregational meeting Sunday."

When young Ockenga, for he was only thirty-five then, received a second insistent appeal, another period of indecision followed. So far had matters now come and so great was his own indecision that a meeting of the congregation was called in the Seattle church. According to the requirements of the church constitution notice had to be given for two successive Sundays prior to the meeting itself. The meeting was called for the 27th of February to act on sending a formal call to the Park Street Prophet from the whole congregation.

The pressure was so heavy on him and the insistence so terrific that at times it appeared to Ockenga that Seattle must be the Macedonian call for him. The Park Street Church had from the first assumed that they were going to lose their pastor and did not lift a finger to stop him from going. Acquainted as they were with the desires of the Seattle church, to them it was a foregone conclusion that their leader would go. The position was so excellent, and the Boston church so much less significant at that time by comparison, that for their pastor to remain seemed impossible. They promised him no increase in salary and no incentives were put before him to keep him from leaving.

On the 23rd of February, four days before the meeting of the congregation and in time to notify the people on Sunday, Ockenga wired Seattle: "Please cancel call for congregational meeting at your evening service. I permitted the call to be issued with the privilege of remanding it." Harold Ockenga could not bring himself to the point, in honesty to them and to God, to allow a congregational call to be sent him; for he had promised that if he permitted this call he would be committed to go. This he now knew he could not do although human considerations strongly pointed to the wisdom of accepting. But this was not the wisdom of God with reference to His will for His servant's life.

This telegram closed the affair. It was never reactivated. By some he was accused of inability to make up his mind. Others wished for a reconsideration. Many were keenly disappointed but took it as the will of God. When his decision came through to retain his pastorate at Park Street, the people rejoiced. A testimonial dinner at the Parker House was tendered their pastor. But for better than two years he got no raise in salary. It could not be said that offers and counter offers and proposals of a human kind kept him in Boston.

The Seattle affair proved a deep spiritual experience for Harold Ockenga. The question that stood out prominently was basic to that and all other decisions: "Shall I drop what I am presently doing every time a better position is offered me in terms of money, and prestige?" To him the answer came clearly, "No."

When he examined his heart to explain the reasons for the negative decision, three major considerations produced the final answer. First, he had no specific leading that he *ought* to go. This absence of *oughtness* made him sure that God, who grants peace of heart to His children, did not wish for him to go. Secondly, the Park Street Church had launched out upon a missionary program of advancement which he did not feel could be interrupted by his departure before it had been carried through.

And finally, in his heart the Holy Spirit whispered: "In your case, my child, it is the Christian thing to do—to deny ambition and keep what seems to be a lesser position for the glory of God."

One unexpected but welcome spiritual result accrued to the pastor out of his decision. The president of the Board of Trustees said to him in effect: "Now what you say will mean more." And from that moment onward it did, because his action and faith were interpreted in terms of his personal sacrifice and refusal of (in human terms) a bigger position.

A curious twist developed from another quarter over the Seattle call. At different times men within the Presbyterian church have made light of the circumstances as though they would lead people to believe that Harold Ockenga was not considered for the church and that no *bona fide* offer of any type came from Seattle. The facts of the case prove otherwise.

Since 1940 other approaches have been made to him. One came from Chicago—again a leading Presbyterian church. Several times outstanding United Presbyterian churches have looked in his direction. On at least two occasions inquiries were made as to his availability for college presidencies. In each and every case he gave no serious thought to making a move. He has become firmly wedded to this beloved New England people and church, but remaining is not an indication of a refusal to go. Always the desire of his heart is to do the will of God and as soon as the Holy Spirit speaks, a response will be forthcoming. For he walks life's pathway acknowledging that this is a pilgrim journey and we are not our own, for we have been bought with a price.

Calls to other places did not disrupt the work of Harold Ockenga at the home base. Indeed, the fourteen years have been productive and fertile. Much effort has been expended and much has been accomplished. The cause of Christ has gone forward and with this unfolds the story of the accomplishments and activities of the years at the home base among this sturdy people of New England.

Chapter

> Work, for the night is coming:
> Work through the sunny noon;
> Fill brightest hours with labor,
> Rest comes sure and soon;
> Give every flying minute
> Something to keep in store;
> Work, for the night is coming:
> When man works no more.
> — *Anna L. Coghill.*
> *Music by Lowell Mason, Organist*
> *of the Park Street Church.*

"They that sow in tears shall reap in joy. He that goeth forth and weepeth, bearing precious seed, shall doubtless come again with rejoicing, bringing his sheaves with him."
— *Psalm* 126: 5-6

Five

AS A MAN SOWS

THE PARK STREET Church membership numbered around fifteen hundred in 1936. Of this number, a portion represented "dead wood." Some of the names included people who had not been at the services of the church for a long time. Some had disappeared so that no one knew where or how to reach them. Some were among those who had become unfriendly to the former pastor. Rather than officially withdraw from the church, they attended other churches but retained membership connections at Park Street.

The new pastor faced the problem of the membership with deep insight into the thought patterns of the people. He realized that those who had left because they were lost in the shuffle of humanity had to be dropped from the rolls. But those who were delinquent in the sense that they were not attending, although still in the Boston area, he would try to win back. The church did not drop their names from the rolls, and over the years many of them returned without their connections being broken and were restored to the church of their earlier days. To this day the church roll still contains names of people who were alienated before the arrival of the new pastor but whom he yet hopes to bring back to the fold, inasmuch as they have not requested letters of dismission nor have they joined the fellowship of some other church.

The sifting process took time and prayer, but it paid dividends in the long run. The pastor began a long-range effort to bring new people into the membership. A downtown church where people must travel to the city from the suburbs demands a different type of ministry. Such a ministry adapted to these peculiar needs is not as productive of visible results numerically as work in a residential area where the people live in the neighborhood of the church itself. These obstacles, however, did not prevent growth in the church, and over the years a rich harvest was reaped with an increased membership.

Thus after fourteen years the Park Street Church has a membership of more than twenty-three hundred people few of whom are inactive.

A survey of the activities of Harold Ockenga as the minister of this church shows the manifold areas in which he has worked and in which God has given him special gifts. The explanation for the healthy spiritual growth and present condition of the church can be traced to the emphasis on these areas of activitiy.

<u>The first and foremost reason for the growth of the church is the preaching or pulpit ministry.</u> Located in downtown Boston, a metropolitan church does not have the same kind of pastoral ministry that a suburban church has. The membership is scattered widely over a geographical area that spreads for miles on all sides of Boston. <u>The decentralization of membership makes pastoral work a virtual impossibility except for sick calls, funerals, and a visit to the members in general on rare occasions. The assistant pastors can average thirty calls a week so that over a period of a year the congregation can be covered.</u> But the pastor himself must guard his time and limit his own calling to the most pressing ones. Immediately this makes the pulpit ministry of supreme importance to the church. Any impact and lasting influence must come from this portion of the ministry and it must weld the people together, build them up in the holy faith, result in conversion of sinners, and forward the work of Christ in general.

It is no exaggeration to say that Pastor Ockenga is strongest in the pulpit, although he is strong in most other aspects as well. The pulpit is his home; he was born to preach, called to preach, and loves to preach. Undoubtedly there is nothing he would rather do than preach the gospel. This great love of preaching explains in part his success as a preacher. But here, as always, he gives God the glory and acknowledges that if there be any treasure in him it is in an earthen vessel that the excellency may be of God and not of men.

Nationally known as a strong preacher of the Word, many people believe that sermonizing comes easily to this gifted man. This is not true. Every sermon that he preaches is born out of prayer, sweat and tears. He works just as hard to create a sermon today as he did fifteen years ago. The same basic work must be done, the same type of hard labor in the study cannot be avoided.

When the words do come they are the product of extensive and intensive preparatory work and do not rise out of any extraordinary gift or facility of being able to pound out messages mechanically. One look at his library will prove this to be true. His collection of books constitutes the tools by which sermons are written. They do not lie dormant, gathering dust on the shelves, but are read, scanned, browsed, digested or discarded as the need may be.

Preparation for the pulpit is not merely mechanical. A minister of the gospel cannot read books and fashion sermons from the reading of books. The God-blessed servant must be a man of "the Book." Essentially, Ockenga is a man of the Book. Even then, being a man of the Book and delving into all of the helps of the ages do not make it possible to create sermons. Divine help is a requisite and to the Lord constantly goes the cry for help that the structure of the message may be divinely given.

Before one word of the message is written there must first be the structure or outline. Rigidly logical in his own thinking, every sermon bears the marks of this logic. Point follows point. There is the gradual erection of a structure leading to an ultimate conclusion that is irresistible. Thus if a man will grant the premises on which each message is built, the listener must also accept the conclusion.

None of his messages is light and frothy. Each is solid and Biblical. Each centers in the Holy Word of God. He has little time for humor, and illustrations are put into the message to illustrate, not to tickle the fancy of the hearers, nor are they there to humor the congregation. Preaching, to him, is serious business and he is deadly in earnest when he walks into the sacred precincts of that pulpit. He is a dying man speaking to dying men.

<u>Expository preaching is the key to a successful pulpit</u> ministry. This is the belief held by the Park Street prophet. <u>Consequently, the Sunday morning services include exposition of the Word.</u> The injunction of the Apostle Paul is his key to sound preaching: "Preach the Word." Thus the expounding of the word of God without the introduction of extraneous elements comprises his major concept of good preaching. The chief motive of this preaching is to convince men and women of the truth he expounds. He aims to convince and then to obtain action based on conviction.

Some people have stated that the preaching of Harold Ockenga is intellectual. They argue that he appeals to the intelligentsia and does not reach the common people. True, he does not speak in the language of the street. In his own pulpit his people have been educated to his type of preaching and all classes gladly hear the words that flow from his consecrated lips. In all of the messages he preserves an amazing simplicity in which theological concepts and ideas that have never been fully plumbed are made clear and plain to all who hear. At times he does use words foreign to the vocabulary of the average Christian but usually with an explanatory note so that the hearer need not lose the trend of the message.

Of incalculable help to the hearer is the clear-cut outline of the message so presented that the major points of emphasis can be absorbed and digested. Preachers often seem to have no beginning and no ending. Not so with this man. He can be followed in his preaching and he delineates his points so forcefully and clearly that the simplest can understand.

In a sense Harold Ockenga is a preacher's preacher. He is a gifted speaker for college forums, commencements and formal academic occasions. When called upon to deliver an address that is not an exposition of the Scriptures themselves, the same gifts which help in the preparation of sermons guarantee the production of a stimulating and effective address for special occasions.

Perhaps the impression is generated that this man is not an evangelistic preacher. He does not rant or rave; he does not tell one emotional sob-story after another of bedside agonies; he does not wave his arms wildly or step from behind the pulpit. He is not evangelistic in the sense of appealing strictly to the emotions, but is evangelistic in making a straight appeal to the intelligence and the will. He has demonstrated this in Boston and in the many special evangelistic campaigns in which he has preached.

Some seven years ago, the Lord laid a burden on his heart to reach the masses in Boston with the gospel story. The Boston Common adjoins the church and on a summer Sunday evening thousands of people gather there on the spacious lawns. When he asked for a permit to preach the gospel on the Common, however, the request was denied.

Of course, a man can bring a soapbox and an American flag and speak without a license on communism or any other ism, but one cannot preach the gospel without a permit. Believing that God had called him to engage in this evangelistic activity on the Common, he used an oak table and went out to preach without a permit. The authorities did not dare molest him or stop his activity. It was not that he wished to disregard law and order, but requests were made again and again for a permit which was granted only after activity without one.

For two years, during the summer months, he preached from the Parkman Band Stand on the Common *after* the usual evening service. He and those who wished to do so began this second evening service with the desire to take advantage of every opportunity and to present to the masses the gospel of redeeming love.

The meetings grew, until clerical pressure was put on the authorities. After two years the permit was cancelled and again he faced what seemed to be a closed door.

Not to be outdone by this wily device to prevent the preaching of the gospel, he spoke from the steps of the church for another year. Then it was that he made a public announcement that before the following spring (1946) when the summer services would normally begin, he wanted an outdoor pulpit as a part of the church itself. This was the same year that the one-hundred-and-fifty-thousand-dollar church restoration program was completed.

God answered prayer about an outdoor pulpit and honored faith. A Roman Catholic who accepted Christ under Ockenga's ministry during Holy Week services owned the Mayflower Hotels on the Cape. He made the church a gift of sufficient funds to erect this balcony pulpit facing Tremont Street above the entrance to the sanctuary. Since 1946, from the end of May until cold weather sets in, this open air pulpit sounds forth the good news that Christ died for our sins.

Originally, the vision was to reach soldiers and sailors who flocked to the Common while in the armed forces of the United States. Now it continues to reach civilians. On other occasions this Mayflower pulpit, having historic connotations of liberty and freedom, is used for noonday Holy Week services and for services during the annual missionary conference, of which more will be said later.

This open-air ministry has been marked with results. Multitudes have heard the gospel and have been saved. Some of the conversions and contacts have been remarkable. One time a man came in to see the pastor after hearing him preach on justification by faith.

"Do you believe what you preached tonight?" he asked bluntly.

"Yes, indeed I do," responded the pastor.

Almost incredulously, he asked him again, "Do you believe that God can take the worst men and justify them in Christ?"

"I believe this and know that it is true," answered the faithful preacher.

"But I have ruined the lives of two women."

"It makes no difference. God can justify the most wicked and he will justify you by faith in His blood."

So with careful dealing and faithful explanation of Holy Scriptures, the man came to a saving knowledge of the Lord Jesus Christ because someone had vision and preached to him on the Boston Common.

A young man chanced to walk by the Common one night and heard the message of life. He had fallen into deep sin, had sold himself in bondage to the sins of the flesh. But the Word of God cut across that life and seared conscience dulled by habitual sin. In his soul came a yearning for the things of the eternal God, and this yearning led to conversation with the preacher.

The upshot of the conversation was the birth of another child into the kingdom of God—another soul was won for eternity. His life was cleaned up following conversion and the young man married a splendid American girl, established a Christian home and is a solid, respectable citizen in his community—because someone was courageous enough to preach the gospel on the Boston Common.

In his own fashion and according to the methods which suit his own gifts and powers Harold Ockenga is an evangelist. Time and time again he has gone on preaching missions, some of which have been city-wide campaigns for reaching the masses with the Word of God. And in his pulpit, week by week, there is the passion of an evangelist in fulfillment of the Pauline command to young Timothy, "Do the work of an evangelist."

The preaching of Dr. Ockenga appealed to members of Park Street Church, but New Englanders are less emotional and certainly more staid than in other areas of America. They must be convinced before they will take action. After his refusal to go to Seattle his preaching meant more to the people than ever before. They knew that it was a living reality to him with no sham and no seeking for the betterment of self materially. Thus it was that within a short period after the Seattle incident, the members rallied round an effort dear to the heart of their pastor from the day he first entered the church. In those desperate days of financial testing when this part of Boston changed from a residential to a commercial area, the church lost ground. Under the leadership of the previous pastor the church premises were renovated and the basement leased out to commercial interests. This was not uncommon, for the magnificent Tremont Temple also had an office building connected with the house of worship.

Never satisfied with having the commercial rental arrangement, however, the young pastor anxiously hoped that it would be terminated. But the income was large enough to arouse severe doubts in the minds and hearts of some folk in the church. The income varied but at least once was as high as twenty-four thousand dollars a year. To cut off such a substantial income was a test of faith.

Ockenga led in a glorious movement to rid the basement of the commercial stores and restore the whole building to its original church use. The church voted to eliminate the stores, and to raise one hundred and fifty thousand dollars as a restoration fund and to go forward in faith.

By 1946 the victory was won. The stores were gone, the restoration of the church building completed. A chapel, offices, assembly hall and a smaller memorial chapel were installed in the basement, a glorious triumph cheering the hearts of the pastor and his people. The loss of income did not curtail the work of the church. Instead, the blessing of God rested on it as never before and it went forward to higher goals.

The printed sermon benefitted Park Street, too. Sensing the need for good literature and realizing that the printed sermon is a potential soul-saver, it became customary to have many of the messages printed for distribution.

Radio, as a medium for spreading the gospel, has been tied into the preaching program and the publication of literature at Park Street. It began in Dr. Conrad's day. It continued into the pastorate of Harold Ockenga and has been expanded and multiplied as the increase in technical knowledge perfected the medium. For more than a quarter of a century the people of New England, and more recently sections of Canada, have been able to hear the Word of God *via* Park Street, Boston.

The extent of the radio ministry depended in part on the amount of money available for it. Over the years it ranged from a low of twenty-four hundred dollars to over fourteen thousand dollars for 1950. In this field, as in all fields, progress has been made and God has blessed the work.

Both morning and evening services are broadcast, each service going out over a station of 50,000 watts. This insures a wide coverage of the New England area and gives the church the finest radio outreach that is available for its purposes.

The radio ministry has not been carried on without problems. On at least one occasion competitors for the hour have offered larger sums of money and inducements to secure this strategic spot on the ether waves. How the Lord answered prayer in the case of one of the stations whose sales manager is Jewish is indeed indicative of God's blessing. He not only refused better offers for the time, but confessed to the pastor that he himself listens to and enjoys the broadcast.

The radio ministry stands on its own feet. It is not included in the regular church budget nor are funds withdrawn from the general church income to make this ministry possible.

It must pay for itself and is carried on as people make it possible. Dr. Ockenga does not wish to dun the radio listeners for money Sunday by Sunday. So he uses a unique plan to make it possible for people to hear the gospel.

He sets aside two Sundays a year to mention the radio work and ask that it be underwritten for the following year. In these two Sundays the needs are underwritten, so that it is not necessary to mention money again for the remainder of the year.

Some unsolicited gifts come in for the radio program but the bulk of the program is paid for by pledges. Here is one case example: One morning an elderly woman came in to pay her radio pledge. She had lived in the Boston area for fifty years and was not a member of the Park Street Church but of another fellowship elsewhere. She said that she believed in the old-fashioned gospel Dr. Ockenga preached and that the old-fashioned gospel included conversion, of which he had much to say.

"He gives me food for the whole week," she said with zest.

Her appraisal of the preacher was undoubtedly the expression of many others. "It is easy to tell when a man is consecrated. I go where I get the most good spiritually."

Dr. Ockenga himself believes without a shadow of doubt that the radio multiplies his pulpit ministry a hundred fold. The response has been wonderful, many souls being won for Jesus Christ over the twenty-six years, and in recent months numbers have knelt beside their radios in tears, confessing Christ. Of these a goodly portion have found their way into the church itself—there to make public confession in accordance with the divine standard, "that if thou shalt confess with thy mouth . . . thou shalt be saved."

Thus has God been faithful in giving fruit springing out of the preaching of the Word of God. And so it is that Sunday after Sunday—morning and evening—the aisles as well as the pews are filled with those who come to hear. They do come to hear Harold John Ockenga; but they know and he knows beyond question that they come to hear him open the Scriptures and preach the Word. Were he to cease opening that Book or refrain from preaching that Word the Spirit of the Lord would depart and the crowds melt away. Whatever success may attend the preaching, that success comes because it is the preaching of the Word of God!

Harold Ockenga's writing ministry cannot be separated from his preaching, because his writing is an integral part of it. A minister who is busy in the pastorate cannot find time to write unless he has an adequately trained staff of assistants in the church to help him. This Dr. Ockenga does have. The spirit of the staff, their competence in the performance of their duties, and their willingness to co-operate and work together as a team has aided in the production of books as well as sermons.

During his present ministry in Boston, Harold Ockenga has published, in addition to his printed sermons and other materials such as articles and addresses, a total of nine books. This production of literary material is no mean accomplishment for a man constantly engaged in a multitude of other activities. The publications have been a part of his total outlook and persistent effort to reach people. In connection with his published volumes the idea is to reach the people of other areas who cannot be reached from his pulpit or by the air. Beyond these people are many ministers who are stimulated and helped by his books.

Consistent with the belief that straight expository preaching from the Bible is best, three volumes are devoted to this purpose. One covers expository studies in the book of Romans, (*Everyone That Believeth*), another in Ephesians, (*Faithful in Christ Jesus*), and still another in II Corinthians, (*The Comfort of God*). They have been well received by reviewers and in every case have been enthusiastically endorsed.

The volume on Romans will serve well to indicate the reception that this type of book received. The *Christian Observer* spoke of it as "analytical preaching at its best." The *Watchman-Examiner* says, "Here the author is at his best." The *Moody Monthly* stated in its review that "he has real skill in analysis and exposition; he combines clarity of expression and thought with orthodoxy of doctrine and spiritual warmth." The *King's Business* succinctly comments that "those who say that the days of powerful expository preaching are past should turn to this volume on Romans . . . "

In these chief expository works one finds again and again the logical clarity of the writer and sees clearly the points as they are made. The homiletical fashion of the author with his introduction and three points provides the skeletal structure on which each message rests. Always can the point of the message be discerned and the application stands out sharply. At no time were these messages written for the sake of the message but for moving the will to action in response to the presentation of eternal unchanging truth.

Another volume of published sermons deals with the Holy Spirit, (*The Spirit of the Living God*). It is a masterful series delineating the person and the work of the Holy Spirit. Filled with choice references to the Holy Spirit from the Old Testaments and unfolding to the believer the deep truths of the third person of the blessed Trinity this work fills a great need in the world of Christian literature. Ockenga himself has been impressed over the years with the truth that the doctrine of the Holy Spirit is the lost dynamic of the Christian church. He knows that the Spirit's power is the birthright, need, and responsibility of the believer. And a life without the power of the Spirit is fruitless and shallow.

Particularly delightful in this work on the Holy Spirit are the references made to the missionary task of the church of Christ. He endeavors to recover for the church the neglected truth that the Holy Spirit is the vice-gerent overseeing the Great Commission as elaborated by the Lord Jesus Christ.

Harold Ockenga's first work, in 1937 was *These Religious Affections*. In this series of sermons the author strikes with great force to support the sound Biblical view that religion is a matter of the heart, and not only the head. For twenty years after World War I the pulpits resounded with the intellectual approach, and forgot that the head also had a heart. In this volume is found the heart that is wicked, hardened, pricked, pure, burning, and believing. The author digs deeply into recesses unplumbed and finds for the reader gems of truth that sparkle the more because they have long been lost or discarded.

In *Our Protestant Heritage* Ockenga can be found dissenting from the moving tide of the day toward organic church union. Realizing fully the implications of this dangerous drift which ultimately looks for a single world-wide church, he demonstrates that the Scriptures do not espouse this cause. Inherent in the gospel is the plea for unity, but it is a spiritual unity, not an organic union of churches into one gigantic church. And the highest to which Harold Ockenga will rise in his thinking on church government is a creedal Presbyterianism.

In 1946 *Our Evangelical Faith* was published. This smaller book contained a series of messages built around the creedal statement of the National Association of Evangelicals. In it the cardinal doctrines of the evangelical faith are more fully explicated. Of this movement and the part played in its formation and development by Harold Ockenga we shall have occasion to say more in another part of this volume. Suffice it now to say that this series served to present to the world the meaning of the creedal statement of the National Association of Evangelicals and to present it to the Christian public from the pen and pulpit of this mighty man of God.

In the thinking of Dr. Ockenga he has never lost sight of the calling of the Old Testament prophets. Bearing in mind that his people do not live in a vacuum, he has preached in such a way as to make his preaching relevant to the times. He has spoken out on the great issues of the day and of his community. He has done this fearlessly and at a price.

In 1939, when war loomed, although the United States was not yet drawn into the vortex, he spoke out from his pulpit about America. In a printed book entitled <u>God Save America</u> he drew the attention of his people to the present crisis. He warned of judgment to come in recognizing that America had departed a long way from the faith of our fathers and our fathers' fathers. But with characteristic directness he did not preach pessimistically but realistically. He ended the series with a Biblical exposition on the way out. America must repent, was the burden of his heart!

So also has he spoken out fearlessly against civic corruption and public ills. The Roman Catholic Church, the strongest single force in Boston life, has been the subject of many addresses. He has had Roman priests in the audience taking notes on what has been preached from the pulpit. And the *Pilot,* a Roman Catholic organ, has tried to refute in print his case against the Roman church. With the thought in mind of his militant attitude toward a dominant segment of society, later charges made by the character assassins of Dr. Ockenga have been ludicrous.

After having been in audience with the Pope of Rome together with leading American religious leaders, it was charged by enemies that he had "betrayed" American evangelicalism by so doing. And when the criticism was being spread over America, a woman wrote him to inquire whether it was true that "he had bowed down and kissed the Pope's toe." This question was directed to one of the few leading American evangelicals who has continually stood up against Rome and who has dared to challenge them in their own precincts.

Thus he could preach and write about separation of church and state and place before the American public his own clear-cut analysis of what Cardinal Spellman wants in connection with education. To charge such an opponent of the Roman Catholic Church with knuckling down before the Pope or any other representative of the Roman Church is preposterous. He has courageously, fearlessly and faithfully borne unaltered witness to the evils of Roman Catholicism and to the danger it presents to the American way of life.

The reaction of the Park Street membership to this portion of their pastor's ministry—his preaching, which finds its further expression in radio and the printed page—is interesting. His preaching wears well. People like to listen to him and come back over and over again. His logical treatment of the theme, his original thinking and splendid vocabulary appear to them as points of strength. Many of them feel that his approach is essentially an appeal to the intelligence and will but that it remains warm and personal. It has a quality of aliveness that keeps the hearer wide-awake.

The general comment is that he loses himself in his preaching. And once he has begun, all else is forgotten; the things of the world are pushed into the background and the eternal truths which perish not grip heart and soul of the preacher. This results in an impact on the audience as they see Ockenga "lost to self" in the presentation of the message of God.

Another aspect of the ministry of Ockenga at Park Street has to do with his organizing ability. Naturally, a good organizer knows his limitations of time, and presence, and does not try to build an organization around himself. He has avoided this pitfall into which men sometimes fall when they make themselves indispensable. Accepting as the highest maxim of organizational precept the idea that one man can do so much, Ockenga has sought for men to supplement himself and to them has entrusted responsibility. This division of responsibility has not meant personal abdication from responsibility, for he knows well what is going on in every segment of that organization.

The Park Street Church has within its fold men and women of potential who respond nobly to the challenge to leadership, and in unity with the pastor move on to higher ground. This congregational response has been instrumental in securing a church that has a momentum of its own. In the absence of the pastor, which absence comes periodically because of his extensive commitments and outside engagements, the church moves on without lag. This ability to carry on without the personal presence of the pastor is a tribute to the minister and in the highest sense is also a tribute to the people who bulwark the work and aid in its forward movement.

The various committees meet regularly and the business moves along with dispatch. No meeting is purely mechanical. Each is preceded by intercession before the throne of God for insight into the problems and for strength to carry out decisions. The pastor himself has attributed much of the organizational success in the church to the "bent knee" before God, which has led to increase in wisdom and has imparted strength for the execution of difficult tasks.

In his administrative capacity Harold Ockenga is ever ready to see the other man's viewpoint. And with this readiness is an equal willingness to accept whatever is involved in changing his own views. Normally he wishes to express his own point of view and convince others of its correctness. But he is sufficiently skilled in human relations to know that coercion does not work; instead he plants ideas. If they take and are acceptable, then the appropriate action occurs.

Times of tension are relieved by humor—a smile, and a quick retort that breaks down reserve and softens dogmatism. At all times he is sincere, with poise and balance that inspire confidence. That confidence has a spiritual quality which he transmits to his people.

Conscious that people respond in kind, he treats them as he expects to be treated—courteously and with deference. Whenever it is necessary to make concrete suggestions for action he has something specific to offer. This rare quality of good leadership makes it possible for the man to stay ahead of his people and give them that kind of leadership which never goes bankrupt.

It is under such leadership that the church has gone forward numerically and financially as well as spiritually. In 1935 just before he assumed the pastorate the church budget for home expenses was not even eighteen thousand dollars. Continuously the income increased year by year until fourteen years later it passed the seventy-thousand-dollar mark. This increase in the amount of money contributed for church expenses is a fraction of the total picture. Along with this increase came the unprecedented increase in missionary giving. This phase of the work demands separate attention and will be dealt with in detail shortly.

The preaching ministry of Harold Ockenga has been supplemented by his teaching ministry. Most frequently his preaching ministry has been a teaching ministry as well. The Bible reveals that men must first be won to Christ and then built up in the holy faith. With the latter thought in mind, Dr. Ockenga is interested in educating Christians. Information that is true will counteract the false. To know what you believe means to hold firmly to those beliefs. Such a concept inevitably led in the direction of an evening Bible school for the city of Boston. Not limited in scope to the membership of the church, it could serve the whole community of Protestants or anyone else who wanted to come.

In the autumn of 1942 God led Howard Ferrin of the Providence Bible Institute and Harold Ockenga to consider prayerfully the matter of inaugurating an evening Bible school as a Christian training center in Boston. Requests for such a school were urgently advanced by laymen and Christian leaders. Laying the proposition before the Lord, an increasing burden for commencing this work came upon these men. Not wishing to operate a haphazard institution of dubious parentage, the experience of the Providence Bible Institute was called into play and a six-year, one-evening-a-week school went onto the planning board. The school was to operate over a period of twenty weeks.

The proposed curriculum was designed to provide a balanced program of study for those who could afford to spend one night a week over a period of six years. Included were courses covering the Pauline Epistles, the Synoptic Gospels, John, Apostolic history, Old and New Testament criticism, the Major and the Minor Prophets, and Archeology and the Bible. Along with these they anticipated offering practical courses in personal evangelism, Christian evidences, Bible memorization, teacher training and Sunday school problems.

In October, 1943, the first classes met. That first year four hundred and seventy-four students enrolled and others were turned away for lack of space. More than one hundred churches in and around Boston had representatives among the students and the initial year amply demonstrated the need which existed for such a school.

The institution operated under the auspices of the Park Street Church in co-operation with the Providence Bible Institute, the latter school offering credit which could be used for further training in that institution, leading to a degree or diploma from the day school.

Year after year the evening school of the Bible continued. Five hundred or more students each year came to study the Word. By the spring of 1949 the first six-year period of the school's life was finished. In the sixth year 563 students enrolled from 221 churches. Boston was getting a rich taste of what could be done when men willingly heeded the call of God, for the work was fruitful.

Beyond the areas of preaching, the radio work, writing, and the evening school of the Bible, Dr. Ockenga has further demonstrated his leadership. The story of evangelical co-operation unfolded in the history of the National Association of Evangelicals is worthy of separate treatment as well as his vision in theological education. But in and out of Boston, outside the major areas which we will consider later, he has made a contribution to American life.

In the civic life of the community Ockenga has played a part. The Roman Catholic Church has made substantial inroads in the affairs of the state and consistently Ockenga has opposed this progress and has encouraged the hands of interested Christians to keep fighting against the goals which the Roman Catholics have in mind. He has urged not only a negative battle to prevent them from gaining ground, but has also sparked efforts to retrieve lost ground and win back concessions which have been granted.

Christian institutions have been helped by his counsel and advice. He has served on numerous boards. Since 1936 he has been a trustee of Gordon College, an institution which has become the leading evangelical college in New England. For five years he was a trustee of Taylor University but had to retire from it because of his inability to carry the load from a distance, with other pressing demands on his time. At one time or another he has been a director of the Union Rescue Mission and of a Chinese mission in Boston. Since 1936 he has served on the board of the New England Evangelistic Association, which has done much to promote evangelism in that region. Also from 1936 he has been associated with the work of the New England Fellowship led by Dr. J. Elwin Wright. He has also helped to promote the Lord's Day League in Boston.

There are several general or non-Christian enterprises to which he has given his time and his help. One is Suffolk University, for which he has served on the Board of Trustees since 1939. On this board he has contact with many leading political and influential citizens in Boston. He is thus able to keep track of inside happenings in the city and brings a witness and a testimony to the members of the board. In 1939 he joined the Rotary Club in his city and has been a member ever since. At frequent intervals he has been invited to make speeches before it and other clubs and has served the civic interest of the city through these media.

Harold Ockenga has an active interest in communism. While pursuing post graduate work leading to the doctorate in philosophy he did research work on it. He kept informed on this subject and has preached and published about it. His strictures against communism in messages all over the land have won him acclaim far and wide.

Intimately acquainted with the writings of Karl Marx and fully cognizant of the aims and aspirations of modern Soviet Russia, he has attempted to expose the basic contradictions of the system and to prove that it is anti-Biblical in all of its outlook. He is opposed to Russian communism in all of its forms and regards its inroads into American democratic life as a tragic consequence of the failure of Christians to be alert.

Convinced that eternal vigilance is the price of freedom, and knowing that Christianity would be a proscribed religion under communism, Ockenga is pledged to wage war against this evil as long as he has breath. In communism, together with Roman Catholicism and secularism, he is convinced that we have a triad of evil that bodes ill for the future of America unless we stand in the gap and prevent any of them from dominating American life.

Some of his convictions about Russian communism have not come from books alone. He was privileged to travel in Europe on numerous occasions. As early as 1933 he went on a preaching mission which carried him to the borders of Russia. With Moses Gitlin and William Fetler as translators he toured Poland, Latvia, Estonia, and Finland for a month holding services with these men as interpreters. On top of this he spent one month inside Russia although he was not permitted to preach while in that country. He had time to gain further insights into Russian life and communist ideology while on this trip.

Traveling inside Russia, Ockenga had difficulty with their police. Without a guide one day he went to worship in a local church in the land. Not having permission to do this, he was promptly arrested by the police and all of his film and his pictures confiscated. Escorted to prison he had the uncomfortable experience of hearing and seeing three prison doors close behind him. Momentarily he did not know if he would get out alive.

He envisioned what had happened to innumerable people who had disappeared in Russia behind prison bars. Fortunately his papers were checked and he was released, but the experience of what a prison is like was a reality and encouraged sympathy for those unfortunates caught in the Russian web but without the protection of the United States Government—people who were sent to Siberia or were slain remorselessly under the Soviet system of espionage.

In 1948 Ockenga was in Europe again for the sixth time. Youth for Christ, International, met at Beatenberg, Switzerland, that summer and Ockenga appeared on the program as one of the speakers. Ockenga has many friends among the leadership of this movement. As in Europe at Beatenberg, so in America at Winona Lake he has addressed International Youth for Christ meetings.

While in Europe for the Youth for Christ meetings at Beatenberg the Inter-Varsity Christian Fellowship conducted an international conference at Lausanne. Ockenga spoke at this conference also.

His attitude toward evangelistic work has been criticized occasionally. He has appeared on programs where modernists have spoken. For this he has suffered reproach by conservatives who think that this is either wrong or unwise. One time he was on a program for a week with E. Stanley Jones. One day he would precede Jones and the next day Jones would precede him.

In the fall of 1949 he conducted evangelistic services in Syracuse—a city-wide campaign involving many churches. The committee constructed a special tabernacle seating several thousand people especially for this series. Thousands of people attended and hundreds of conversions resulted. The committee extended the meetings for an additional week when the response appeared to warrant it.

Dr. Ockenga speaks plainly about his actions. He will preach the gospel of Christ any place he is permitted to do so. He believes that Christ came to call the sinners, not the righteous to repentance. And he believes the evangelistic opportunity is greater where he speaks in a liberal church than at a Youth for Christ meeting. In the latter case most of the audience will be Christian. In liberal churches they need to hear the gospel and the fish are there to be caught.

Up to this point no one has ever suggested that he tone down his message or that he not preach the blood atonement of Christ. If the modernists are without salvation as the fundamentalists understand it, then preachers should try to reach them with the true message. For Christ died to save the modernist as well as the bum on the Bowery, and the modernist needs to hear the message of the blood proclaimed, too.

Before God and the bar of his conscience Ockenga knows that he is justified in his efforts to reach liberals. He would rather stand approved before God than be overly concerned with what human critics think. Jesus was snubbed because he ate with publicans and fellowshipped with sinners at meat. If the Son of God did so and encourages us so to do, Ockenga feels he must heed His command, knowing that he need not compromise his convictions nor water his message.

Despite his being a conservative he does not lack for opportunities, as the summer of 1949 demonstrated. He went to a summer camp meeting among the Methodists. He preached as he always preaches and the hungry hearts of the people who came were filled. They had not tasted of the kind of food he gave for better than thirty years. With warmed souls they gloried in his message and joined in praise to God that He had sent a messenger to give them something after so long a period of drought. They obtained help because somebody cared.

Where fearful fundamentalists will not tread, this man will go with *the message*. And with the message he brings his Saviour, too! Let the chips fall where they may, he will obey the call of God to his soul regardless of what people may say.

This man's theology has undergone some changes in the past thirteen years. By this is not meant any switch from the cardinal doctrines of the Christian faith. He subscribes to the Apostles' Creed, the Westminster Standards, and the creedal statement of the National Association of Evangelicals. Born in a Methodist environment and trained in a collegiate institution of that persuasion one might expect him to be more Arminian in his theological emphasis.

He is a moderate Calvinist in the sense that he is not a monergist but a synergist. It appears to some that in his earlier ministry he believed in a double predestination and held to a strong view on election. Today he holds to a position which includes freedom of the human will to accept or reject the offer of salvation. His view on the perseverance of the saints remains unchanged. He has a strong belief in a critical experience for the Christian with reference to the work of the Holy Spirit. Realizing that theoretically a man should be surrendered to God fully from the moment of his salvation he knows experimentally that most Christians come into this position of surrendering their lives to God at a later date than when they first are saved. He holds that a critical experience is involved when a man says his great "Yes" to God. He does not hold this to be a second work of grace and differentiates it in terms of the logical and the chronological. This aspect of his theological thinking has been productive of fruit wherever he has preached on the Holy Spirit. He believes it to be a neglected emphasis on which more needs to be said than the average preacher says.

To some he seems more tender now than in the younger years. The Calvinism of the classroom probably has been molded to a degree by the experiences of the pastorate and by intimate contact with people. He does not have the problem that troubles some of the Calvinists of the higher type with respect to inviting the unsaved to find Christ. Gladly and freely he beseeches men everywhere to be reconciled to God with the assurance that if they will believe in their hearts and profess with their mouths they will be saved.

There is no bookish argumentation as to whether he can invite all or speak only to the elect. He speaks to all and beseeches all to come. And come they do. This theological mellowing, if we can properly define it as such, is the result of contact with people and with the practical.

The position to which Ockenga has come has brought with it academic recognition from educational institutions in America. He has been the recipient of degrees besides those for which he labored in residence in college, seminary and graduate school. He holds the doctorate in philosophy, and earned degree which entitles him to a place of recognition in the field of learning, and yet colleges and universities have conferred on him honorary degrees as well.

In 1937 his Alma Mater honored him with the D.D. degree. This came, no doubt, in connection with his rise to leadership at the Park Street Church. In 1939 this was followed by the conferring on him of the Doctor of Letters degree by Suffolk University in Boston, indicating that he had already made his mark in the New England area and was recognized for his outstanding gifts and accomplishments. In 1944 Bob Jones College conferred on him the degree Doctor of Humanities for his work done in the Christian world. And in 1949 Houghton College, of which Dr. Stephen Paine is the president, and who later became the president of the National Association of Evangelicals, conferred upon him his fourth honorary degree, Doctor of Laws.

He holds these academic distinctions lightly, perceiving that divine approbation, in the last analysis, is the mark and distinction that all the earned and honorary degrees in the world cannot replace.

Somehow the spiritual quality of a man is tested when the honors of the world are heaped upon him, and it is a dangerous period—for the man who can be led astray into thinking that there is something within himself intrinsically valuable and worthwhile. Harold Ockenga knows this and he carries these honors with humility and grace; for he has his eyes fixed on Jesus, the Saviour of men.

Chapter

> We grovel among trifles and our spirits fret and toss,
> While above us burns the vision of Christ upon the cross;
> And the blood of God is streaming
> from His broken hands and side,
> "As thou hast sent me into the world,
> even so have died."
> —*Unknown*

> "How then shall they call on him in whom
> they have not believed? and how shall they
> believe in him of whom they have not heard?
> and how shall they hear without a preacher? And
> how shall they preach, except they be sent?
> as it is written, How beautiful are the feet
> of them that preach the gospel of peace and
> bring glad tidings of good things!"
> *Romans* 10:14, 15

Six

Fields White Unto Harvest

HAROLD OCKENGA HOLDS deep and abiding convictions about how to develop a successful church on a Biblical basis. He is convinced that a spiritual church will be a missionary church, and that a missonary church will be a spiritual church. To be a spiritual church, in his opinion, means to put first things first. And first place is given in the Bible to missions.

The visible church of Jesus Christ has a twofold task assigned to it. The first is to win people to a saving knowledge of the Lord Jesus Christ and the second is to build them up in the holy faith until they be conformed to the image of His dear Son. But before the sheep can be built up in the faith they must become members of the flock through the new birth. This means that the gospel must be taken to them.

Deeply conscious of his own personal responsibility for foreign missions in the light of the Scriptures, the Park Street Prophet has led his people into the same realization of their responsibility. Together they have fashioned under God a missionary program that has rarely been equaled in the annals of the modern church. This congregation knows that there are five hundred million people who have never heard the name of Jesus. They know that one half of the world, beyond this number, do not profess him as Saviour and Lord. They know that missions mean sacrifice; missions mean obedience to go and to give and to pray. And the pastor and people of this church are determined to be obedient to the great commission of their Lord.

Harold Ockenga has a philosophy of the misionary enterprise which he has obtained from his study of the Word of God. He holds that Matthew 24:14, "this gospel of the kingdom must be preached to all the world for a witness and then shall the end come," is valid today. He does not hold that this passage rests on dispensational grounds and is applicable to the Jews during the Great Tribulation after the Church has been raptured. Rather he believes firmly that this applies to our age and to our people and is related to the second coming of the Lord. The Great Commission, in his opinion, is to the church and to no one but the church.

Ockenga believes that the Great Commission has an intensive and an extensive application. It is at this point that he confesses to be without exact knowledge from the Bible about the missionary enterprise. He definitely believes that the coming of the Lord is imminent and that the gospel is already in the nations. Yet so long as Jesus tarries the Great Commission has not been completed and we are to hasten the coming of the Lord by completing that commission. He is confident that the commission can and ought to be fulfilled as to its extensive and intensive elements in our day. God wants the world to be evangelized but men must respond to the invitation of God to join Him in the completion of that task.

Himself no stranger to missionary feelings and passion, Ockenga traces his own interest in missions back to his college days. During those days the Lord spoke to his heart about missions and he was willing to let God have him for missionary service if it was the will of God. When in seminary at Princeton he felt called to the mission field and yielded his life to God for that form of Christian service. He joined the Student Volunteer Movement indicating his wish to become a missionary and was prepared to do so.

When Ockenga left Princeton to finish his work at the newly formed Westminster Theological Seminary under the leadership of men like Dr. J. Gresham Machen, a new factor entered into the picture to convince him that God wanted him to remain at home and to strengthen evangelical Christianity. At Westminster tremendous emphasis was laid upon the obvious truth, that at that moment men were needed to hold the churches at home or there would be no missionaries on the field. The turn of affairs in the Presbyterian Church was such that the whole denomination was rocked over the conservative-modernist controversy.

Young Ockenga was strongly advised to hold the fort at the home base since the foreign missionary picture is simply a projection to the foreign field of what the church is at home. It was with this thought in mind and with specific encouragement from some of the leaders that Ockenga accepted the appointment as assistant to Dr. Clarence Edward Macartney in Pittsburgh.

Never has he differentiated, however, between the foreign and the home fields. He holds them to be part of one world, but sees that the foreign field has added claims in the light of the greater need numerically and in the light of the greater opportunities to hear the gospel at at home. This, added to the Biblical assertion that the evangelization of the world is the ultimate goal, keeps his eyes fixed on foreign missions.

Two years after he settled in the Park Street pastorate Ockenga began to think in terms of a missionary conference. This idea sprang from his own dissatisfaction with the missionary work of the church. When he landed in Boston in 1936 the church budget for missions was less than twenty-five hundred dollars for the previous year. In 1936 the budget jumped to slightly better than four thousand dollars. When God laid the vision on his heart for still greater things in missions, the 1939 budget jumped again and this time to almost ten thousand dollars.

The Park Street Church had been a great missionary church in its past. Shortly after its founding, in the year 1817, missionary-minded Christians established the Monthly Concert of Prayer. This sparked the first missionary revival in the history of the church and led to the founding in the vestry of the church the Near East Mission, and in October, 1819, of the Sandwich

Islands Church, out of which impulse has come the flourishing Hawaiian Islands churches of today.

It was a missionary church, but the changing metropolitan conditions in and around Boston after 1900 quenched that movement in no small degree. Now God was working to bring the church back to its first love and to make that church a beacon to challenge not only the churches of the area but of all America. To this hour, springing from the work of Ockenga under God, few churches in America can match the generosity of the Park Street Church in missionary giving.

One thing Ockenga learned quickly in New England: It is not easy to make a movement successful in its first year. In New England, he says, a project needs five years to determine whether it will really catch on fire. In the spring of 1940, after two years of prayer and thought, the first missionary conference opened. Ockenga planned to give the conference five years, in the hope that at the end of that time it would be a marked success.

Desiring to spark the first conference so as to give it every chance to succeed, Harold Ockenga was led of the Lord to approach Oswald Smith of Toronto, Canada, to lead the conference. Dr. Smith was pastor of the famed Peoples Church in that Canadian city and under God had wrought wonders for missions. Dr. Smith's experience had given him much technical knowledge of value to a church beginning a similar enterprise.

The purposes of the missionary conferences in the mind of Dr. Ockenga were clear. He wanted to have an informed people. To know is to act. And without knowledge people are not likely to act.

He also wanted to arouse within himself and his people a passion for the fields of the world. He also desperately wanted to challenge young lives to devotion to the cause of Christ in the foreign fields of the world. He believed that the missionary conference would do this and that from the church many young people could commence training to go unto the uttermost parts of the earth.

Prayer is a weapon which when properly employed can do more for missions than almost anything else. Ockenga knew that an informed people who had heard and seen living missionaries and who had the opportunity to see moving pictures and slides of the fields of the world would become a praying people. Information gave Christians a chance to enter into the problems, challenges, tribulations and trials of missionaries from every corner of the earth. A concert of prayer for individuals who had touched the hearts of the church people would be productive of tremendous good for missions once the people at home had missionaries and their labors laid on their hearts.

Money makes the missionary machine operate and function. God has divinely ordained that missionary endeavor shall be supported through the gifts of God's people. Harold Ockenga had in mind that the church should support more missionaries by an increase of giving to the work. To what extent this and the other aims of the conference might be successful he could not know when the first one was in prospect.

Individuals in the church early supported this enterprise and their co-operation strengthened the pastor's hand. The planning of the conference which they hoped would be a yearly affair, included noon meetings, afternoon meetings, evening meetings, booths and displays for the visiting mission boards, and inspirational messages by Dr. Oswald Smith of Toronto.

The first missionary conference was successful. Hearts were challenged; lives were yielded to God; prayers were made to Him; and money was consecrated to God for missions. The first year witnessed an increase in missionary giving of better than 100 per cent over the previous year. In 1940 the Park Street Church contributed to missions more than twenty-one thousand dollars. This is especially significant when one consider that the expenses are not deducted from the missionary pledges but are taken from the local budget. Offerings are received during the week for the expense of the conference but nothing is deducted from the offering and pledges made for missions.

When the initial conference proved what could be done, the hearts of the pastor and people were encouraged to continue. It was after this first conference and during the second one that the Seattle call to the leading Presbyterian church brought temporary problems to the Park Street Prophet. One of the reasons he did not feel he should accept the offer of the Seattle church was that he had only embarked on the missionary conference and it was not yet firmly established as a tradition. To leave the New England area then might well have meant defeat for the larger missionary picture in the heart of the young pastor.

For six long years Oswald Smith returned again and again to help Ockenga and the people of the church. The second conference brought in better than twenty-nine thousand dollars; the third saw the total giving swell to more than thirty-three thousand dollars; the fourth saw another rise to more than forty-seven thousand dollars; the fifth witnessed an increase to fifty-three thousand dollars. And this meant that for two years running the missionary giving of the church had risen higher than the church budget for home operations. With the help of Dr. Smith in the sixth conference the giving of the church rose to almost sixty-two thousand dollars—ten thousand dollars more than the contributions to the home budget!

In 1935, the year before Ockenga came to Park Street, the total budget for the local church and for missions was a shade over twenty-one thousand dollars. By 1945, at the end of the first six years of missionary emphasis, the giving of the people was better than one hundred and thirteen thousand dollars for the year!

In 1946 Harold Ockenga felt that he had sufficient experience to handle the conference himself without calling in outside help. Together with the loyal Park Street staff this change in policy was inaugurated and the church itself began operating the conference on its own. The Lord signally blessed this step of faith and in that year the missionary giving jumped again.

This time the people contributed close to ninety thousand dollars. The total giving of the church went up to more than one hundred and forty-three thousand dollars, a peak of giving which astonished both the people and the pastor. They were doing something undreamed of a few short years before that. It hardly seemed likely that further increases could be expected. The peak seemed to have been reached.

But 1947 saw a slight advance. That year giving for missions rose to over ninety thousand dollars, but the increase over the previous year was less than a thousand dollars. Giving was levelling off and the peak was in sight—or so they thought. But again the people and pastor were challenged to expect God to do mighty things in their midst. Well did they lay hold on the axiom of former missionary leaders to "expect great things from God."

High expectancy hung over the Park Street Church when the 1948 campaign came around. Folks did not know what to look for but their hopes were high. When the pledges were totalled and the year ended they had brought into the Lord's treasury more than one hundred and five thousand dollars. To them it was a sweet savor of victory unto the Lord and hearts were quickened. Once again the pastor and people felt they had gone as far as they could go, humanly speaking. But again God challenged their faith and asked them to look to Him—the God of the impossible. So 1949 dawned and with it came increased expectation that God would work.

By 1949 the church supported in whole or in part ninety missionaries of their own. Their ministry now was world-wide. Their stake in the work of Christ knew no bounds and the sun never set on their spiritual horizons. In every nation of the world men and women were singing praises in the name of our blessed Redeemer because the people of the Park Street Church cared for their souls. The year 1949 was important for it represented a decade of missionary effort. This was the tenth anniversary of the program. What God had wrought in nine years! But what was God going to do in the tenth year?

Appropriately enough in 1949 the conference was called "Vision and Victory. The vision of years ago was a reality and victories had been won. Were they to lay down their arms at this stage or seek to go on? A wonderful program was arranged, following in substance the programs of previous years. Beginning on Monday, April 25, the conference ran for seven consecutive days to Sunday, May 1. No respite was taken on Saturday. A splendid morning, afternoon, and evening program was arranged for the day. Each day at 11:45 speakers ascended the then famous Mayflower Pulpit from which the gospel was proclaimed every summer. And to the passing crowds the gospel was widely proclaimed.

Morning, noonday, afternoon, and evening services were held. There were devotional Bible study periods each day; round-table discussions in the morning at 10:45; testimonies of missionary volunteers; representatives of mission boards from all sections of the world; and leading missionary speakers to encourage the hearts of the listeners. Names that shall in glory be honored for dedication of life and fortune to the missionary cause studded the daily programs. Ralph Davis, general secretary of the Africa Inland Mission; David Johnson, general director of the Evangelical Alliance Mission; Leland Wang of China; J. O. Percy, secretary of the Sudan Interior Mission; Eugene Nida of the Wycliffe Bible Translators and Version secretary for the American Bible Society; and Howard Ferrin, President of the Africa Inland Mission were there. The Voice of the Andes leader, Clarence Jones, and the leader of the Latin American Mission, Kenneth Strachan, and many others came.

It was a spiritual feast with blessings for all interested in obtaining them. Enthusiasm reached a new high. Personal testimonies attesting to the blessings of God were frequent. The Holy Spirit worked in power in the hearts of the people. And His working manifested itself as He laid hold of individual hearts and as He worked in and through the conference in every regard.

Highly expectant of what God might do for them, the moment for making pledges came. Already the Lord had touched lives and now He asked individuals what financial part they wished to have in helping to fulfill the Great Commission. Prayerfully and carefully the Christians wrote out their pledges; the workers gathered the cards; tellers recorded the totals. Excitement reached a high point as the gifts came in and went up to fifty thousand, then sixty, then seventy, then eighty thousand dollars. When the giving by pledge reached one hundred thousand dollars the church was literally afire with power. The giving was not just a matter of course; believers sacrificed gladly in most cases. Slowly the pledges rose to equal the 1949 figure of better than one hundred and five thousand dollars. Then dramatically the gifts went beyond the previous high until one hundred and ten thousand dollars was reached; and then on and on until 1949 promised at least one hundred and eighteen thousand dollars! A new high for Christ came after ten long, hard years of unremitting toil and labor by pastor and people. The God of Abraham, Moses, and Elijah demonstrated again that He is the God of the impossible.

The pledging of money does not end the task by any means. It must then be taken in day by day and week by week. It is easy for people in moments of spiritual excitement and enthusiasm to make promises they will not fulfill. Not so here. The spiritual lift they got had sustaining power and the money came in to meet the pledges the people had made.

When Christians hear of the wonderful missionary work at the church, they comment that the people must be well-to-do. Such is not the case. There are a few people of real means in the church; but most of the members are middle class. The highest single gift in 1949 was for two thousand dollars. Most of the gifts are sacrificial and even the higher ones involve definite elements of sacrifice. A case or two in point will enable the reader to see how true this is.

One woman who gives sacrificially operates a rooming house of sixteen rooms. She runs it for the glory of God, and from the fruits of this labor has built a Bible school for Christ in Addis Ababa worth twelve thousand dollars. She does her own work and never takes a vacation. But she loves the Lord and willingly does this as a service for Him in obedience to the Great Commission.

An older unmarried lady with a small income wanted to give her "mite" to God for missions. With reckless abandon she determined to earn a living and devote her otherwise small income to missions. To do this she supported herself by making jig-saw puzzles. It entailed sacrifice but brought with it commensurate spiritual rewards.

One young man was converted. In finding Christ he heard the challenge of God to service and finally accepted that challenge. Upon the death of his father he received a legacy. The Lord led him to give seventeen thousand dollars to missions in addition to giving himself for service. Soon this man will go to the field of God's choice for him. But here is a case of consecration of money and self because the Park Street Church is a missionary beacon light in the community.

One young lady in the church taught Sunday-school class of girls. This class of girls came to the place where they entertained a vision of what God wanted them to do for missions. As a class they pledged a substantial sum of money. The teacher of the class, a secretary, spent her own vacation working as a waitress in Howard Johnson's eating establishment to help her girls meet the pledge they made.

In 1949 the Spirit of God moved in such a remarkable fashion that Mrs. Ockenga made a missionary pledge which left her own husband gasping for breath. People and pastor alike are in this thing and together they have made it what it is today. Obviously Dr. Ockenga has provided leadership but the people themselves have responded to the leadership, have been partakers and helpers along the way, and have upheld the arms of the one they selected to be their pastor.

From a human rather than the divine viewpoint it appeared as though the church in 1949 reached the high point to which it could attain financially in giving for missions and the local church work, yet in 1950 its missionary arose to $150,000.00. These eleven years have been years of growth. Blessings have come to church and people in an amazing way. Souls are being saved and the work of Christ flourishes. While they do not know how it will be possible for God to do still greater things for them, they have, nevertheless, a spirit of keen anticipation that God *will do* mightier and more glorious things in the second decade of their missionary labors.

The forward-looking attitude of the church brought another vision unique in modern denominational life. During October, 1949, the first Christian Education Conference met in the church. This conference purposed to acquaint the Christian public with the Christian grade schools of America, the academies, colleges, summer camps, and conference grounds. Prospective students had an opportunity to meet and counsel with representatives from the institutions in which they expressed an interest. Display booths provided literature; motion pictures were shown; eminent speakers like Clarence Roddy, Charles Woodbridge, Clarence Bouma, and Frank Gaebelein appeared on the program. The interested people made pledges designated for various educational institutions for sixty-three hundred dollars. The second conference raised $12,432.00. Recalling to mind the missionary budget of the early years of Dr. Ockenga's ministry it is safe to predict that this successful conference will produce more and more income for Christian education as the years go by.

In all of the missionary endeavors, foreign and home, this church and its leadership are pressing on to higher goals with consequent spiritual blessings accruing to themselves as they walk in obedience to the divine commands of Christ.

Chapter

"As thou hast sent me into the world, even so have I also sent them into the world. And for their sakes I sanctify myself, that they also might be sanctified through the truth. Neither pray I for these alone, but for them also which shall believe on me through their word; That they all may be one; as thou, Father, art in me, and I in thee, that they also may be one in us: that the world may believe that thou hast sent me."
— *John* 17: 18-21

Seven

THE NATIONAL ASSOCIATION OF EVANGELICALS
A WIDENING HORIZON OF CONSERVATIVE CO-OPERATION

THE STORY OF The National Association of Evangelicals is a modern miracle. Without the personage of Harold John Ockenga the story is incomplete. He has been one of the key figures in this effort for evangelical co-operation and his part in the picture gives a deep insight into one of the most hopeful but tragic situations in the present Christian world.

Fifty years ago in American life the religious outlook differed vastly from what we see today. The inroads of unbelief and German rationalism were beginning to be felt in American religious life but the churches on the whole were soundly evangelical. The nineteenth century had witnessed the most significant missionary advance since the apostolic era eighteen hundred years before the "great century." Out of this missionary advance came the impulse toward the unity of believers. This eventually led to the modern Ecumenical Movement. In the strands which make up the Ecumenical Movement must be included the great missionary conferences at Edinburgh, and Madras and Jerusalem in the last fifty years. Also included are the Faith and Order, and Life and Work conferences held in key cities like Lausanne, Stockholm, Geneva, Oxford, and Amsterdam. At least in their origins, the seeds of unity were evangelical. But into the picture crept much that was not orthodox.

Before the first decade of the twentieth century passed, the American Christian world was deeply touched by the same yearnings for unity which were to find expression in the great missionary conferences and the Life and Work, and Faith and Order conferences embracing the whole world. It was part of a general world movement and it was evangelical or conservative in its theological emphasis. The first tangible, concrete step in the direction of unity in America came in the formation of the Federal Council of the Churches of Christ. The purpose of the Federal Council was to bring the major communions in America together so that they could act in concert on critical issues facing them. The idea was excellent for it embraced the principle that in unity there is strength. And what could not be done separately might be done by the many working in harmony.

Following the formation of the Federal Council of the Churches of Christ in America there was a pronounced drift away from the old theological concepts, a drift heightened by the first World War.

In fact, during the second decade of the twentieth century all of the old line denominations were plagued by the problem of theological liberalism. In the struggle that ensued, which became a fight for the control of the ecclesiastical machinery, a militant fundamentalism arose within the ranks and outside the ranks of the denominations. Seminary after seminary capitulated to the modernists and in the course of time spread the infection into the churches, since their students were indoctrinated with their ideas and then channeled into the churches.

Among the Baptists, the Chicago Divinity School, Colgate-Rochester, and Crozer seminaries drew farthest away from the conservative position and represented modernism. The Methodist seminaries also capitulated; among the Presbyterians, inroads were made, although the process here was less swift than in others. Andover-Newton was lost both to the Congregationalists and the Baptists. Inter-denominational and non-denominational schools like Yale, Harvard, and Union in New York became strongholds for liberalism.

In the battle of modernism *versus* fundamentalism every group was affected. Liberalism had an ugly way of raising its head in quarters least expected and its fifth column movement was so insidious that it remained under cover for some time. Key spots in the political arena were coveted and won by the liberals with the fundamentalists fighting a rearguard battle and losing all along the line.

The same mixture of liberals and fundamentalists which became common to all of the denominations was seen in the Federal Council of the Churches of Christ in America. Infected with the same disease, the purposes for which it was originally founded were lost sight of. It became in turn the battleground for opposing theologies with fundamentalism on the losing side.

The capture of the Federal Council by the liberals led to the change in its outlook and program. It espoused the cause of the social gospel so well propounded by the Baptist Rauschenbusch of Rochester Seminary, and departed from the cardinal doctrines of the historic Christian faith. To all practical intents and purposes the virgin birth, blood atonement, the physical resurrection, and the deity of Christ were scrapped. Few in the leadership of the Federal Council believed in them. It was neither popular nor expedient so to believe when the temper of the times was all in favor of modernism.

Thus the original purposes of the Federal Council were subverted and it became the organ of the modernists with the fundamentalists inarticulate inside and firing their guns helplessly from the outside.

During the 1920's the American picture did not improve. Instead, conditions got worse and the Federal Council deteriorated considerably from a conservative viewpoint. Now all of this was happening when the world-wide movement for unity among Christians was prominent and securing attention. It was not unnatural that the evangelicals of the land, pursued by similar thoughts of unity (not organic) should think about the possibilities of gathering themselves together for fellowship and the propagation of the theological convictions which they held. Not finding what they wanted in their own communions which were spotted with modernism and which were oftentimes controlled by modernists so far as the ecclesiastical machinery was involved, and not being adequately represented by the views of the modernist Federal Council of the Churches of Christ in America, they looked elsewhere. What the elsewhere was, in the 1920's, few fundamentalists could picture.

The partly conscious and partly unconscious longing for a larger fellowship of evangelicals was not limited to the conservatives within the larger denominations. After World War I many new religious organizations came into being to minister to various groups. These groups were positively evangelical in their theology and remarkably successful in their evangelistic endeavors. They grew apace and became sizable segments on the periphery. In rare cases did they attempt to join the Federal Council, which did not resemble their views theologically. Thus they too had conscious and unconscious leanings toward a larger fellowship beyond their denominational boundaries.

Against a background like this, the fourth decade of the twentieth century opened, and agencies and organizations which tangibly expressed the desire for unity among evangelicals based upon common theological agreement in essential points of dogma came into being. One of the organizations born for this hour was the National Association of Evangelicals and among its leadership was the prophet from Park Street, Harold John Ockenga.

Active in the formation of this new organization and the one man who most helpfully secured the services of Harold Ockenga for the movement was J. Elwin Wright. Since 1929 Dr. Wright has been the guiding hand in the affairs of the New England Fellowship which he was encouraged to begin by the constructive efforts of Dr. A. Z. Conrad of the Park Street Church.

The New England Fellowship actually began at Park Street, although not organically related to the church itself, as an interdenominational endeavor on the part of the evangelicals in that area. Its aim was to do together what could not be done as well separately.

With the passing of the years, the work grew. It had a ministry which embraced the opening of closed churches, daily vacation Bible schools, the instruction of students in Christian truth in the day schools, and summer conference work at Rumney, New Hampshire. This summer work included boys' and girls' camps, special conferences for laymen and for pastors, and general conferences for Christians.

Assisted for years by the Evans sisters and a corps of consecrated workers, the New England Fellowship grew steadily and supplied a positive witness for Christ in a way that transcended denominational boundaries and emphasized the unity of believers in areas of life where co-operation could be worked out effectively.

The experience which Dr. Wright obtained out of the work of the New England Fellowship did two things for him. It enlarged his vision for some co-operative enterprise on a national scale and eventually on an international scale, although the latter was a development of a later date. And second, he gained a fund of knowledge relating to co-operative endeavor which was to serve him in good stead in the larger work that under God was about to be projected into the contemporary American scene.

By 1940 the evangelicals had written off the Federal Council as a hopeless enterprise. To be sure, some sincere evangelical believers continued to hope that redemption for the Federal Council was a latent possibility and they honestly tried to work within the framework of that organization in the belief that something might be done. But the greater number of evangelicals with deep insight perceived that the deliverance of the Federal Council was unlikely. With that thought in mind the National Association of Evangelicals was created and brought into the open. A meeting of key evangelicals was set for Chicago in October, 1941, at the Moody Memorial Church.

A similar movement was called for in September, 1941, by what was to become the American Council of Christian Churches, closely associated with Carl McIntire, editor of the *Christian Beacon*. The American Council group was invited to meet in Chicago with the Wright movement. The American Council then laid down conditions under which they would meet with the group that was to become the N.A.E. Chief among the conditions was one which stipulated that only churches outside the Federal Council of the Churches of Christ in America would be considered for membership. In effect this condition meant only those churches outside the large denominations like the Presbyterian Church, U.S.A., the Northern Baptist Convention, and the Methodist Church.

The stipulation of the American Council group did not fit into the plan which men who hoped to form the National Association of Evangelicals had visualized. They hoped for an association of Bible believers in a co-operative framework whether the churches and the men were in or out of the major denominations. Furthermore, the aspirations of the N.A.E. differed in that it was to be a fellowship broad enough to include whole denominations, schools, individuals, and missionary organizations. In other words it was to be large enough and broad enough to make room for all and any organizations or groups, or individuals in the evangelical camp who wished to be identified with such a witness for Christ in our generation.

The American Council, on the other hand, intended to provide competition for the Federal Council in the sense of creating an organization comparable to that body, with membership from whole denominations, with no room immediately for individuals, institutions and other groups.

Another essential difference between the N.A.E. and the American Council in the formative period was in the methods by which they were organized. The American Council began as a small group to which other groups were added from time to time. The N.A.E. explored the possibility of an organization and then called a national meeting to organize the same in a democratic fashion so as to begin operations with as large a group as possible.

The ideology behind the N.A.E. was to create an organization for the following purposes: to provide a fellowship for brethren like-minded in the things of Christ; to secure some form of representation for those who were not represented so far as voice was concerned in the Federal Council; to raise a united testimony to the evangelical faith in a time of much apostasy; to secure united action in areas where the work could be done better together. In this area they sought co-operative action for foreign missionary work and passports, separation of church and state, Christian education, gospel radio broadcasting, and allied endeavors.

Dr. Wright played a major part in the drama before the organization was formed and during its subsequent history. Much credit is laid at his door for effective and faithful service to a cause to which his heart is committed. And to him goes the credit for interesting actively Dr. Ockenga in the same cause.

In 1942 the new movement planned a meeting in St. Louis. Dr. Ockenga was asked to participate in it and he delivered one of the major addresses on that occasion. As a result of that message, Dr. Ockenga was invited to become the provisional president of the organization that was to be created a year later in Chicago.

The American Council received an invitation to the St. Louis meetings. Some of its leaders were present and the problem of the relationship of the American Council to the proposed National Association of Evangelicals was discussed.

Again disagreement prevailed, following which the American Council extended an invitation to the N.A.E. men to come into the American Council of Christian Churches; otherwise, there would be two separate and distinct groups. Furthermore, any of the men in denominations affiliated with the Federal Council, were expected by the American Council to withdraw from these denominations. Inasmuch as the men at St. Louis were from the leading denominations, it would have meant virtual abandonment of the N.A.E. idea.

At this time the Pentecostal brethren were not in the N.A.E. movement, so the final fruit of the suggested arrangement would have been the dissolution of the N.A.E. movement, leaving the field of evangelical co-operation exclusively in the hands of the American Council. The N.A.E. refused to concede this development.

At the conclusion of the St. Louis meetings, a small group of men toured the United States to speak about and inform people of the projected National Association of Evangelicals. Dr. Ockenga himself journeyed thousands of miles for this purpose.

Wherever he went he spoke about the coming constitutional convention and the hopes of the new organization. Briefly he revealed that the new organization hoped to become the clearing house for the articulation of the evangelical viewpoint. It desired to end conservative isolation which existed in and out of the old-line denominations. The leadership longed to open an era of positive as against negative co-operation along common lines. The organization did not wish to be divisive, however. It did not have for its immediate or ultimate goal the splitting up of denominations.

On his tours over America, Ockenga sounded out evangelical opinion and found it favorable to the creation of the N.A.E. Everywhere he was met with an enthusiastic response as God had prepared the hearts of conservatives for many years to this end. The grass roots campaign portended the success of the constitutional convention.

From May 3 to 6, the Constitutional Convention of the National Association of Evangelicals met at the LaSalle Hotel in Chicago. A large number of the leading evangelicals in American Christianity were present. Men like Harry Ironside, Robert McQuilkin, Robert Munger, Stephen Paine, Christie Innes,

The N. A. E.

Cary Weisiger III, H. J. Taylor, Bishop Marston, Harry Hager, John McCall, R. L. Decker, Albert Sidney Johnson, John Bradbury, Paul Rees, T. Roland Philips, Robert Shuler, Carey Thomas, J. Elwin Wright, Howard Ferrin, Clarence Bouma, Bob Jones, William Ward Ayer, and a host of other well-known conservatives attended.

Of their meetings and their significance to American life Bishop Leslie Marston declared, "America's revival is breaking!"

Harold Ockenga had a prominent part in these meetings, and in the spade work which preceded them. The newly created National Association of Evangelicals elected him president formally instead of provisionally, an honor that came to him unwanted but which he accepted due to his enthusiasm and approval of the enterprise.

In the publication issued after this historic meeting in Chicago the purposes and the stand of the National Association of Evangelicals were elaborated. In *United We Stand* the avowed composition of the fellowship included "evangelical denominations, churches, and associations of churches, mission boards, educational institutions, and other Christian organizations, and individuals in matters of mutual interest an concern."

The objectives were listed as follows:
1. To encourage evangelism in all its forms and assist in the promotion of evangelistic effort.
2. To provide a service to mission boards in securing passports, visas, the rapid transmission of funds and supplies to the fields, and the extension of missionary interest. To protect the missionary enterprise from undue restriction and regulation.
3. To act as a clearing house in chaplaincy matters for denominations and groups not now represented by other organizations at Washington.
4. To protect the freedom of gospel broadcasting.
5. To maintain and defend the American doctrine of the separation of church and state.

6. To assist in the correlation of the work of the churches: promoting understanding and co-operation among its organizations.
7. To encourage and promote Christian education in all its fields.
8. To provide information, leadership, and assistance in every way to all organizations engaged in propagating the gospel message.
9. To provide an interdenominational medium of spiritual fellowship and inspiration for Bible-believing Christians.

The National Association went on record regarding the Federal Council of the Churches of Christ in America. The feeling of the membership was that a negative statement condemning the Federal Council and a constant attack on it was ill-advised. They preferred to state their own program positively and rally around this standard rather than to indict other organizations, erroneous as they might seem to be.

The National Association of Evangelicals did indicate its position on the Federal Council in these words: "The Federal Council, because of its lack of a positive stand on the essential doctrines of the Christian faith, its inclusion of leaders who have repudiated these doctrines, and its active support of programs and institutions which are non-evangelical or apostate, does not represent the evangelicals of America. The National Association of Evangelicals was organized because of this fact and its creation is a testimonial to the conviction of its constituency that the Federal Council does not represent Bible-believing Christians."

One of the differences between the N.A.E. and the American Council came over the membership of the Pentecostal groups in the N.A.E.

Harold Ockenga has distinct views about speaking in tongues and the doctrine of eradication which teaches sinless perfection. He does not believe that these doctrines find adequate support in the scriptures, but the groups that hold these doctrines are otherwise in perfect harmony and agreement respecting the primary doctrines of the faith. The matters of eradication and speaking in tongues Ockenga considers to be peripheral problems which would not make fellowship impossible or undesirable. He classes these views on speaking in tongues and eradication with other differences existent among Christians who are agreed on fundamentals but who differ quite radically on questions of baptism, church government, and the meaning of the Lord's table. And so far as he personally regards the matter he does have fellowship and can easily co-operate with Christians who differ with him at these points.

Hopes were not yet dead that the American Council and the N.A.E. groups could come together in some way acceptable to both of them. The door was kept open and Mr. McIntire of the American Council constantly reiterated that in his opinion two groups were unnecessary. And he also stressed the point that his group was in the field first and the N.A.E. should give way to that chronological primacy.

At the annual meeting of the N.A.E. in Columbus, Ohio, in 1944 when Ockenga was still president, the question of union with the American Council was raised again. Some felt that one organization was the solution to the evangelical crisis.

The leadership of the two groups canvassed the issue thoroughly and from that canvass certain conclusions emerged: McIntire's idea of a compromise arrangement meant to disband the N.A.E. and retain the American Council and its framework. All of the denominations in the N.A.E. were to apply to the American Council for membership and would be admitted except for the Tongues and Pentecostal Christians. Men like Ockenga, Barnhouse, Munger and all others associated with the work and among the clergy or in the fellowship of the so-called apostate denominations (Northern Baptist, Presbyterian Church, U.S.A., Methodist, etc.) would be admitted to the American Council on an associate basis with no voting privileges.

God had already blessed the N.A.E. and had shown that His divine favor rested with the movement; so no one felt inclined to meet the demands of the American Council. From that time onward the two movements were increasingly divorced from each other and it appeared less and less likely that cordial relations could be established.

At the Columbus meeting in 1944 the presidency was again urged for Dr. Ockenga. Convinced in his own thinking that it was an unwise precedent for the same man to continue in office, and that a one-man leadership was dangerous in such a splendid movement, he expressed his opinion that he should not assume that executive function again. He firmly believed that a succession of leadership was indispensable to the future of the organization.

Bishop Leslie Marston replaced him, in turn to be succeeded by Dr. R. I. Decker of Kansas City and then by Dr. Stephen Paine of Houghton College.

On his retirement from the presidency of the N.A.E., the full board of administration invited Dr. Ockenga to become executive vice-president and thus to guide with some degree of permanence the destinies of the Association. He declined this invitation largely on the grounds that he had no presumptive leading from the Lord to assume this position. So far as he could tell, the will of God for him to continue as the pastor of the Park Street Church had not changed.

Harold Ockenga has retained his intimate connections with the N.A.E. on its boards and committees, however, after the presidency passed into other hands. From its beginning he was a member of the Board of Administration. He worked on the policy committee, and was chairman of the commission on evangelism. For two years he was chairman of the chaplain's commission and served willingly in any capacity where he was able to do so. He is now chairman of the N.A.E. commission on international co-operation of evangelicals.

THE N. A. E.

With the expiration of his term of office, he did not lose zest for the N.A.E. and its work. He bulwarked it whenever and wherever he could. He traveled to Europe in 1946 for the N.A.E. and its further expansion. In April of that year he met and talked with the evangelical leadership of England in and around London. <u>He preached for Dr. Martin Lloyd-Jones in the historic Westminster Chapel.</u> The purpose of this European trip was to inform the evangelicals about the work of the N.A.E. in America, looking to the future when Bible believers outside the continental United States might wish to ally themselves with brethren of like mind in America.

The European trip clearly evinced Harold Ockenga's faith in a Biblical ecumenicity, resting upon Bible believers everywhere whether in or out of the major denominations. His type of ecumenicity is based upon the strong certainty that doctrinal sameness with respect to the fundamentals of the faith is the cord that binds Christians together. Christ and His doctrine present the hope of the hour.

It is not that Dr. Ockenga repudiates separatism in itself. To do this would jeopardize the Reformation of Martin Luther and John Calvin. He agrees that there is a Biblical separatism which true believers must practice when events and circumstances warrant it. He knows that the Reformation was justified. Consequently John Calvin was neither schismatic or heretical when he withdrew from the Roman Catholic Church. It had ceased to be a true church and one cannot break up that which does not exist.

It was the last thought in the mind of John Calvin and is far from the thinking of Ockenga to be schismatic. This is one of the most serious sins against the true church and is fraught with danger. It can be stated, then, that Ockenga agrees with the American Council idea that when a church becomes apostate Christians must withdraw from that church. Where he does not agree is on the indictment that all of the present denominations in America which the American Council speaks of as being apostate are actually that.

Always a man must be ready to face the facts and observe the conditions. That a denomination which Ockenga today does not think is apostate may tomorrow become apostate is a possibility. And he is always ready to leave any group which ceases to be a true church. So also should every true Christian be of the same mind and spirit as men like Calvin and Luther who bravely followed conscience and the Bible in their day.

Historically, no man identified with a Protestant group can state that separatism as understood by Calvin and Ockenga is wrong. To do so would be to conclude that Protestants must return to the Roman church, a movement which is hardly likely in the light of historical facts. Serious and devout Christians in our difficult period of church history to disagree as to which, if any, of the present churches are apostate among the Protestant groups. Had Ockenga, while in their ministry of the Presbyterian Church, U.S.A., believed that it was apostate in the sense that John Calvin felt the Roman Catholic Church to be apostate, he would have severed his ties immediately. This does not mean that any denomination is perfect, but simply that up to this point he is not convinced that many of the so-called apostate churches are actually apostate.

He holds this view firmly and can defend it trenchantly, but he is not willing to condemn anyone else who for reasons of conscience may disagree with him. He also expects in return liberty of conscience and often is keenly disappointed to find that others will not grant him similar liberty of conviction.

On the international horizon, ecumenically, Dr. Ockenga believes that all Bible-believing Christians ought to unite in a fellowship of a non-organizational type. He believes that Biblical ecumenicity is spiritual, not organizational, and that we ought not to compete with a world organizaton like Rome or any other one similar to it.

We do not need a second World Council of Churches for evangelicals but a fellowship of like-minded believers who will fulfill the wish of Christ that we may be one—not in organic union but in spirit and heart. His 1946 trip to Europe and his conversations with English evangelicals convinced him that Christians everywhere are hungry for this kind of spiritual unity in the knowledge that we are all brethren in Christ.

Again in 1947 Ockenga went to Europe for the N.A.E. This time the United States Government sponsored and conducted the tour, the personnel of which included leading representative religious leaders from America. It was designed to show them post-war Europe and to report to America on conditions among the people and among our occupation forces.

From the picture painted thus far it is possible to conclude that Ockenga has been a leading figure connected with the N.A.E. from its inception. He represents its aims and spirit. He has worked in the organization and for it. He believes in it with all his heart. He hopes that it will concern itself with the issues that trouble our country today. And he holds that the N.A.E. has a message for this critical juncture in the history of our people and of the world.

Dr. Ockenga knows that his cause is in the hands of God. At least he feels confident that the position held by the N.A.E. while it may be called one of compromise by those who disagree, is at least one in which they practice what they preach and one which they try to live up to without fear or favor. To paraphrase the famous quotation from Emerson. "What you are speaks so loudly I cannot hear what you say."

Dr. Ockenga reprobates endless divisions and longs for the day when all of the evangelicals can unite for the purpose of propagating the faith once for all delivered unto the saints. He believes it must be done constructively and in a positive rather than a negative framework. It is not the best strategy to scold and condemn; it is far wiser to be positive and to stand *for* something than to stand always *against* something. This does not mean that he will not take a position against an idea or state his disapprobation of whatever he thinks is wrong and evil. The Congregational and Christian Churches are going forward steadily with their merger movement against the protest of many churches. Despite the objections the merger with the Evangelical and Reformed Church probably will be consummated sooner or later. Dr. Ockenga has protested this merger and has served notice in conjunction with the Park Street Church that neither of them will become a part of the new denomiation when it is formed and that when the merger is consummated the Park Street Church will then become an independent church which is its right to do. At the time this occurs Ockenga himself would be loathe to concede that it makes him a "come-outer" in a negative sense. Rather, he identifies himself and the church with the historic stream of such movements and not with a side eddy.

In his place of leadership in the N.A.E. since its formation, Ockenga has been the target for abuse and attack. He has not shunned his responsibility and has willingly borne the opprobrium which has been heaped upon him. As strongly as when he first began he believes today that the position of the N.A.E. is a Biblical position which does not involve compromise, and that it is the evangelical hope of America. He will not concede defeat to the enemy but will ever fight the good fight in the way he sees to be right and according to the powers that God has granted unto him in this life. And God alone can be the judge for He knows the heart and mind. Having committed his cause unto Him who is able, he fearlessly faces the unknown future like Christian in *Pilgrim's Progress,* with his back to the world, his Bible in his hand, and his face toward heaven.

Chapter

As go the seminaries so go the churches.

"And the things thou hast heard of me among many witnesses, the same commit thou to faithful men, who shall be able to teach others also."
— *II Timothy* 2:2

Eight

THE FOUNTAINHEAD OF THE CHURCH

A VISION IN THEOLOGICAL EDUCATION

THEOLOGICAL SEMINARIES determine the destinies of churches. As goes the seminary so goes the church. No one can deny that the present tension in the major denominations over modernism, conservatism, and neo-orthodoxy is organically related to theological education. If any one factor is responsible for the decline of true religion in the past fotry years it has been the decadence of the theological seminary.

The churches of America are staffed by the graduates of the numerous seminaries of our land. Eventually the churches take on the theological hue and color of the under-shepherd of the flock. These two factors working in harmony have helped to cause the decline of orthodox Christianity. The manner of it is simple. Liberals captured the citadels of learning, the seminaries. Then they steeped their students with their unbelief and modernism. By higher criticism and unending attack on the Word of God as the only infallible rule of faith and practice, the faith of the students was undermined. Conditioned in such an environment with no emphasis on the new birth or need for a real spiritual experience, the men went forth to the churches to put into practice what they learned or did not learn in the seminaries. Gradually the churches were filled with people devoid of a spiritual experience but learned in the things that do not produce everlasting life.

Not all the seminaries were affected by this intrusion of liberalism into the halls of learning. Nor did the subversion of the institutions occur simultaneously. Some schools continued to stand long after most others had capitulated. Harold Ockenga was familiar with the process. He knew the trends. And when he entered into the pastorate the problem of advising candidates for the ministry concerning the choice of a seminary was thrown into the arena of his thinking.

Primarily a pulpit man himself, and exhibiting a great love for preaching, Ockenga always gave thoughtful consideration to Christian educational institutions. He accepted a trusteeship on the board of Gordon College and served on the board of Taylor University. From time to time inquiries came to him about assuming the presidency of one or another of America's Christian colleges. Never did he feel any inner constraint to consider these approaches seriously. He had an interest in academic preparation, and unknown to him God was preparing the circumstances to make his vision of well-trained men for the ministry a reality.

In the fall of 1946 Dr. Charles E. Fuller of Old-Fashioned-Revival-Hour fame, a man who preached to millions of people through the medium of radio for more than two decades, approached Harold Ockenga. Dr. Fuller had in mind the establishment of a school of evangelism and missions with a student body, in the future, of five hundred. He did not come to Ockenga because they were intimate friends. In fact, their relations to each other up to this point were nominal. Dr. Fuller had generously visited meetings which Ockenga held on the west coast and Ockenga helped in meetings which Dr. Fuller held in Boston. Each knew a great deal about the other through reputation and mutual friends and acquaintances.

In 1946 Dr. Fuller revealed to Harold Ockenga that God had laid a burden on his heart for training men to preach the gospel. However, Harold Ockenga did not think that training on the collegiate level was the answer to the problem. He was convinced that men today must be highly trained, with the best none too good in our present world. Even though Dr. Fuller, through his father, had some property and some money with which to begin the institution, Dr. Ockenga did not feel led to identify himself with the project on what would have been a collegiate level.

About the same time, Dr. Roy L. Laurin of the Westmont College Board of Trustees, wanted Ockenga to visit Westmont in the hope that he might assume the presidency of that school. This visit was combined with the delivery of the Griffith Thomas lectures at Dallas Theological Seminary in Texas. He met and talked with Dr. Fuller in February of 1947 and during the conversation expressed a conviction that a seminary of the highest academic calibre, with spiritual standards second to none, was the answer to the need of the hour. Informally approached about the presidency of Westmont at that time, he stated that he could not possibly leave the Park Street Church. This same answer he gave to Dr. Fuller when discussing the question of a new institution.

Both Dr. Fuller and Dr. Ockenga made the issue of a theological seminary a matter of prayer. Both knew that Dr. Ockenga would not and could not leave Boston, however. After much prayer Ockenga was led to make a commitment to the extent that he would accept a place on the board of trustees for the new institution if it was founded. Thus it was that in the spring of 1947, on the way home from the annual meeting of the N.A.E. in Omaha, Dr. Ockenga stopped off in Chicago to talk with Dr. Fuller, and Dr. Wilbur Smith of the Moody Bible Institute who had been brought into the picture. Ockenga and Fuller approached Wilbur Smith as to his availability for a teaching position on the faculty. Smith was widely known over America for his annual publication of Peloubet's Sunday School Lessons and also as a dynamic and aggressive defender of the evangelical faith. Author of a number of books, and a veritable dynamo of energy, he was believed to be a good choice for the first faculty member in the prospective institution.

Wilbur Smith heard the men and after prayerful consideration gave them his answer. He was willing to help inaugurate the enterprise provided three other men could be obtained. If three other first-rate men were willing to hazard their lives and their fortunes in the venture he was also agreeable. At the same time Dr. Smith wanted to know the exact relation of Harold Ockenga to the institution. At that point Dr. Ockenga indicated that he would take the presidency *in absentia,* and accept the academic responsibility of planning the curriculum, choosing the faculty, and whatever else needed to be done. Dr. Smith himself was not interested in the administrative side of institutional work but was truly concerned over the preparation of men for the ministry.

They originally planned to open the doors of the new school in September of 1948. But God was moving in a mysterious way to force the hands of all involved. Ockenga and Smith had correspondence and conversations with a number of other men. Carl F. H. Henry of the Northen Baptist Seminary of Chicago was added as a vitally interested man in the new project. Everett Harrison of Dallas Theological Seminary in Texas was named and he decided to cast his lot with the other men. Others were mentioned for a fourth man, without whom it was agreed that the institution would not begin. Dr. Ockenga engaged in extensive correspondence with Dr. Fuller and outlined what it would cost, what the problems were, and what might come from the move. Rising out of this correspondence, another meeting was called for May of 1947 in Chicago at the Christian Workers' Foundation offices.

At the May meeting Dr. Fuller was able to present the men with a building as a site for the seminary. He had purchased a large estate in Pasadena at a fraction of the original or reproduction cost. At this meeting the question of the opening date was again discussed and events moved so rapidly that it appeared impossible to wait until 1948. Everything geared into a perfect picture for opening the school the fall of 1947. Delay seemed unwise in the providence of God. The building was available, a faculty of three was gathered; only a fourth man remained to be secured. The fourth man was obtained in Harold Lindsell of the Northern Baptist Seminary faculty who agreed to become registrar and professor of church history and missions.

The decision to open the new theological institution on the professional or graduate school level was made at the end of May, 1947. By the first of July it was possible to make a public announcement about the school and to encourage men to send in requests for applications. Many inquiries came from interested people. A goodly number of those inquiring were not academically prepared to step into an institution requiring a collegiate diploma as a prerequisite. Many wanted only literature. But some had both the qualifications and the desire to come to the new school.

Carl F. H. Henry and Harold Lindsell met with Dr. Ockenga in his study high in the Park Street sanctuary that July. At this meeting the course of study was outlined by the new president and steps taken to print a catalogue and the registration and application forms. The work had to be completed rapidly and since the Registrar was spending the summer in New Hampshire the work had to be done in that area despite the lack of adequate facilities. God gave added grace at a time when it was needed and in a relatively short period the application forms and catalogues were ready for public distribution.

A real problem was liaison between the East and the West. An office staff was set up on the west coast comprising people who had never met those on the east coast but who had to work together as a team. Providentially God stepped into the picture and supplied the office of the Registrar with a woman of ability and skill who worked into the picture beautifully. At best it was a difficult situation; for the application forms were sent by the prospective student to the California location and from there to New England for appraisal and acceptance or rejection. Then the forms were shipped back to the coast and further instructions sent to the accepted students from there. Dormitory accommodations had to be arranged, school equipment like chairs, desks, typewriters, furniture for the students' rooms and hundreds of other items purchased.

The first men who came labored under adverse conditions because of the housing shortage. Three of the first year faculty could not get to California before September due to other commitments and when they did get there, only one of them had a place to live. The other two had to "camp out" in Seminary rooms pending the acquisition of a home of some kind.

The presence of Dr. Ockenga was missed from the beginning, but he had promised to be there for the first convocation and then for several weeks of the second semester. The Seminary was widely publicized and reactions came from all over America. Some reactions were favorable; others expressed fears. One journal said that the school might have a faculty of "stars" but questioned whether the "stars" would be able to work together harmoniously. By and large the reactions were decidedly good. Some pressures were brought to line up the seminary in one or another of the movements in American religious life.

Those who favored breaking with the old-line denominations knew that the presence of Ockenga, an N.A.E. leader, obviously meant that he would adhere to the same principles which he enunciated so clearly in his N.A.E. connections. For this reason some people claimed that the seminary was to be an N.A.E. school. This was not true, although members of the faculty and the president as individuals had close connections with the N.A.E. The strategy of those who favored breaking with the denominations and who wanted the institution to follow a similar pathway was to create friction and tension between the president and the founder, Dr. Fuller. In this way they felt they could force the issue. Fortunately the strategy at no time was successful.

Undoubtedly Harold Ockenga was fully aware of the efforts to undermine him with the seminary and the founder. The opponents of the N.A.E. had attacked him for a long time. He had suffered much misrepresentation at their hands. Perhaps this in part explains the reference he made to "come-outism" in the first convocation address for the institution. This convocation was held in the Civic Auditorium in Pasadena, California, the week the school opened its doors. A multitude of well-wishers filled the auditorium to see and hear the official launching of the seminary. Dr. Ockenga gave a masterful address.

What Dr. Ockenga said in the first convocation address was simply a restatement of what he had maintained for many years. He believed with Calvin that when a church ceases to be a true church men ought to leave it. But he was not convinced that all of the churches spoken of as "apostate" by some people were all actually apostate or that the time had come to leave them. He did not intend then or now to reflect upon any man or movement which had separated from a church or other group for conscience' sake. That, he recognized to be a man's inherent right in the belief that a man can worship God according to the dictates of his own conscience. He opposed then and he now opposes the type of negativism which constantly attacks other groups and other positions rather than engaging in a positive presentation of the gospel and a constructive ministry.

His remarks about "come-outism" were isolated by some from the rest of his speech, although they should have been interpreted in accord with the remainder of it. A hue and cry was raised all over America by those who opposed Ockenga and the N.A.E. The short paragraph was taken out of its context and spoken of as a "betrayal" of separatist forces, with the idea that the convocation address was designed to curry favor with the Presbyterian Church, U.S.A.

All over America people were encouraged to believe that the seminary was not theologically sound; that Dr. Fuller was being deceived; that the Old Fashioned Revival Hour was not worthy of the support of Christians after its many years of unremitting proclamation of the gospel; that young men ought not to be encouraged to attend the seminary.

Dr. Fuller was deeply grieved over the attacks and more so when some people who had professed friendship over the years deserted the cause. This servant of God, for almost a quarter of a century, had proclaimed the unsearchable riches to Christ to countless millions of people. Perhaps God intended this to be a sifting process like that experienced by the men who followed Gideon. The Old Fashioned Revival Hour went on its way. For every desertion God had a replacement. Once again the Lord plainly brought home the lesson that the broadcast was His work and that He had ways and means of sustaining it. Little did Charles E. Fuller know then that the new medium for reaching people with the gospel—television—after this time of testing would be opened to him and that God would lead along this way.

Everything Dr. Fuller ever did for God has been subjected to attack. It is in the nature of the Christian warfare that those who labor for Him shall suffer tribulation and endure hardship. Inured by his long years of previous testing and fully confident of the guidance of God he did not turn back, but once more laid all on the altar of sacrifice—to be rewarded in a few short years by seeing men go forth from the institution he helped to create to add to the number of those preaching the gospel.

Eternity alone will reveal the extent of the damage that was caused by these unwarranted attacks. Unquestionably the Devil spent many an enjoyable time contemplating the progress he had made by dividing Christians who were otherwise agreed on the fundamental doctrines of the Christian faith. Well had Satan learned across the years that Christians in agreement on doctrine can be instrumental in damaging and ruining the work of Christ in other ways. Well did the Devil remember the rebuke of Jesus to his own disciples regarding sectarianism in Mark

9: 38-40: "We saw one casting out devils in thy name, and he followeth not us: and we forbad him, because he followeth not us. But Jesus said, Forbid him not: for there is no man which shall do a miracle in my name, that can speak lightly of me. For he that is not against us in on our part."

The faculty of the institution in conjunction with Dr. Ockenga considered the advisability of making a statement regarding the misrepresentation on "come-outism." After full debate it was decided that the policy of the institution in this and in all such matters, wherever they might originate, should be to remain quiet and give God time to work on our behalf. Reminded that God has ways of defending His own children when they put their trust in Him, and that deep waters would be the lot of His children, the faculty readily claimed the promises of God. Totally apart from this was the human knowledge and consideration than anything said in reply would be distorted beyond recognition, as experience had already taught. The Lord Jesus himself suffered in silence before Pontius Pilate and His disciples could afford to do the same.

Silence during those days of continuing attack paid off richly in spiritual dividends. The faculty was drawn closer together and closer to God. His strength became the well-spring from which to draw. Daily He supplied every need. The attack diminished and the school discovered that strong supporters were added who were evangelical and who did not care for the attacks or the methodology underlying them.

During the first year the institution had to face severe problems in other directions. One of them involved the zoning ordinances of Pasadena. Looking to permission from the zoning authorities to convert the premises purchased by the school into an administration building, the faculty was surprised to learn that it probably would not be granted. The zoning problem of the whole street was involved with a complexity of factors which made it highly unlikely that suitable changes would be made for some time. Fortunately the Lake Avenue Congregational Church opened its Sunday-school plant to the institution and this arrangement was admirably advantageous to both parties.

A good library was obtained for the new seminary. More than ten thousand volumes were acquired, and in addition to these which belonged to the seminary itself was added the personal library of Dr. Wilbur M. Smith. Possessing more than thirteen thousand volumes, he made this large private collection available to the entire seminary. At least the classes did not lack reading material, since other professors added to the stock their own collections of more than seven thousand volumes.

The president planned the institution with the provision that only first-year men would enter the opening year. In the second year a new class would enter and the first year's class would then be the middle class. This class would be ready for the first commencement in May of 1950. The plan was to build the seminary logically and in an orderly fashion. It made possible the addition of necessary faculty personnel year by year instead of all at once when it might have been a substantial difficulty.

The students that first year were fine men. Most of them were war veterans who had seen action in World War II. They were mature, responsible and ready for work. The spirit was good, the fellowship close, and the whole year pleasant. For the faculty the teaching load was light the first year but this was more than made up by the small matters constantly demanding attention. A new organization was being created and the "tooling up" process kept faculty members busy with assignments outside their teaching. Committee appointments were particularly heavy since there were only four men to share them all for the first year.

One reaction from denominational sources created the possibility of strife. The Los Angeles Presbytery overtured the Pittsburgh Presbytery to forbid Harold Ockenga to labor at the Fuller Seminary. The charge against the institution was "divisiveness." On one hand the school was criticized because it did not take a divisive position and on the other for being divisive.

Harold Ockenga had received ordination in the Presbyterian Church, U. S. A., by the Pittsburgh Presbytery. When its sister Presbytery, Los Angeles, overtured the Pittsburgh Presbytery, it was recommended to President Ockenga, without official Presbytery action, that he transfer into the denomination with which he was working through Park Street: the Congregational group. This he did and the reason for so doing was his distaste for fighting—especially since it would involve the institution itself and do no good. Always Ockenga had covenanted with himself that he would never split a local church and that if a situation ever arose at Park Street he would leave the church rather than split it.

With the dawning of the second year seventy new students and three new faculty members joined the family. Dr. Edward John Carnell joined the faculty. Dr. Gleason L. Archer, holding numerous degrees and honors, including the doctorate from Harvard, came in the field of Old Testament. And Dr. Arnold Ehlert came as librarian.

Dr. Ockenga spent nearly four weeks at the seminary the middle of the first year. He returned for the convocation at the opening of the second year. Bringing a tremendous message on the theme, "This is the Hour," he stirred and challenged hearts to the task that lies before the Church of Jesus Christ. The new faculty members were installed in their chairs and the splendid new class officially welcomed into the seminary family. The pioneer days of the school were not over but God had blessed. More tests lay ahead but a rocky road had been traversed; experience had been gained; and time was of the essence.

The second year of the seminary moved along without unusual incidents. Externally the situation was much quieter; internally there was faculty harmony and student unity. As a unit, forward progress was made. A large number of books were added to the library, the academic program was enriched, and the preaching outreach of the faculty increased considerably. Approval by the state of California which resulted in federal benefits for the veterans was gained.

When the time came for bringing in the third class, the school had added housing facilities for single and married students and had begun a campaign to raise funds for the main administration building. This building was to be in honor of Dr. Charles E. Fuller, the seminary having been named for his father who had left some trust funds for purposes like this. The Christian public was invited to have a share in erecting this building; for the funds left by the father of Dr. Fuller could not do everything. The ground on which the building was to be erected had been obtained but the construction of the building waited for gifts from God's people who wanted to have a part in the training of young men for the Gospel ministry. The campaign was launched informally before the end of the second year, at which time the trustees, faculty, and students, pledged thirty-five thousand dollars toward the building. This was accepted as a token from God that having done their best they could with clear consciences ask others to help.

The third year opened with a new junior class which brought the enrollment to more than one hundred and fifty students. Three new faculty members joined the staff, making ten full-time men in addition to four part-time workers. And with the advent of the third year some old problems were solved and some new ones added. By this time the institution was placed on the Attorney General's list, which permitted foreign students to come to the school on a student's visa instead of on a visitor's visa, which required renewal every six months and which did not permit a foreign student to obtain gainful employment while here. The Department of Education in Washington accepted the institution for listing in its biennial publication, and steps looking toward membership and accreditation in the American Association of Theological Schools were inaugurated.

At the opening of the third year the president brought his third convocation address. This time speaking on the subject "The Sons of the Prophets," he brought a superb address to the several thousand people gathered in the Pasadena Civic Auditorium. At this meeting Harold Ockenga had the pleasure of beholding with Dr. Fuller an institution which had reached maturity under their combined leadership and that of the trustees. One hundred and fifty students and a faculty of ten were there. The first class looked to graduation the following May. The field had been sown and a harvest soon was to be reaped.

It was not without some insight into the life of an institution that Emerson said so aptly: "An institution is the lengthened shadow of one man." Truly in the case of the Fuller Theological Seminary, a product of the vision of two men, Harold Ockenga and Charles Fuller, it could be said that this institution is the lengthened shadow of these men. Both had the same vision and wanted to attain the same objective—that of training men for the home pastorates, for the mission fields of the world, and for strategic teaching postions at home and abroad to bring to the world the glorious tidings of salvation as found in the life, death, and resurrection of the blessed Lord Jesus.

Harold Ockenga is serving temporarily as president *in absentia*. People often ask whether he will come to California to serve the institution full time or whether he will abdicate in favor of someone else, remaining at the famous Park Street Church. He himself does not know the answer to that question. He has not been called upon to face the issue and decide one way or the other yet. Above all he wants the will of God for his life. And when he reaches that fork in the road he confidently knows that God will reveal to him His perfect will and confirm that to him unmistakably so that he can make his life count best for the cause of the Master.

Chapter

" . . . O Lord, revive thy work in the midst of the years, in the midst of the years make known; in wrath remember mercy."
— *Habakkuk* 3:2

Nine

Revival Comes

THE HEART OF Harold Ockenga yearned and longed for revival for many years. His library contains well-thumbed volumes on this subject. Finney's great lectures on revival are there. Volumes on the work of men like Whitefield, Tennent, Edwards, and the Wesleys have yielded their rich spiritual treasures to this man whose soul is ceaselessly burdened for the special outpouring of God's Holy Spirit in this generation.

Ockenga knows that the Holy Spirit of God moves, at least partly, in response to devoted prayer. For fourteen long years at Park Street prayer went up to God as incense beseeching Him for revival. Had not Park Street Church been the scene of mighty works of grace? Had not men like Finney, Moody, and Biederwolf stirred God's people in past days? Had the God of Elijah left them forever? Were there no more mercy drops from heaven available to them? Years had passed and Park Street knew no special visitation of God's power. But in the valley years when the road was long, and hot, and dry, pastor and people persevered in their ceaseless intercession for a manifestation once again of mountain-top experiences and the refreshing showers of spiritual blessing.

Harold John keeps a prayer book. In this little book he writes down his personal requests and when the prayer is answered he puts in the date of the answer. When circumstances demonstrate that certain requests no longer require prayer and apparently the prayers have not been answered so far as human sight can tell, they are scratched out. But for fourteen years the prayer for revival remained. Blessings came; the work of the church prospered; the missionary program moved forward—but the great revival did not come. And still the shepherd and the flock prayed on for revival.

In 1940 the two hundredth anniversary of the Great Awakening dawned. Ockenga secretly hoped and fervently prayed that this was the year for a new outpouring. People and pastor prayed on but the looked-for blessing did not materialize in the great revival. Missionary blessings came; souls were converted; prayer meetings flourished; weekly cottage prayer meetings were not uncommon. The whole church was geared for the anticipated spiritual blessing—but it did not come.

Park Street Church emphasizes prayer strongly. Every Friday night for years the weekly prayer meeting assembled. Except for the summer months, three hundred or more people gathered together. Usually three hundred and fifty to four hundred and fifty people came together to lay hold of God. Half a dozen cottage prayer meetings were active the year round. For several months prior to the annual missionary rally twelve or fourteen cottage prayer meetings met weekly to insure the success of the missionary venture. Surrounding communities like Belmont, Watertown, Cambridge, Melrose, Brighton, Needham, and Wollaston had cottage prayer meetings to give the membership living outside the city limits an opportunity to meet for prayer. Preceding the regular Friday night prayer meetings a dozen groups often gathered in various portions of the church plant to engage in the holy ministry of intercession.

For months before the annual missionary conference, prayer meetings were held on Sunday afternoons. And all of this prayer effort resulted in blessing. The church restoration was an answer to prayer; the Mayflower pulpit was an answer to prayer; conversons came through prayers; backslidden Christians were restored through prayer. Always prayer opened the door to the expanding ministry and influence of this church.

In his own personal experience Harold Ockenga came to know something about prayer. For a season a throat ailment gave him much trouble. Expert medical advice with the finest treatment, including an operation, did not effect a cure. For weeks and months he was laid aside. Despite an aching soul which cried out to preach, he simply marked time. Anxious and fretting, he desired above all else to resume actively the ministry to which God called him. It was an enigma to him why God cut off his effectiveness when, so far as he knew, his life was right with God, the work was going forward, and limitless opportunity opened before his eyes. Those were days and months of severe testing. Prayer bathed in tears of importunity rose to heaven, but nothing happened.

One day God did something in the soul of the Park Street prophet. While Harold John emptied and humbled himself before the Lord in an open woodshed in New Hampshire, the still, small voice of Jehovah-Jireh spoke. His voice questioned, "Harold, are you willing never to preach again? Will you accept even this as my will for you?"

The murmurings of self were silenced before the voice of the Lord. The anxiety of heart and fretfulness of spirit stood clearly revealed. Ockenga saw now that he was impatient; that *he* wanted to preach again; that *his* plans were important—but that now all of these considerations faded into oblivion before the light of God's presence. His heart pondered the question over and over again, "Are you willing never to preach again if it is God's will?" No special experience came; no tears flowed; no exotic outbursts occurred. In the quietness of that hour before the Lord, Ockenga lifted his heart and answered that question. No wordy, verbose sentences sprang from lips or soul. Rather in the simplicity of faith and like a child he said to God, "Lord if you do not want me to preach again, it's all right with me." That was all there was to it—surrender to the will of God. If he never preached again it would be all right with him.

From the moment that prayer of surrender to God's will was uttered, healing began. God moved in on a human predicament and worked on behalf of this yielded servant. Under the miracle working power of God, Ockenga preached once more and from that day to this God has marvelously sustained him and enabled him to meet his heavy speaking commitments without the loss of voice or efficiency. No one, hearing him today, would ever suspect that he had experienced any difficulty at any time with his voice. Thus it was through this and other numerous experiences that Harold Ockenga came to know the power of God in answer to prayer.

The knowledge that God works in answer to prayer he had experienced personally. Books in his library bore striking testimony in the lives of others. Revival he knew to be directly related to faithful and persevering prayer—but revival still did not come.

From time to time the Park Street Church called in outstanding men to minister to the church and to Boston. Bob Jones, William Ward Ayer, Gordon Brownville, Paul Rees, Harry Hager, Oswald Smith, Howard Ferrin and others came, were heard, and left without the great revival breaking. Mercy drops fell, but not the showers of revival. These men preached fearlessly and faithfully. Much good was done, souls were won, but still the great revival did not break.

When the National Association of Evangelicals was formed in the early forties, some of the brethren believed that revival was on the verge of breaking out. Somehow forces operated to prevent it from happening. Ockenga believed with all his heart that the N.A.E. then was meant to be the vehicle through which God was going to break through. Yet it did not happen. Bishop Marston could say, "America's revival is breaking." And still the great revival did not break. As God, when one channel is closed, finds another channel, so it was that another channel was found.

The channel God has used to bring the longed-for revival to New England and to Park Street is the Youth for Christ movement. Begun at a time when America's spiritual life was at low ebb this mighty movement born of God reached out to attract the youth of America. Saturday night after Saturday night thousands and thousands of young Americans met and today meet all over our land. And youth found Christ. Criticized, maligned, lambasted by many for its "unorthodox" approach to youth, and a program "geared" to youth, no man can deny today that God has used Youth for Christ to stir America and to reach out through Youth for Christ to the mission fields of the world.

Out of Youth for Christ came Billy Graham. And today Billy Graham is one of God's chosen men for the hour of revival. As the voice of one crying in the wilderness, God has raised him up for a testimony that Elijah's God is not dead nor does He sleep. So it is that the evangelistic and revival passion of Harold Ockenga linked to the mighty Spirit-drenched preaching of Billy Graham brought what Ockenga has sought for many years: revival.

In the middle of 1948 Harold Ockenga contacted Billy Graham to hold meetings with him in Boston. Ockenga endeavored to get the pastors of Boston interested in a city-wide campaign, but he encountered locked doors. The pastors stated that they did not know Billy Graham (and they *did not* know him, nor did it imply any criticism of him) and did not want to gamble on a man they did not know. Ockenga countered with the proposition that he would bring in Graham for a ten-day meeting and if the pastors of the area were satisfied they would then hold a city-wide campaign another year. To this proposal general assent resulted.

It is well to remember that Billy Graham, at this time, had not held the Los Angeles tent meetings which opened a new era in revival work. But Ockenga believed that Billy was the man for this Boston testimony and somehow came to know that God would do a new thing for the people of New England.

Ockenga wanted a testimony for Christ in Boston on New Year's Eve. The ten-day campaign he scheduled in the Park Street Church, but for New Year's Eve Harold John wanted a larger testimony. In December of 1948, on the strength of the promises of two men, Allan C. Emery, Jr., and Malcolm Calder of the Park Street Church that they would stand any financial loss. Ockenga dared to rent the Mechanic's Hall in Boston for New Year's Eve of 1949. This hall in Boston seats more than six thousand people. Surely if they filled this hall on the eve of the New Year it would be a testimony for Christ!

Upon completon of the arrangements in February of 1949, Billy Graham already having assented to come, Ockenga again approached the ministers of the area to inquire if they would join him in this one service. The evangelicals of Boston enthusiastically agreed to participate in the projected New Year's Eve rally. During this same time Ockenga again pushed for a future city-wide campaign. It so happened that Graham was engaged to hold a Baltimore meeting and the Boston brethren agreed that a committee should attend that meeting and if satisfied with Graham then the evangelicals of Boston would unite for a city-wide campaign in the near future. When they heard Graham the committee endorsed him, talking in terms of a city-wide campaign for November of 1951 and even voted to approach Billy Graham to hold meetings at that time.

Looking toward the 1949-50 meeting which included the projected one-night stand in the Mechanics Hall, two committees were set up. The first committee was a Park Street Church committee headed by Allan C. Emery, Jr., a Boston merchant whose father has been a staunch supporter of New England evangelical movements for decades and under whose labors Billy Sunday put on a Boston campaign some years ago. The second committee served for the Mechanics Hall meeting and included many of the Park Street committee members in addition to others representing interested evangelical churches and believers. On the whole it was preponderantly a Park Street affair even in the Mechanics committee.

For the New Year's Eve meeting the Gideons consented to handle the ushering and the assistant city editor of the

Boston *Herald* became publicity chairman. This latter individual performed yeoman for service for the cause, which, in fact, resulted in perhaps the finest newspaper coverage any revival movement has ever had in the New England area.

The committee made extensive, detailed, and careful preparations for Billy Graham's coming. They checked finances, organizations, prayer meetings, advertising and other matters carefully. The first meeting was scheduled for the Park Street Church, Friday evening, December 30. This meeting was in the nature of a preparatory one for the Park Street congregation so the committee did not advertise it widely. When the night of the first meeting came, the ten-day revival campaign got off to a thrilling start with a packed auditorium.

The central feature of the ten-day rally was the New Year's Eve service. By this time reports of the wonderful Los Angeles meetings of Billy Graham percolated throughout the United States and Christians took notice that God had done something out of the ordinary. From eight o'clock in the evening to midnight on December 31, the Mechanics Hall meeting was in session. Grady Wilson, Beverly Shea, Cliff Barrows, folks from the New England Evangelistic Association, the New England Fellowship, the pastor of the famed Baptist Tremont Temple in Boston, and other pastors and churches were there. The public packed the hall with no standing room and with hundreds turned away for lack of seating or standing space. One hundred and fifty people accepted Christ at this meeting and personal workers from Park Street Church and other co-operating churches dealt with them about salvation.

This glorious evening broke the ice and did something which had never been done in New England before. Never in the history of this city had such a wonderful service been held on such an unauspicious night—New Year's Eve. God broke through and worked in a marvelous manner. The Boston press caught hold of the meeting and gave it front-page treatment.

Deeply moved, Ockenga caught a vision of what could be done. On the spur of the moment, fourteen hours away from the projected meeting time, he proposed to Billy Graham and Allan C. Emery, Jr., that they hold another Mechanics Hall meeting the following afternoon, which was Sunday. Checking to see if the hall could be rented and finding it free, they engaged it, and the co-operating pastors agreed to announce it to their people at the church services. With almost no advance publicity whatever and only a few announcements here and there the Mechanics Hall on Sunday afternoon, January first, was almost completely filled. Fifty-five hundred people came to hear and one hundred and fifty men and women found Jesus Christ as Saviour and Lord.

On Sunday evening Billy Graham preached at the Park Street Church. Twenty-five hundred people packed the main auditorium and overflowed into other portions of the church to hear the service by loud speakers. Two thousand people were turned away from the meeting. The manifest moving of God's Spirit was apparent to all. Twenty-five or thirty more people found Christ in that evening service.

Ockenga himself never saw anything like it in his years of gospel ministry. His prayers and those of his people had not been in vain. The Spirit was moving and revival was not breaking—it had broken! What it would become and where it would lead to he did not know. But his own spirit was so challenged that caution was thrown to the wind and he promised himself to move out in any direction God indicated.

On Monday night, January 2, the Park Street Church was filled again. Twenty-five hundred people jammed the edifice and as many more encountered closed doors for lack of space. The leadership covenanted with God that Monday evening was the test night. They put out the fleece with the promise that if God did something and indicated they ought to seek larger space it would be done in simple faith. When the Monday meeting was over, the leading of God's Spirit was clearly discerned by all. Inquiry revealed that the Mechanics Hall was available for the next four nights. In faith they rented it for those nights and publicized the meetings.

By now the revival stirred the city of Boston, and Christians laid hold of God as they sought for showers, not just drops of rain. On Tuesday evening the hall was filled except for possibly two hundred and fifty seats. On Wednesday only a hundred seats were vacant. On Thursday five hundred were unoccupied. On Friday, the 6th of January, every seat was taken and again God worked. In one week of meetings, beginning with the initial Park Street meeting on Friday, December 30, roughly nine hundred people professed to accept Christ as Saviour and signed cards. Boston had not seen, if ever, such mighty power from God for many years. Nine hundred conversions in one week!

On Tuesday, January 3, Edward Dunn, editor of the Boston *Post* called Ockenga. "Why don't you have a meeting in the Boston Garden?" he asked. Ockenga replied that he had tried to get the Boston Garden but it was taken for six months on weekends and for three solid months on week nights. It could not be obtained. Tersely Dunn asked Ockenga a pointed question, "If I get you the Boston Garden, will you take it?" And then he said, "I'll get behind you." With fear and trembling Ockenga responded, "If you get the Garden we'll take it."

In a few moments Harold Ockenga contacted one of the leading pastors of Boston, asking his advice about the Garden. This brother cautioned him against rushing in and making a fool of himself. In his opinion he recommended "No" as the answer. Ockenga next called Allan C. Emery, Jr., a hard-headed young businessman, and a Park Street deacon. Emery said, "Take it." Then Ockenga called the church treasurer, for the meetings were under the control of the church and the financial problems belonged not to an individual but to the corporation. The treasurer advised calling the trustees of the corporation. Before God, Ockenga covenanted that if these trustees, unknown to each other, said, "Yes" they would go ahead. He placed eleven phone calls and in turn each man, without knowing what the others had said, replied, "Yes." Businessmen, they were moved by God to reach out in faith on this magnificent evangelistic enterprise.

The cost of the Boston Garden for one night was thirty-seven hundred dollars. But on the approval of the trustees Ockenga moved ahead. He engaged the Garden for Monday night, January 16. In the meantime they needed other places for their meetings.

When Ockenga secured Mechanics Hall for four days in that first week of January, he knew that if the meetings continued until the 16th another place would have to be secured. On Thursday, January 5, he looked at the Boston Opera House which seats 3400 people. Checking with the head man he learned that only a call to New York would avail. Contacting the Schubert office in New York, he was told that for six hundred and fifty dollars a night the evangelistic party could have the Opera House for the following Monday through Friday. They took the step in faith and at one time the financial commitments for rentals on different halls amounted to more than ten thousand dollars. They truly were moving out in faith, trusting God.

Every evening that Billy preached the Opera House was filled with standing room only. From January 11, no matter where the meetings were held, no hall had enough seats to accommodate the crowds that came. It was a long walk from the balconies and the longest to the stage of the Opera House and yet hundreds made that walk to find in Christ life everlasting.

When the Opera House was no longer available, the Mechanics Hall opened to them once more. They moved into this hall again on Friday, the 13th, and stayed there through Sunday. People gladly stood to hear the message although the hall itself could accommodate more than six thousand people. Hundreds stood those three days, and on Sunday, the 15th, in the afternoon, thousands of people were unable to enter the hall at all. Hundreds again responded to the invitation to accept Christ as Saviour.

Reports began to flow back to Park Street of how God blessed other churches and areas through the meetings. One pastor who had labored long with never a conversion went back to his church and on Sunday preached to his people with such unction that forty-five men, women, and children accepted Christ. Even deacons were saved. On Sunday, the 15th, Ockenga himself preached in the Park Street Church morning and evening while Billy Graham preached in Mechanics Hall in the afternoon. At the morning and evening services together between sixty and seventy people professed Christ as Saviour in the Park Street Church. Ockenga himself felt the blessing of God's Spirit and the showers continued to pour down mightily.

While all this was happening, the Boston press gave the revival meetings widespread publicity. Everyone now looked forward to the Boston Garden meeting. No one felt that the meeting in the Garden should close this work of God. Consequently, Ockenga checked everywhere to see where they could go when the Garden meeting ended. Mechanics Hall was out; the Opera House was not available; the Rockwell Cage of the Massachusetts Institute of Technology could not be had. They put the fleece out again. If God wanted the meetings continued He would have to open the doors. So they waited expectantly for the biggest rally of them all, the Boston Garden conclave.

The committee called for an all-day prayer meeting at Tremont Temple for the Garden revival. Evangelical churches and pastors joined in the effort, although Dr. Ockenga himself was chairman of all the meetings. Loyally the ministers backed this work of God. Truly they saw God breaking through. Radio, newspapers, men, everything, geared together by God's grace to produce the maximum effort to reach souls for Him. At Tremont Temple daily prayer meetings had been held. And now on the day of the Garden meeting this all-day prayer meeting in the Temple convened. Between two and three thousand people made their way at different times during the day to this Baptist stronghold to make intercession to God for the evening meeting.

At 4:30 P.M., January 16, people clamored to get into the Boston Garden. At 5:00 P.M. the doors opened. At 6:55 P.M., fifty minutes before the meeting was supposed to commence, sixteen thousand people crowded inside the Garden. It was so packed that the police closed the doors and refused to permit any more people to enter. Twenty-five hundred people stood in the lobby just to hear what was going on. Ten thousand more people filled the streets. There was no room! Busloads of people came from Vermont, New Hampshire, western Massachusetts, Rhode Island, and even Connecticut. Revival truly had broken!

In the Garden that night they put up no signs, no banners, no decorations. The committee made no special appeal to the eye. It was a meeting of God with people. Billy Graham spoke for thirty minutes on Noah's Ark. He did not have to press or plead. But sinners were on the march. The inquiry room seated six hundred people. Every seat was taken. Hundreds stood after they walked down the aisles to find Christ. Between twelve and fifteen hundred people made decisions for Jesus. No one wanted to leave the Garden even when the services were over and the last sinner had made his choice. At last at 11:30, attendants turned off the lights and slowly the crowds began to file out of the Boston Garden.

In the space of eighteen days more than three thousand souls made their peace with God. Every outstanding bill was paid and some money was left over. No meeting place opened for the continuance of the revival campaign, but the Spirit of God seemed to say, "Halt the meetings temporarily, do not close them." And this is exactly what they did—suspend the meetings, covenanting again with God that in the spring they would seek to shake, not only Boston, but all of New England for Jesus Christ.

Graham and Ockenga discussed continuing the meetings in the spring. Billy was agreeable to returning but he laid down two conditions. He wanted Harold Ockenga to direct the campaign as a whole and to be present and to help in the meetings. In fact, Ockenga was to talk on revivals before Graham preached. Unquestionably Billy Graham sensed that God has given Ockenga splendid organizational abilities and he knew that under that kind of leadership the preliminary steps leading to a larger New England campaign would be taken care of. Ockenga himself had gained valuable experience about the conduct of an evangelistic campaign by his own labors in Syracuse the previous fall.

When Ockenga contemplated holding meetings in Syracuse he laid down several conditions. He asked for a neutral meeting place; for the inauguration of prayer meetings prior to the campaign; and for the churches to guarantee the financial underwriting of the campaign in advance so that no pleading for money would be needed during the campaign. When the Syracuse pastors agreed to these stipulations, the deacons of the Park Street Church released their minister for the meetings. No neutral hall was found in Syracuse and the committee was shut down to the idea of building their own tabernacle for the meetings. A lot in the heart of the city became available; twelve men signed a fifteen-thousand-dollar note; materials were purchased, and except for the salary of the building supervisor the labor unions contributed their services in the erection of a tabernacle seating thirty-four hundred people.

In Syracuse Ockenga had twenty days of marvelous meetings with more than three hundred decisions for Jesus Christ. In this campaign he found out what ought to be done, and his own soul was set on fire for more evangelism. This series of meetings ended on November 25, 1949, and fresh from them he came into the Boston meetings with Billy Graham with the passion as well as the know-how.

For the second phase of the New England revival Ockenga initiated some changes. Now the work of the Holy Spirit made it plain that God was not working on behalf of the Park Street Church alone. All interested evangelicals who wanted to make a revival impact on the area now could join hands in this venture of faith. A New England-wide committee was formed as requests poured in from all over New England asking that Billy Graham come in the second phase. This enlarged committee obtained the services of Mr. Luckman from Gordon College who became the executive secretary. The nucleus of the area-wide committee came from Boston and included George McNeill of the New England Fellowship, Wesley Huber of the New England Evangelistic Association, George Murray of the First United Presbyterian Church, and the Vaughn Shed of the Lord's Day League, as well as others.

Rising out of the suggestion of Wesley Huber, a co-chairmanship was established with Harold Ockenga and Sidney Powell acting in concert. The larger New England committee came out of this and included local committees from all over New England. In turn these local committees built up the widest possible representation from among the evangelicals of their local areas so that all who wished to co-operate in this strategic effort for Christ might have ample opportunity to do so.

The men selected major New England cities for the itinerary which meant that hundreds of requests had to be declined. Time and physical limitations made it impossible to do more than the plans provided for. Specific financial arrangements guaranteed the integrity of the campaign and served to prevent criticism. Each committee in the area where a meeting was scheduled was responsible for local expenses. In the event the local area ran a deficit the main committee agreed to pay fifty per cent of that deficit with the local group paying the remainder. No love offerings were taken for Billy Graham in any of these non-Boston rallies and the expenses of the evangelistic party of seven men (Billy Graham, Cliff Barrows, Ted Smith, Jerry Beaven,

Grady Wilson, Beverly Shea, and Carlton Booth) were paid by the central committee.

Any funds turned in to the central committee from local rallies were used to help defray the expenses of the team, the advertising, the executive secretary, the expenses of the press relations man, and to remunerate the various men on the evangelistic team. The five men on the evangelistic team, not including Billy Graham and Cliff Barrows, at the end of their period of service, received a total of twenty-nine hundred dollars by way of remuneration. In the light of their services the total sum paid for this work was very small indeed. For Billy Graham and Cliff Barrows, a love offering was taken the last night in the Boston Garden. This Harold Ockenga believed would be a token to these men for their services, and while the amount of that offering was not made public Ockenga himself declared that it was not excessive nor can any charge of money-making be levelled at these men of God who labored on behalf of the gospel.

The funds left over from the first phase were invested in the second phase, and the Park Street Church to which this money belonged, donated it for the second phase. From the last report it appeared that the income from the various rallies in the second phase was not sufficient for the total expenses so that some of the money left over from the early meetings was absorbed.

Harold Ockenga knows the dangers connected with revival movements and he is conscious of the ethical temptations rising out of large-scale movements where money is collected. It is for this reason that every precaution was taken and every avenue safeguarded lest the work of God be hindered or impaired by the charge that money was the motivation or that those connected with it were serving for financial gain. Ockenga was the spark plug and the key man in the whole undertaking; he spent innumerable hours over the multitude of details that accompanied the effort—and he gave himself, his time, and his enthusiasm without taking for himself a single penny. And for this, God has richly rewarded him in spiritual benefits and in the knowledge that the work of God has prospered. Men have come to Christ, and the spiritual lives of Christians have been bettered a thousand fold.

Another contribution which Harold Ockenga made to the revival movement in New England and all over America, for that matter, involves the pattern or the method of the revival. Remembering the scripture which speaks of Paul as preaching in Ephesus and all Asia, Ockenga concluded that Boston was the central city and that from Boston they should "fan out" as it were into all of New England. This principle Billy Graham used in South Carolina between the first and the second phases of the New England campaign. And it worked in South Carolina as it worked in New England and as it will work in succeeding campaigns with Billy Graham and other evangelists as God leads.

With this background of extensive and intensive preparations, with hundreds of God's choicest people laboring all over New England, the campaign opened. From the closing part of March into the latter part of April the campaign moved forward with visits to leading New England cities. From Boston the evangelistic party went to Maine, stopping in Portland, Waterville, and Houlton. In New Hampshire Billy preached in Portsmouth, Manchester, and Concord. Twenty-seven thousand people heard him and sixteen hundred conversions were recorded. From New Hampshire he went to Vermont for a one-night stand in Burlington. Then the party moved into Massachussetts, Connecticut and Rhode Island, with stops at Springfield, Danbury, Bridgeport, West Harwich, Fall River, Woodstock, Providence, Fitchburg, Gardner, Concord, Worcester, Lowell, Hartford, and Waterbury.

Hundreds and thousands of people crowded place after place. Hundreds and thousands were turned away night after night. People traveled far and wide to come under the hearing of the gospel. Conservative and accurate estimates for the second phase, not including the final glorious rally on the Boston Common, place the number of people who heard Billy Graham at one hundred and fifteen thousand. And in this second phase of the great revival, six thousand and forty-six people signed cards accepting Jesus Christ as their personal Saviour. Thus in both phases of this unprecedented campaign more than nine thousand people signed confessions of faith. No cards were signed for the meeting on the Common, but from the number of hands raised, hundreds more came to a saving knowledge of Jesus Christ on that occasion.

Not so dramatic but perhaps more effective because it involved the student world, Graham addressed a large meeting of Brown University men and women. In Boston he addressed five thousand students in the Rockwell Cage, the largest Massachusetts Institute of Technology auditorium. Here admission was by ticket only.

The publicity accorded this campaign was also without precedent. Headlines appeared constantly throughout the campaign, and no less than four hundred and seventy-six newspaper articles were printed about the meetings. Even the Boston papers ran front page headlines almost daily. Local papers went all out to give journalistic coverage to the greatest series of meetings that had hit New England since the days of George Whitefield.

Police escorts met the team in almost every city. At each rally the committees hired two extra halls and wired them to care for possible overflow crowds. In Portland, Maine, folks jammed the extra halls and five thousand people lined the streets. In Hartford, Connecticut, people jammed the extra halls and thousands sought entrance in vain. Even an airplane hangar many miles from teeming cities was filled to hear this man of God speak.

Harold Ockenga went with the team to some of the cities and spoke on revival before Billy preached. When asked what he thought is a fair and adequate estimate of Billy whom God is using in our generation he thoughtfully replied. "Billy has a transparent passion and love for souls. He feels everything, but he feels first of all the great need for men to come to Jesus Christ. He is also a tremendous strategist. He sees opportunities and lays hold of them. When preaching he dramatizes and makes real to the people the truth he is mediating. The people actually "see" what he talks about. It is remarkably effective, for when people have laid hold of the truth they are then responsive to it and act accordingly. Billy is sincere and consecrated. He has humbled himself before God and God has exalted him. It is an unblemished sincerity and is not colored with self or its by-products. He also has a personal magnetism as evidenced by the universal approbation accorded him by the reporters who made the tour with the evangelistic party. On the morning of his departure from Boston when the campaign was over, a breakfast was held for Billy with the reporters present. Many of them wept unashamedly over his departure. And finally, Billy has a consecrated wife who is willing to let her husband follow the will of God and be absent from home and its enchantments when he has every reason to be there."

So Billy preached; Cliff Barrows led the singing; Beverly Shea and Carlton Booth sang; Ted Smith played the piano. And God's Spirit used these men to bring revival blessing to New England. Everywhere the same old story was re-enacted. Under the preaching of this fiery evangelist hundreds sought the front of auditoriums all over New England to confess their sins and find refuge in the Rock of Ages. No special pleading was necessary. As soon as the call came people moved forward under the dynamic of God's spirit. Tears flowed; confessions poured forth; wrongs were made right; sinners became saints; homes were transformed by the power of God; and all Heaven rejoiced in the salvation of men, women and children.

After the triumphant tour of New England the meetings closed with four rallies in the Boston Garden. But Ockenga was not satisfied with only this. He conceived of a final rally on the Boston Common where Whitefield had preached more than two hundred years before. He suggested to Billy Graham that they have a tremendous peace offensive based on the truth of Genesis 6, which states that where corruption covered the earth violence reigned. Using this in conjunction with the book of Romans, Ockenga concluded that wherever you have righteousness you have peace, which is the fruit of righteousness. And the way to peace is through repentance, revival, and righteousness.

On the Sunday of the mass rally on the Boston Common the weather was disastrously bad. It was cold, raw, and rainy. But the multitude gathered hours in advance for this wonderful meeting. When the rally began, the rain ceased and in place of the rain God sent His divine showers of blessing.

Boston is predominantly Roman Catholic. This group did not wish to permit a successful meeting of Protestants on the Common. Consequently, when the police estimated the number of people attending the meeting their estimate was influenced by Roman Catholic pressures in this city. The estimate was given out that ten thousand people were there. It was so obviously inaccurate with five hundred people along the rope, four hundred deep, tapering off in the rear, that the newspapers struck a half way estimate between the figures of the police and other estimates. The papers proclaimed that forty thousand people were there. Harold Ockenga believes that the crowd was closer to seventy five thousand but speaks in terms of fifty thousand people. It is not that numbers in themselves mean anything, save as they witness to the mighty power of God and reveal how God is working in our generation.

In this mass meeting Ockenga called for a peace offensive with fifty million Americans joining in it. Billy spoke briefly on his own five-point peace plan, the last point of which called for a revival of real heart religion. It was a spiritual answer to the Russian five-year plans. Then Harold Ockenga led the mass of people in a prayer for peace which the people repeated phrase by phrase after him. Following the outline of the peace plan and the prayer for peace, Billy preached on the subject "Prepare to meet thy God." Hearts were touched and souls saved. And the campaign for Christ in New England concluded gloriously on this high note and in demonstration of power and might.

Mass evangelism has many critics. Some have proclaimed that the day of mass evangelism is over. Los Angeles, South Carolina, and New England have disproved this and the critics have had their mouths stopped by the power of God. Other critics have stated that mass evangelism rests on an emotional appeal and that the "converted" masses return to their old condition as soon as the evangelistic meetings are over. This criticism has valid aspects if nothing is done to insure the permanence of the results. Normally no evangelist can be held responsible for this aspect of the problem. Once the evangelist has come in, and has obtained conversions, the work of construction following the experience of the new birth must be the responsibility and the obligation of those who remain when the evangelist has departed. This work of construction logically belongs to the churches and to the ministry and in its own right is vitally important although less conspicuous. It is a labor which requires time and patience and lasts over the lifetime of the new convert as he becomes assimilated outwardly, following the inward change of heart and life by conversion.

Acutely conscious of the need to conserve the results of the evangelistic campaign and this great revival, Ockenga laid down a consistent plan to retain the converts and to assimilate them into the churches. In the first phase of the campaign a personal letter signed by Ockenga, individually written (not printed or mimeographed), was sent to each convert. The signed cards were sent to the churches indicated on the decision cards for follow-up work, and on Graham's return for the second phase of the campaign two months later, twelve hundred of the converts came to the Park Street Church by special invitation to hear Billy Graham encourage them to continue in the Christian life.

In the second phase the signed cards were handled by the local groups, since it was impossible for the Boston committee to do much with those outside its geographical confines. To those from the Boston area the Committee sent letters although this time they were signed by the committee rather than by Ockenga, who, in the first phase, was in sole leadership, since it was a Park Street Church matter. A weekly series of six meetings followed, convening in the chapel of Gordon College, involving the expenditure of five hundred dollars. This series was designed for the converts of the first and the second phases with the view to conserving them and working them into the fellowship of the local churches.

In direct results accruing to the Park Street Church the blessing of the Lord was evident. In the first four months of 1950, one hundred and eighty-six people came into the fellowship of that church, bringing its membership up to twenty-three hundred and twenty-five.

Additions to the church were not the only gains made at this time. The annual missionary rally of the church came during the period of the revival campaign. The whole church was on fire over evangelism and this reflected itself in the zeal of the believers for sending out the light to regions of darkness. In 1949 the actual amount pledged during the week of missions was one hundred and ten thousand, seven hundred dollars. Eventually the pledges and income ran higher so that when the year was ended the church received from its people one hundred and thirty-three thousand, seven hundred and two dollars. Now in 1950 the missionary rally came at a moment when the people of God were on fire with revival enthusiasm.

At the end of this week of missionary emphasis, again the people were asked to make their annual pledges to God for the work of missions at home and abroad. Again the presence of the Holy Spirit in mighty power was seen. The pledges kept coming in and the figure climbed higher and higher. Rapidly it went over the one-hundred-thousand-dollar mark and kept moving upward until it hit a new total for Park Street Church—a total of one hundred and forty-three thousand, four hundred sixty-five dollars and ninety-five cents

($143,465.95). In the light of the previous experience this gave pastor and people every reason to believe that before the end of the year the actual amount received would exceed one hundred and fifty thousand dollars for missions alone.

But the work of Park Street is not complete. Its numbers and its influence have increased; its missionary program seeks higher levels each year; revival has come at last. However, much land remains to be possessed. Its missionary outreach can become greater; revival can be the common experience of the church—there is no limit to what our sovereign God can do with this people and this church.

So we come now to the closing portion of this book. We have seen what God can do with a life yielded to Him. And from the past in that life we can evaluate the future, unknown as it is. Yet, all predictions historically must be rooted and grounded in the experiences of the past relative to the life and ministry of this prophet of God. What, then, shall we say about the future?

Chapter

"He calleth to me out of Seir, Watchman, what of the night? Watchman, what of the night? The watchman said, The morning cometh . . ."
Isaiah 21:11, 12

Let us labor for the Master from the dawn till setting sun.
—*J. M. Black*

Ten

The Future as Bright as the Promises of God

WHAT THE FUTURE has in store no man can answer. The world in which we live today stands at the crossroads. If ever a man could believe pragmatically in an apocalyptic this is the day. Our world is passing through one of the severest crises in two thousand years. One culture is dead or dying; another is emerging. All mankind is on the march and which ideology will shape the slowly emerging world we do not yet know.

The chaos of World War II is slowly being dissipated but a third World War is already on the planning boards of the military in most nations of the world, and the war itself is being fought in limited spheres as a prelude to the major titanic struggle around the corner. China and the Balkans are two danger zones where the opening phases of the third war are being fought. The communist dialectic of history inescapably forecasts that the battle for world domination now fought in these two areas will be extended in a desperate effort to bring all nations under the yoke of Russian totalitarianism.

Not alone in the political life of the nations are the lines closely drawn, but also here in America the lines are closing in. Increasing regimentation marks the contemporary scene. This is true for the nation, for religious life, for economic life, for the tendencies toward Statism. Roman Catholicism has made tremendous progress in its efforts to undermine the principle of separation of church and state and is seeking to lay hold of America as a bulwark for the Papacy in its own fight for existence.

The Christian faith is just as much under attack today by anti-Christian forces as ever. True it is that a decadent liberalism seems to have made partial surrender in its fight against orthodoxy; true it is that neo-orthodoxy appears to be turning toward orthodoxy (although it is doubtful that with its present epistemology it can ever approximate orthodoxy); true it is that in desperation people seeking a solution to the present seeming impasse now talk in terms of a return to spiritual values. But the hopeful signs are more than offset by rising tides of unbelief and secularistic movements throughtout the world.

In such a chaotic world as this, pregnant with opportunity for success as well as failure; at a time when men search for something outside themselves to lean upon, for adequate leadership, what of the future for Harold Ockenga? In what way is he likely to play a part in this battle? Does he have hope for the future and is he willing to provide leadership by the grace of God in this dark hour?

Dr. Ockenga knows one truth which is pivotal in his thinking and which truth is the only basis for hope in the future. This truth has to do with the vital question of the revelation of God. It is his firm and undying conviction that God has spoken to man through the Bible. When men everywhere seek for something outside themselves to lean upon; when they search for certainty in an uncertain era, in such an age the question of revelation and inspiration with reference to the Word of God is basic. Neo-orthodoxy speaks about the Word of God being contained within the Bible. It speaks of Biblical truth in terms of that whch is witnessed to an individual from within the Book. But Ockenga realizes that this position is weak and that if the Christian has any solution for the problems of today that solution must be found in the context of the fully inspired Word of God. The entire Bible is objectively true and contains verities which are absolute although they may be verified in experience when seeking souls kneel before the Christ of God.

The Future

That Book which turned the Roman Empire upside down; that Book which has made America great; that Book which has been the chief ingredient of the finest elements in western culture; that Book in its totality, the once for all faith delivered unto the saints, is the key to the future. Whatever hope there is must be found through its light, its message and its Redeemer.

Eschatology is no foreign study to the Park Street prophet. Conditions at the end times he knows as well as the next man. However, he will not take a pessimistic view and assume that because it is to come he must then be fatalistic and throw up his hands without seeking to stem the tide. The greatest weakness of an otherwise militant and aggressive orthodoxy in this tendency to assume that nothing can or should be done by earnest Bible believers to put off the end times. Knowing that the inevitable will come, he still believes that he is divinely constrained to fight against lethargy and to uphold the cause of Christ positively. Then having done all, if the last days come while he still is in the flesh he will have satisfied himself that he has given everything in the war against the onslaughts of the devil.

Furthermore Harold Ockenga believes that Christians must not only believe what the Bible teaches but that they must relate their faith to the hour in which they live. They are to stand for the right and fight for it too. <u>Evangelical humanitarianism, he believes, is the need of every orthodox heart.</u> We must bring faith into the home, into the labor movement, into business, into the race question. Christianity cannot be divorced from life. And the faith of a man should be made relevant to all of life, not just a fragment of it on Sunday when he sits in a pew. He does not think that this or any other culture can ever be distinctively Christian in the sense that the post-millennialist thinks the Golden Age will come in before the coming of Christ. On the other hand, the fact that the opposite will occur does not mean that we should not try to make an impact on all areas of life with the Gospel of Christ. To this end he has fought for years, and for years he will continue to fight.

An instance will serve to demonstrate what he has in mind. In Massachusetts the Roman Catholic Church has made appreciable gains financially from the state over the years. Ockenga has always felt that the preferred position they have obtained (contravening his view of the relation of church and state) should be taken away. Colleagues have argued that it is hopeless to fight against Roman Catholicism and that since no changes can occur the effort is wasted time. But Harold Ockenga continues to wage war against the evil in the hope that in *can* be corrected and he will fight despite the inability to secure redress presently. Maybe he will never see success crown his work but he will fight in the hope that some day success will attend these labors.

Deep in his consciousness Ockenga feels that the future demands missionary commitment by every believer. He has yielded his own life here in the hope that through his ministry the cause of Christ can be furthered all over the universe. He believes that the key to the coming of the Lord is related to missions. Consequently he is anxious that his church, in prayer, giving, and the raising up of young people to go to the fields of the world, be a dynamic force for Jesus Christ. Human intuition would make men conclude that financially Park Street Church has reached its zenith but the pastor of the church has faith to believe God can do still greater things in the coming years.

Along with his leadership in missions for the foreign field is an intense interest in evangelism for the home base. Evangelism at home and missions abroad go together in his thinking. The future of America lies in the hands of an aggressive and effective evangelistic effort. People must be reached with the gospel and shaken out of their secularism, atheism, and indifference. Only God can do it, but the channel through which it will be done is evangelism. The day of mass evangelism is not over in his opinion and he is willing and eager to play whatever part God would have him play in such endeavors. This enterprise cannot be subjected to narrow and selfish interests or aborted by disagreements among men of like theological beliefs. He will preach anywhere and under different auspices providing he is not restrained from preaching the true gospel.

The future for him has no limitations in the production of men through the Fuller Theological Seminary. Solidly behind this effort to produce men trained for the purpose of becoming evangelists, missionaries, and teachers, he has a contribution to make here. Instrumental in gathering under one roof an excellent array of theolological educators the groundwork has been laid for an enduring yearly addition to the religious life of America through the men who graduate. The literature of this faculty is rapidly closing the gap which has existed for several decades between the theological convictions of conservatives and the production of books to defend those beliefs and answer the competing systems of thought.

Dr. Ockenga has envisioned a twentieth century apologetic second to none rising out of conservative circles. Objecting strenuously to the consistent policy of evangelical retreat in the face of liberal attacks, he thinks the hour is ripe for a positive attack and assault upon the positions of the opposition. If the position we hold is not defensible we should not seek to propagate it. But so firmly does he hold that it is a reasonable system and that it has been and can be vigorously defended against all comers that his heart yearns for a new generation of men to replace the giants of yesteryear like Wilson, Warfield, and Machen. Succeed or fail, it cannot be said by later generations that the attempt was not made. And the future is bright with promise. A start has been made; results have already come. The struggle has cost much and the soldiers in the struggle have come away with scars of battle. Criticism, slander, oppostion, and strife from without cannot conquer men who have an inner unity and drive and whose lives are co-ordinated for a purpose. So real is the sense of commitment of this man and those whom he has gathered to labor together that death would be preferred to failure, with the destiny of men and nations hanging in the balance in this fateful hour. Never has the peril been so grave nor the opportunities so manifold. And at this point God has given men to stand in the gap.

One question about Harold Ockenga and his relationship to the Fuller Theological Seminary is asked in many quarters. Will he eventually leave Boston and the Park Street Church for the west coast and the Seminary, or will he remain at Park Street and retain his connections as President *in absentia* as long as it appears desirable from his viewpoint and from the general interests of the institution? The answer to this query is simple, so simple that few people can believe the answer. Harold Ockenga does not know what the outcome will be. He has not had to face this issue and when he made his commitments to the Seminary he did so on the basis that he would act as president *in absentia*. All he wants is the will of God in this as in all phases of his life and ministry. When the time comes for him to make a decision one way or the other he will face it and decide as he understands and knows the will of God. He lives one day at a time and does not cross his bridges before he comes to them.

Forecasters have made predictions what he will do when and if he must face the question of choosing between Boston and Pasadena. Most predictors do not realize the implications in the picture which make it far more complex than at first sight. He has spent fourteen years in Boston and has come to love it. He has a small retreat in the mountains of New Hampshire which has helped him in his hours of vacation and leisure. It is not too far distant from Boston and accessible to his home within a few short hours. His roots have settled deep in this New England soil and the progress of the work of the church would make it difficult for him ever to leave it whatever the circumstances. His people love him. They would do anything to hold him. The ministry in that church and city is significant.

A metropolitan pulpit like this has national importance and means much to him.

It is almost impossible to think of Harold Ockenga without a pulpit. He was born to preach and without his preaching he would be lost. He loves his people and this church. He consistently believes this church is unique and wonderful. That mutual reciprocity between pastor and people and the harmony and good feeling which exists is not fictional but real and tangible. Still in the flesh he must have some detractors in his church but one hunts hard without finding them. On all sides he has the general approbation and approval of his people. They realize that the church today stands where it does because of his contributions to it in his ministry.

The missionary work of the church strongly holds Ockenga in Boston. Beginning with two missionaries, today they have one hundred and ten on their list for support; it is as great a work for its size as can be found anywhere in America. Ockenga is not ready to believe that the peak has been reached and he foresees a larger outreach as he continues to bear down on the primacy of missions for the success of the church.

Over against the ties of the Park Street Church which are so real and vital to him, are the challenges of theological education. A man multiplies his ministry when he helps in the training of other men. An institution graduating forty or fifty men each year in its maturity can make a substantial impact on the religious life of a nation across the years. The accumulated impact of hundreds of men is bound to result in the accomplishment of more than a single man can do in a church in his own lifetime. The challenge of this geometric progression which springs from the stream of theological graduates going into the churches of the land cannot be overestimated.

Ockenga is also a scholar in his own right. He sees clearly the important theological issues disturbing our generation. If the fight for orthodoxy is won it must be won at the hands of men who are equipped to defend the faith once for all delivered to the saints. The production of theological and other works to fill in the gap and to provide textbooks and reading material for men of like faith will alter the complexion of religious life too. In his own background he profited from the labors of giants like Machen.

Ockenga has had to forego scholarly research work himself in the interests of the pastorate and calls which come to him.

He has had to forego scholarly research work himself in the interests of the pastorate and the calls which come to him. But he has the ability to do this kind of thing and make a contribution himself to the academic life of the theological world. In a seminary, literary production is more of a probability than it is when a man's time is taken by the work of a large urban church, no matter how wide its outreach and impressive its ministry.

Also, the form of evangelism he has an interest in would parallel that of men who do not hold pastorates in local churches but who devote most of their time to travel and evangelistic meetings. In residence as president he would be able to do more evangelistic work than presently.

Having said all this, the answer does not change—Harold Ockenga himself does not know the final decision. And if he has to make a decision the strings of his heart will be wrenched; for he has won his way into the lives and destinies of two groups of people separated by three thousand miles of land but all closely knit to the heart of the loving Father. And until and unless the hour of choice comes he is co-laborer in both groups for the glory of God and the increase of His Kingdom.

The whole future of evangelical co-operation remains as a problem to be resolved in our day. Again the future in some ways is obscure although added light comes in daily with respect to certain movements. Evangelical co-operation today has its two major streams in America. One stream is the National Association of Evangelicals; the other is the American Council of

Christian Churches. Harold Ockenga has a real part in this struggle.

Conceivably four alternatives exist in the effort to unify conservative voices. Both the American Council and the National Association of Evangelicals could lose their power and cease to be a voice for evangelicals. This would be tragic. A second option is that either one of them die, leaving the field to the other. A third possibility is that both of them will continue and both exercise an influence in whatever way and to whatever constituency they can. A fourth option is that the American Council and the National Association of Evangelicals will get together, resolve their difficulties, and put forth a united effort in the representation of evangelicals. What are the possibilities of these options and what part will Harold Ockenga play in the years ahead?

So far as it is humanly possible to tell, neither the American Council nor the N.A.E. is going to retire from the field either by reason of internal collapse or complete defeat. This rules out two of the four alternatives immediately. It leaves either the possibility of uniting the two groups for one witness or both of them operating independently of each other. The former possibility appears remote and probably both of them will go their respective ways.

Ockenga himself is not against harmony and unity among brethren of like faith. He cannot favor it, however, at the expense of basic convictions nor can it come without making past wrongs right.

Harold Ockenga believes that the N.A.E. is in a strong position. Great numbers of key evangelicals are counted among its staunch supporters. Forward progress is noted each year. Continually this organization has gained and is gaining strength.

Approaching his forty-sixth birthday, the Park Street prophet can look for twenty more years of active service for Jesus Christ. These years will be spent in a period which may well determine the destiny of America and the world. The shape of things to come is unknown, as we have observed, and truly into the kingdom for such a time as this God has sent this man.

Outwardly few additional honors are left for him to obtain. He has demonstrated his own academic achievement; he has received honorary degrees; he is pastor of one of America's great churches; at forty-five he is president of a theological seminary; he has traveled widely and preached on two continents with effectiveness; he has spearheaded a movement for evangelical co-operation among the constituency of the N.A.E.; he has developed a marvelous missionary zeal, enthusiasm and interest in New England; he has served on the boards of numerous Christian organizations and schools. Surely the work of the Lord has been strengthened by the life commitment of this prophet, and if, in the providence of God his days of service ended now, the life he has led would still be marked by accomplishments more notable and service more valuable than most men render in their three score and ten.

His path has been marked by incalculable difficulty. Opposition has faced him consistently along many fronts. Enemies have risen to smite him. But his course is unshaken; his vision is undimmed; his hopes never falter; his leadership continues firm and unabated.

As the description of the Apostle Paul of the warrior's armor indicates, Ockenga has no provision or protection for his back. He faces the enemy with the divine armor God has provided. It is the whole armor of God, which guarantees that a man shall stand against the wiles of the wicked one.

If ever a man was conscious of the war between good and evil, heaven and hell, God and the Devil, light and darkness, Ockenga is that man. He knows that "we wrestle not against flesh and blood, but against principalities, against powers, against the rulers of the darkness of this world, against spiritual wickedness in high places." This knowledge drives him to the Source of light and life and to the secret place where strength is found. His private spiritual life is not one for public display. From that

THE FUTURE

inner sanctuary of refuge where first each battle is fought before God before it is fought before men he has found strength and courage and power for the waging of the good fight which lays hold of life eternal. And he comes out to fight as a giant before men because he has first humbled himself before God.

As Hudson Taylor learned to sing in China in rude inns where he sought communion with God and willingly suffered the loss of all things for Christ's sake, so Dr. Ockenga has learned the meaning of the song that filled Taylor's heart:

> I am resting, simply resting
> In the joy of what Thou art;
> I am finding out the greatness
> Of Thy loving heart.

The Uneasy Conscience of Modern Fundamentalism

by CARL F. H. HENRY, M.A., TH.D.

This is *not* a revolt against the great Biblical varieties of the Fundamentalist position. The author, as an evangelical himself, is pleading for an application of these very fundamentals of the faith to the solution of world problems.

"The church needs a progressive fundamentalism with a social message."

In this deeply thought-provoking book Dr. Henry puts his finger on what is troubling us. He calls for an evangelical ecumenicalism and for unity to face social, world-wide needs. He believes that by contributing to the uplift of humanity, and the eradication of the common evils of society, as far as possible, many more people will be brought to receive Christ as Saviour.

"Fundamentalism, to the present world mind, is almost non-existent on the great social issues." However, the scene is changing. There is an awakening, a realization in their midst that an assault on global evils is demanded by its proper world-life view. The time has come to speak with an ecumenical outlook and voice; if it speaks in terms of historic Biblical Christianity, it can refashion the modern mind. But if Protestant orthodoxy holds itself aloof from this present world predicament, it is doomed to a much reduced role.

"To the extent to which any society is leavened with Christian conviction, it becomes a more hospitable environment for Christian expansion."

A Christian world and life view embracing world questions, societal needs, and personal education, ought to arise out of Matt. 28:18-21, as much as evangelism does.

A new reformation is imperative within the ranks of evangelical Christianity. It should result not only in a new passion for souls, but in power to overcome evils in every realm.

The Uneasy Conscience of Modern Fundamentalism

Rev. Emmett V. Johnson

> Carl F. H. Henry's *The Uneasy Conscience of Modern Fundamentalism*, 1947 (especially chapter three, "The Most Embarrassing Evangelical Divorce") seemed scarcely listened to. Perhaps it was 20 years too soon.

Carl Henry, author,

The Uneasy Conscience of Modern Fundamentalism

By
CARL F. H. HENRY, M.A., TH.D.

*Professor, Philosophy of Religion,
Northern Baptist Theological Seminary,
Chicago, Illinois*

WM. B. EERDMANS PUBLISHING COMPANY
GRAND RAPIDS   1947   MICHIGAN

THE UNEASY CONSCIENCE OF MODERN FUNDAMENTALISM
By Carl F. H. Henry, M.A., Th.D.

Copyright 1947, by
Wm. B. Eerdmans Publishing Company

All rights in this book are reserved. No part may be reproduced in any manner without permission in writing from the publisher, except brief quotations used in connection with a review in a magazine or newspaper.

PRINTED IN THE UNITED STATES OF AMERICA

TO T. LEONARD LEWIS
Christian Friend and Former Colleague

T. LEONARD LEWIS
B.D., Th.D., Ph.B., president of Gordon College of Theology and Missions, Boston; formerly on faculty of Northern Baptist Seminary.

Contents

Preface 9

Introduction by Harold J. Ockenga, D.D............. 13

   I. The Evaporation of Fundamentalist
      Humanitarianism 15

  II. The Protest Against Foredoomed Failure...... 25

 III. The Most Embarrassing Evangelical Divorce.... 35

 IV. The Apprehension Over Kingdom Preaching.... 47

   V. The Fundamentalist Thief on the Cross........ 59

 VI. The Struggle for a New World Mind........... 67

VII. The Evangelical "Formula of Protest".......... 75

VIII. The Dawn of a New Reformation.............. 83

Preface

SOME of my evangelical friends have expressed the opinion that nobody should "perform surgery" on Fundamentalism just now, thinking it wiser to wait until the religious scene is characterized by less tension.

I do not share this view that it is wiser to wait, for several reasons.

It is a sober realism, rather than undue alarm, that prompts the fear that, unless we experience a rebirth of apostolic passion, Fundamentalism in two generations will be reduced either to a tolerated cult status or, in the event of Roman Catholic domination in the United States, become once again a despised and oppressed sect. The only live alternative, it appears to me, is a rediscovery of the revelational classics and the redemptive power of God, which shall lift our jaded culture to a level that gives significance again to human life. It was the rediscovery of classic ancient philosophy that gave incentive to Renaissance humanism with its disastrous implications for Western culture. The hour is ripe now, if we seize it rightly, for a rediscovery of the Scriptures and of the meaning of the Incarnation for the human race.

Further, Fundamentalism is a constant object of surgery anyway. One can hardly move about the campuses of the large universities and secular colleges — let alone some religious schools — without awareness of the constant assault on our position. Numbers of clergymen who minister to university students repudiate the doctrine of substitutionary atonement as doing violence to man's moral sense. [To us who insist on the abnormality of man's religious affections, there is no infallibility of man's moral sense. The latter leads away from redemption's path those who walk in the confidence of man's inherent goodness. One of the things which modern man most needs to be saved from, is a moral sense which is outraged at a divine provision of redemption.] But it is not this doctrinal assault on the central affirmations of our faith that here distresses me; it must always be, preceding that future day when we shall no longer move by faith, that revelational and non-revelational views shall stand in sharp conflict. What concerns me more is that we have needlessly invited criticism and even ridicule, by a tendency in some quarters to parade secondary and sometimes even obscure aspects of our position as necessary frontal phases of our view. To this extent we have failed to oppose the full genius of the Hebrew-Christian outlook to its modern competitors. With the collapse of Renaissance ideals, it is needful that we come to a clear distinction, as evangelicals, between those basic doctrines on which we unite in a supernaturalistic world and life view and the area of differences on which we are not in agreement while yet standing true to the essence of Biblical Christianity. But even beyond this, I voice my concern because we have not applied the genius of our position constructively to those problems which press most for solution in a social way. Unless we do this, I am unsure that we shall get another world hearing for the Gospel. That we can continue for a generation or two, even as a vital missionary force, here and there snatching brands from the burning, I do not question. But if we would press redemptive Christianity as the obvious solution of world problems, we had better busy ourselves with explicating the solution. I am not unmindful of constructive efforts along this line, as Dr. Earle V. Pierce's *The Church and World Conditions*, but I cannot set aside the conviction that we have not as a movement faced up with the seriousness of our predicament.

Moreover, I am well aware that some who have no sympathy for a supernaturalistic viewpoint, will likely distort and misrepresent the sentiments voiced in these pages. But

I do not consider it needful on that account to hesitate. Those who read with competence will know that the "uneasy conscience" of which I write is not one troubled about the great Biblical verities, which I consider the only outlook capable of resolving our problems, but rather one distressed by the frequent failure to apply them effectively to crucial problems confronting the modern mind. It is an application of, not a revolt against, fundamentals of the faith, for which I plead.

That it may be somewhat optimistic to speak of a widespread uneasiness, I also recognize. Many of our Bible institutes, evangelical colleges, and even seminaries, seem blissfully unaware of the new demands upon us. My hope is that some, who were not troubled at the outset of these pages, will become concerned before they finish.

One last word is almost superfluous. It will be almost too evident that the formulation of a solution requires much more constructive treatment. At times, I have been content with a minimal statement, seeking to provoke a united effort, rather than to dogmatize. I address my words to fellow evangelicals, in the hope that they shall not make every faltering word an occasion of calumny, but rather inviting them to stand firm in the recognition that, while we are pilgrims here, we are ambassadors also.

These chapters were delivered, in a somewhat briefer form, as a series of popular lectures in Gordon College of Theology and Missions.

CARL F. H. HENRY

3026 WASHINGTON BLVD.,
CHICAGO, ILLINOIS

INTRODUCTION

RECENTLY, when preaching a sermon on "The Influence of the Church in the Labor Crisis," I evoked a comment from a Christian soldier. Said he, "I became a political liberal on my knees, though I am a Fundamentalist in faith. Why must the church be on the wrong side of every major social issue?" Another soldier wrote, "That is a new note in Fundamentalism."

If the Bible-believing Christian is on the wrong side of social problems such as war, race, class, labor, liquor, imperialism, etc., it is time to get over the fence to the right side. The church needs a progressive Fundamentalism with a social message.

If Acts 15:13-18 outlines God's program and premillenarianism is correct, the church will not preach on Paris Conferences or liquor, yet it will not be indifferent to these pulse-beats of the world's life. If we vacillate between Fundamentalist isolationism and cooperation with the World Council of Churches, it is because we cannot be fatalistic on ethical problems. Yet Fundamentalism is precisely that. Dr. Henry has put his finger on what is troubling us. May this brief thesis be the harbinger of a new articulation of the growing revolt in evangelical circles on ethical indifferentism. It is impossible to shut the Jesus of pity, healing, service, and human interest from a Biblical theology. The higher morality of redemption does not invalidate moral consistency.

That there is little agreement concerning the Kingdom is shown from the contrast between writings of Stanley Jones and A. C. Gaebelein. It has always been easiest for me to think of the Kingdom as one, but with several forms —

theocratic, church, millennial — but *all* the Kingdom of God. Unless the continuity and the breaks, along with coterminous principles and ends, of the forms of the Kingdom are recognized this question becomes a hopeless puzzle to men.

A Christian world- and life-view embracing world questions, societal needs, personal education ought to arise out of Matt. 28:18-21 as much as evangelism does. Culture depends on such a view, and Fundamentalism is prodigally dissipating the Christian culture accretion of centuries, a serious sin. A sorry answer lies in the abandonment of social fields to the secularist.

Here then is a healthy antidote to Fundamentalist aloofness in a distraught world. Dr. Henry may well call for an evangelical (Fundamentalist) ecumenicalism and for unity to face social needs.

Dr. Harold John Ockenga

Pastor, Park Street Church,
Boston, Mass.

Chapter I

THE EVAPORATION OF FUNDAMENTALIST HUMANITARIANISM

I.

The Evaporation of Fundamentalist Humanitarianism[1]

THE present tendency of conservative Christianity is to make much of the embarrassment of religious modernism.

The modernist embarrassment is serious indeed. The shallow insistence on inevitable world progress and on man's essential goodness has been violently declared false. Not only sound Bible exegesis but the world events of 1914-1946 indict optimistic liberalism.

But contemporary Fundamentalism is not without its own moments of guilt. For the world crisis serves to embarrass Fundamentalism also. The uncomfortableness of evangelicalism cannot be palliated by an emphasis on someone else's uneasy predicament. Even if it could, the device would hardly escape attention from the alert modern mind.

The predicament of contemporary evangelicalism can be set forth from two vantage points, that of the non-evangelicals and that of the evangelicals themselves. From whichever direction the problem is approached, it is serious enough.

Against Protestant Fundamentalism the non-evangelicals level the charge that it has no social program calling for a practical attack on acknowledged world evils. True, other

---

1. The word "humanitarianism" is used in the sense of benevolent regard for the interests of mankind.

complaints are made against Christian supernaturalism. Representative spokesmen for religious liberalism, for ethical idealism, for religious humanism, and for pessimism, are linked by a common network of assumptions which clearly differentiates their philosophic premises from the orthodox Hebrew-Christian view. Non-Christian groups have no dealings with a supernaturalistic metaphysics. But nonetheless — though they regard contemporary orthodoxy as a vestigial remnant of traditional obscurantism — they theoretically recognize the philosophic right of the evangelicals to hold any doctrinal framework they may desire. But what is almost wholly unintelligible to the naturalistic and idealistic groups, burdened as they are for a new world order, is the apparent lack of any social passion in Protestant Fundamentalism. On this evaluation, Fundamentalism is the modern priest and Levite, by-passing suffering humanity.

The picture is clear when one brings into focus such admitted social evils as aggressive warfare, racial hatred and intolerance, the liquor traffic, and exploitation of labor or management, whichever it may be.

The social reform movements dedicated to the elimination of such evils do not have the active, let alone vigorous, cooperation of large segments of evangelical Christianity. In fact, Fundamentalist churches increasingly have repudiated the very movements whose most energetic efforts have gone into an attack on such social ills. The studied Fundamentalist avoidance of, and bitter criticism of, the World Council of Churches and the Federal Council of Churches of Christ in America is a pertinent example.

Now, such resistance would be far more intelligible to non-evangelicals were it accompanied by an equally forceful assault on social evils in a distinctly supernaturalistic framework. But, by and large, the Fundamentalist opposition to societal ills has been more vocal than actual. Some concerted effort has been attempted through organizations like the National Association of Evangelicals or the American Council of Churches. Southern Baptists have a somewhat better record, coupled with rejection of the Federal Council. But evangelical social action has been spotty and usually of the emergency type.

The situation has even a darker side. The great majority of Fundamentalist clergymen, during the past generation of world disintegration, became increasingly less vocal about social evils. It was unusual to find a conservative preacher occupied at length with world ills.

In a company of more than one hundred representative evangelical pastors, the writer proposed the following question: "How many of you, during the past six months, have preached a sermon devoted in large part to a condemnation of such social evils as aggressive warfare, racial hatred and intolerance, the liquor traffic, exploitation of labor or management, or the like — a sermon containing not merely an incidental or illustrative reference, but directed mainly against such evils and proposing the framework in which you think solution is possible?" Not a single hand was raised in response. Now this situation is not characteristic only of one particular denominational group of Fundamentalists; rather, a predominant trait, in most Fundamentalist preaching, is this reluctance to come to grips with social evils.

There are Fundamentalist groups, admittedly, which have not lost a keen world reference, especially those alert to their Reformational lineage in John Calvin. Their interest in ethics is demanded, rather than precluded, by their doctrinal fervor. Holding fast to an ideology of supernaturalism, these groups have sometimes been tempted to dissociate themselves from the Fundamentalist camp because of the widespread notion that indifference to world evils is essential to Fundamentalism. And, after all, social irresponsibility was not the only trend that was imputed to Fundamentalist circles. Modern prejudice, justly or unjustly, had come to identify Fundamentalism largely in terms of an anti-ecumenical spirit of independent isolationism, an uncritically-held set of theological formulas,[2] an overly-emotional type of revivalism. There is also the tendency to replace great church music by a barn-dance variety of semi-religious choruses: some churches have almost become spiritualized juke boxes. It was the recognition, by the ethically alert Fundamentalist minority, that such tendencies do not express the inherent genius of the great evangelical tradition that prevented their desertion from the Fundamentalist camp. Spokesmen particularly for orthodox Reformed groups saw that the title of "Fundamentalism" was applied initially with doctrinal fidelity, rather than ethical irresponsibility, as the frame of reference. Fundamentalism was a Bible-believing Christianity which regarded the supernatural as a part of the essence of the Biblical view; the miraculous was not to be viewed, as in liberalism, as an incidental and superfluous accretion. It was from its affirmation of the historic evangelical doctrinal fundamentals that modern orthodoxy received its name, and not from its growing silence on pressing global problems. This was clearly seen by spokesmen for contemporary Fundamentalism like the late J. Gresham Machen, who vigorously insisted that Christianity has a message relevant to the world crisis, however staggering the issues.

The average Fundamentalist's indifference to social implications of his religious message has been so marked, however, that the non-evangelicals have sometimes classi-

---

2. Many newspapers have inaccurately applied the Fundamentalist tag to cultists (like the Mormon polygamists) whom the evangelicals would be the first to disown.

fied him with the pessimist in his attitude toward world conditions.

Of all the seemingly incongruous weddings in philosophy, this is the most striking. That Christian supernaturalism, which as a matter of historical record furnished the background and in some sense the support for the modern humanisms and idealisms, should be accused of having lost its own devotion to human well-being, is indeed a startling accusation.

But, from the standpoint of not a few religious modernists, ethical idealists and humanists, the common strand that runs through Fundamentalism and pessimism is that both are viewpoints from which the humanism, or humanitarianism, has evaporated.

This is not to suggest that Fundamentalism had no militant opposition to sin. Of all modern viewpoints, when measured against the black background of human nature disclosed by the generation of two world wars, Fundamentalism provided the most realistic appraisal of the condition of man. The sinfulness of man, and the exceeding sinfulness of sin, and that God alone can save man from his disaster, are insistences that were heard with commonplace frequency only within the evangelical churches. But the sin against which Fundamentalism has inveighed, almost exclusively, was individual sin rather than social evil.

It is not fair to say that the ethical platform of all conservative churches has clustered about such platitudes as "abstain from intoxicating beverages, movies, dancing, cardplaying, and smoking," but there are multitudes of Fundamentalist congregations in which these are the main points of reference for ethical speculation. In one of the large Christian colleges, a chapel speaker recently expressed amazement that the campus newspaper could devote so much space to the all-important problem of whether it is right to play "rook," while the nations of the world are playing with fire.

And yet it ought not to be overlooked that, in its attack on personal sins, there is an indirect coming to grips in Fundamentalist churches with some of the major contemporary problems. The bitter opposition to intoxicating beverages is, in a localized sense, an attack upon the liquor traffic, even though it does nothing to curb the menace itself and concentrates upon schooling the believer to circumvent it. Again, while the Fundamentalist's opposition to the theatre is sometimes so deep-rooted that it is forgotten that the camera may also serve to the glory of God, he nevertheless is expressing a vigorous protest against the secular and often pagan standards of value which Hollywood film producers have consistently enthroned and glorified. At this point, in fact, the Fundamentalist has often been more sensitive to the danger of undermining Christian convictions by propaganda means than has the religious modernist with his selection of "best, good, and unrecommended films." And yet, the Fundamentalist appears to pursue a rather foredoomed approach, schooling his constituency against all movies, as if they are inherently evil, so that there is no direct attempt to change the external picture itself.

The problem of personal ethics, moreover, is complicated no little by the shifting standards in various sections of the country, among Fundamentalists themselves. Among evangelicals, for example, smoking is hardly considered the sin in the southern tobacco-growing states that it is in the north.[3] And the northern Baptist pastor who would join his wife for mixed public swimming would be called before his board of deacons in many a southern church.

---

3. Although the Southern Baptist Convention in 1937 affirmed "that the prevalence of smoking among Christian people, especially among preachers, church leaders, and denominational workers, is not only detrimental to the health of those who participate, but hurtful to the cause of Christ in that it weakens the messages and lowers the influence of those charged with the preservation and spread of the Gospel."

Now, the purpose of such examples is not to promote a plea for laxity in personal morals. It is simply to emphasize that such personal issues are themselves frequently in a state of environmental flux which, if anything, adds to the predicament of the Fundamentalist pastor on the score of ethical preaching.

Even more serious is the mounting repudiation in evangelical circles of Fundamentalist standards for the practical moral life. This testifies to more than a growing estrangement from traditional ways of living. As seen by those who are not evangelicals, this movement away from the evangelical evaluation of life and duty, in the personal as well as social code of behavior, is an inevitable consequence of an ideology which refuses to relate itself to the cardinal issues of the global dilemma. The non-Christian idealists and naturalists know, of course, that their outlooks demand an evaluation of life which differs from the Fundamental appraisal, but they trace the growing Fundamentalist revolt against stringent personal prohibitions, to the peculiar strategy of evangelical ethics, as much as to the penetrative dissemination of anti-Christian moral theories. It remains a question whether one can be perpetually indifferent to the problems of social justice and international order, and develop a wholesome personal ethics.

In mentioning the typical ethical insistences of Fundamentalist churches, it would be unfair not to allude to the strict attitude taken toward divorce, as contrasted with the increasingly loose secular view of family relations. The insistence that only death or adultery can sever the marriage bond is maintained nowhere today with such a conviction of absoluteness as in Fundamentalist circles, although there are here, as everywhere, exceptions. The contribution of this viewpoint to the integrity of the family, and its significance in precluding juvenile delinquency, is of no small moment in its social consequences. From a certain perspective it can be said that the effort to remedy the disintegration of the American home, pressed by social reformers, does not get at the heart of the problem as directly as the Fundamentalist proclamation of the divine sanction of a monogamous family life.

But here again it must also be conceded that the defection of American culture from a vital Christianity means that the problem of the home and of juvenile delinquency is unconfronted in countless family circles where remedial measures might create a more favorable soil for the preaching of the Gospel. By such argument even those who have disagreed with a supernaturalist ideology have sought to enlist evangelicalism in reform programs.

The failure of the evangelical movement to react favorably on any widespread front to campaigns against social evils has led, finally, to a suspicion on the part of non-evangelicals that there is something in the very nature of Fundamentalism which makes a world ethical view impossible. The conviction is widespread that Fundamentalism takes too pessimistic a view of human nature to make a social program practicable.

This modern mind-set, insisting that evangelical supernaturalism has inherent within it an ideological fault which precludes any vital social thrust, is one of the most disturbing dividing lines in contemporary thought. In the struggle for a world mind which will make global order and brotherhood a possibility, contemporary speculation has no hearing whatever for a viewpoint which it suspects has no world program. It dismisses Fundamentalism with the thought that, in this expression of the Great Tradition, the humanitarianism has evaporated from Christianity.

Chapter II

THE PROTEST AGAINST
FOREDOOMED FAILURE

II.

The Protest Against Foredoomed Failure

NO complaint against Fundamentalism is, from the Fundamentalist viewpoint, more untrue than the contention that the Biblical estimate of man involves a social impotence.

An evangelical message vitally related to world conditions is not precluded by New Testament doctrine.

Indeed, conservative Protestantism insists, *only* this estimate of the sinfulness of man and his need of regeneration is sufficiently realistic to make at all possible any securely-grounded optimism in world affairs. Any other framework can offer only a "bubble and froth cure."

And yet, evangelicalism is disturbed. There is a growing awareness in Fundamentalist circles that, despite the orthodox insistence upon revelation and redemption, evangelical Christianity has become increasingly inarticulate about the social reference of the Gospel. The conviction mounts that the relationship of the church to world conditions must be reappraised, even if the doctrinal limits are regarded as fixed within which solution is likely to be found. While the modern mind wrestles with its global dilemma, the evangelical conscience is troubled because the historic Christian message is dismissed arbitrarily as a dead option for dissolving the ills of Occidental culture. Fundamentalism is wondering just how it is that a world changing message narrowed its scope to the changing of isolated individuals.

The evangelical predicament is not a simple one.

For one thing, evangelical Christianity views the non-evangelical movements which vigorously promote world social uplift as competitors for the ideological loyalty of the masses. They proclaim rival and contradictory doctrines. The ethical societies, the world brotherhood movements, the united nations organizations, the war prevention agencies — insofar as they seek to attain their ends without an insistence on man's specific need, as a sinner, of individual regeneration — are regarded as hostile to the historic Christian tradition.

This hostility the Fundamentalist refuses to minimize. The whole Biblical viewpoint appears to him at stake. The non-evangelical movements, however desirable their goals, encourage their followers to place their trust in what, from the orthodox viewpoint, is the *wrong method* for attainment of such ends. The Fundamentalist does not think that the ends can be reached by various means, and that his method is better; if he did, the hostility would not be as serious.[1] Rather, the evangelical is convinced that the non-evangelicals operate within the wrong ideological framework to make achievement a possibility. He believes they stimulate a naive and misplaced confidence in man, growing out of a superficial view of reality. He believes the liberal, the humanist, and the ethical idealist share a shallow sense of the depth of world need and an over-optimism concerning man's own supposed resources for far-reaching reversal even of admitted wrongs.

Only an anthropology and a soteriology that insists upon man's sinful lostness and the ability of God to restore the responsive sinner is the adequate key to the door of Fundamentalist world betterment. Any other approach is a needless waste of effort and, in effect an attack on the exclusive relevance, if not on any relevance, of the historic redemp-

---

1. In point of fact, neither do the non-evangelicals think that Fundamentalism is one among many possible methods. The non-evangelicals are in hearty disagreement over the best method; they agree mainly in the conviction that it is not Fundamentalism.

tive Gospel. The globe-changing passion of the modern reformers who operate without a Biblical context is, from this vantage point, an ignoring of Jesus' insistence that "all these things shall be added" only after man has sought first "the kingdom of God and His righteousness." Non-evangelicals tend to equate the "kingdom" and the "these things," reflecting a blindness to the significance of the vicarious atonement of Christ. The non-evangelicals have a non-evangelical methodology.

Yet the rejection of non-evangelical solutions does not involve — at least, logically — a loss of the social relevance of the Gospel. A globe-changing passion certainly characterized the early church, however much it thought within a redemptive pattern centering in Christ's substitutionary death and bodily resurrection. Had it not been so, Christianity would not have been the religion of the then-known world within three centuries. Some sort of a world passion had made the Christian message pertinent enough for rulers to want to bring their subjects in subjection to it. A Christianity without a passion to turn the world upside down is not reflective of apostolic Christianity.

Consequently, modern Fundamentalism is wondering by what peculiar manipulation of circumstances the Great Tradition has seemingly lost its world relevance. This is doubly marked in our day, when problems often are no longer settled on a community or even national basis except by reference to broader international decisions. For evangelicalism has cautiously avoided any alignment with non-evangelical groups, yet has failed to develop the broad social implications of its message.

The problem is even more complicated for the premillenialist and amillenialist. They are convinced not only that non-evangelicals cannot bring in the perfect social order in their methodological context, but also that the evangelicals will not bring it in by their proclamation of the Gospel.

This latter conviction is grounded in the belief that the inauguration of the kingdom awaits the second advent of Christ in His visible return. The amillenialist does not believe in a thousand-year earthly reign, but he shares the despair over the present social order apart from the return of Christ. In this respect, the premillenialists and amillenialists, who together form the largest segment in modern Fundamentalism, are aligned against the postmillenialists, who labor to bring in the kingdom of God by human redemptive effort and anticipate the return of Christ will follow a golden age of world conversion.

It should be emphasized that this despair over the present world order grows, for contemporary Fundamentalism, not out of any lack of confidence in the ability of the supernaturalistic Gospel. Rather, it issues from the fact that the Scriptures, as interpreted by premillenarians and amillenarians, hold forth no hope for the conversion of the whole world, and center upon the second coming of Christ as crucial for the introduction of a divine kingdom. The despair over the present age, then, is grounded in the anticipated lack of response to the redemptive Gospel, rather than in any inherent defect in the message itself.

This Gospel of hope coupled with a prophetic despair has posed, during the past two generations, a problem which Fundamentalism was unable satisfactorily to resolve. Before the rise to power of modern religious liberalism, it was possible for Fundamentalism to proclaim redemptive regeneration as the only solution for world problems, and yet not appear to have lost its social passion. The reason was that most of the creative idealism was within the church itself. But liberalism minimized the necessity of a specifically supernaturalist framework, religious humanism enthroned a thorough-going naturalism, and these movements together launched a vigorous attack on great social evils of the modern world.

The recoil of Fundamentalism from such moralism cut loose from Biblical redemption, might have been pursued without a divorce between evangelical doctrinal and evangelical ethical insistence. Historically, Christianity embraced a life view as well as a world view; it was socially as well as philosophically pertinent.

But, almost unawares, Fundamentalism became increasingly absorbed in resistance to non-evangelical humanism as a deceptive competitor for the committment of multitudes, and because of its prophetic cheerlessness about the present age came more and more to narrow its message for the "faithful remnant" that would be called out of the godless world context. The die was cast, not so much because God had made present world conditions inevitable as because of the foreseen hardness of men's hearts, so that the nonsupernaturalistic idealisms could all be abandoned to future disillusionment. Whereas once the redemptive gospel was a world-changing message, now it was narrowed to a world-resisting message. Out of twentieth century Fundamentalism of this sort there could come no contemporary version of Augustine's *The City of God*.

In protesting against non-evangelical ideologies, Fundamentalism came to react also against the social programs of the modern reformers. This grew in part, as already indicated, out of the conviction that desirable ends were being sought in an undesirable or ineffective context. But, in addition, Fundamentalists came to see that world peace, the brotherhood of man, democracy, and the new economy hardly meant for religious liberalism and humanism what they meant for evangelicalism; that is, Fundamentalism insisted that its ends, as well as its methods, were distinct from the non-evangelical movements. The non-evangelicals were striving for *inadequate ends*.

For example, the non-evangelicals were working for a just and durable peace which, in theory, was to be achieved by any possible formula whatever but which, in practice, ruled out specifically Christian regeneration as its conditioning context. The end in view was a global peace without any reference to the vicarious atonement and redemptive work of Christ. To one who was realistic about human nature, this appeared but a luxurious dream.

The brotherhood of man, too, had shriveled from New Testament redemptive proportions. Democracy had meant, for early Americans, the right to worship God as patterned in the Scriptures, without the obstruction of earthly powers; between the two world wars it had narrowed down to the four freedoms, including the right to worship God any way and if one wanted to do so. That sort of brotherhood, the evangelical was aware, made brotherhood impossible, because it obscured man's relationship to God.

The problems of management and labor were now referred not to a regeneration-conditioned submission to the divine will, but rather to the leftist precepts of political Socialism or Communism. It was implied in the doctrinal genius of evangelicalism that it must resist such non-evangelical ends, as well as a non-redemptive methodology. For here existed two definitions of man's true nature and destiny, the one looking for a perfect material order and the other mainly for a perfect spiritual order.[1]

---

1. John C. Bennett discusses the relationship of the liberal Social Gospel to the Christian social imperative and concedes that the Social Gospel "appeared in the context of theological assumptions that were vulnerable and that are now dated" (*Christian Ethics and Social Policy*, p. 2. New York: Charles Scribner's Sons, 1946). But he objects to discarding the term because this "might mean a loss of that vital sense of the social imperative that the Social Gospel means for everyone" (p. 3). The criticisms which a repentant liberalism today makes on the Social Gospel almost invariably are still within a higher liberal framework, making no room for such apostolic doctrines as substitutionary atonement and supernatural regeneration; social sensitivity still runs far deeper than theological sensitivity.

The reaction against non-evangelical ends manifested itself in a two-fold way, one the way of vocal denunciation and the other the way of silent resistance. The trend toward Communism, as reflected in denominational committees on social action and especially in the Federal Council of Churches, became the topic of vigorous attack. On the other hand, Fundamentalists were quite sure that the disruption of the liquor traffic would hardly put an end to world godlessness, and came to regard the campaign against intoxicants as an inexcusable occupation with a secondary evil; temperance forces sometimes found it harder to present their work in Fundamentalist than in liberal churches. Evangelicalism saw in such moralistic movements the subtle proclamation of a higher, more respectable way of life that stood nevertheless at a far remove from the redemptive regeneration of the New Testament, which the church was commissioned to proclaim to the nations. The moralism of pagan idealism was being substituted for the Biblical "good news."

While the non-evangelical groups captured the propaganda centers for their ideology, the evangelicals reacted against the humanistic enthusiasm. The modern reformers in their assaults on aggressive warfare, political statism, racial intolerance, the liquor traffic, labor-management exploitation and other such focal points of tension, had little encouragement from Fundamentalist quarters. Fundamentalism in revolting against the Social Gospel seemed also to revolt against the Christian social imperative.

It was the failure of Fundamentalism to work out a positive message within its own framework, and its tendency instead to take further refuge in a despairing view of world history, that cut off the pertinence of evangelicalism to the modern global crisis. The really creative thought, even if in a nonredemptive context, was now being done by the non-evangelical spokesmen.

The evangelicals were being locked up to the uncomfortable alternative of an attack on contemporary social reformers, seeking solution to admitted ills, or of going along with those whose ideology they did not endorse. Many evangelicals finally were caught up in the social gospel effort, which progressively obscured an evangelical doctrinal context and identified itself correspondingly with ends of the non-evangelical definitional type. But the great majority cut loose deliberately from the social reform movements of the times, denounced as futile and deceptive the world-changing efforts on a non-Biblical formula, and redoubled their efforts to rescue the minority from an increasingly hostile environment.

Now and then came a more visionary Fundamentalist attack on world conditions, predicted on the apostolic passion to change the world by changing the individuals in it. Even the Fundamentalists most interested in prophetic speculations were uneasy over the fact that, however much the early church linked up the consummatory kingdom to the return of Christ, the apostles labored nevertheless with uncompromised passion to carry the Gospel to men everywhere in obedience to the great commission. Spasmodic and isolated efforts were made to link the evangelical message effectively to contemporary world conditions. The uneasy conscience of modern Fundamentalism was stirring. But to become articulate about evangelicalism and its social implications was not an easy task. There is the danger that it might involve an unstudied and superficial analysis of the specific modern evils. For example, one recent Fundamentalist discussion of the social program of the Federal Council of Churches bitterly condemns the Communist leftist trends in that group, while exhibiting a contrasting silence about the evils of a Capitalistic system from which the redemptive reference is largely abstracted.

There is a rising tide of reaction in Fundamentalism today — a reaction born of an uneasy conscience and determined no longer to becloud the challenge of the Gospel to modern times. It is a reaction to which the best minds of evangelicalism are bending their effort these days, convinced that no synthesis is more relevant than modern frustration and Biblical redemptionism.

It was remarked earlier that, during the past two generations, creative ethical thinking was done by those whose ideology was divorced from New Testament supernaturalism, often invading the church itself with the Renaissance humanism of modern philosophy. But that does not necessarily mean truth was on their side. Nothing is clearer today than that the Fundamentalist was dismissed with an almost perverted lightness, when he warned that the non-evangelicals were not delving deeply enough into the nature and destiny of man to prevent a dark disillusionment. After all, the judgment of the two world wars stands now with the appraisal of the Fundamentalist.

The troubled conscience of the modern liberal, growing out of his superficial optimism, is a deep thing in modern times. But so is the uneasy conscience of the modern Fundamentalist, that no voice is speaking today as Paul would, either at the United Nations sessions, or at labor-management disputes, or in strategic university classrooms whether in Japan or Germany or America.

Chapter III

THE MOST EMBARRASSING
EVANGELICAL DIVORCE

III.

The Most Embarrassing Evangelical Divorce

FOR the first protracted period in its history, evangelical Christianity stands divorced from the great social reform movements.

That Christianity has not always been fired by a maximum social passion must be conceded. Despite the fact that the difference between the Oriental and Occidental worlds must be explained to a large extent in terms of Christianity — for the New Testament world-life view lifted the ancient world out of pagan barbarism — it remains true that there have been earlier eras in European history when the church was devoid of measureable social concern. The Roman Catholic Church in the middle ages tended to substitute political for spiritual revolution, and also staunchly supported the feudal system; even today Roman Catholic humanitarianism often appears dictated by expedience, as witness the contrast between Catholic action in Spain, and Latin America, and in the United States. But even in the Lutheran Reformation, Martin Luther too deserted the people in the Peasants' War for social and political improvements which, however much in advance of their day, seem remarkably minimal to us.

But in proportion as the world passion was absent from Christianity, the latter ceased to be an apostolic or missionary Christianity of the type which the Reformation sought to recapture for the western mind. Manifesting its true genius, Christianity furnished an idealistic atmosphere of judgment upon its environment in any age, and precipitated most of the successive reform movements within previous cultures.

However, Fundamentalism today denies that Christian ethics is in any sense to be identified with the humanistic moralism of modern reformers. Yet it is specifically the humanism of the day that is most vocal and vigorous in the attack on admitted social ills. As a consequence, Protestant evangelicalism without a world program has largely relegated itself to a secondary, or even more subordinate, role of challenge to the prevailing cultural mood.[1]

One of the ironies of this predicament is that some important benefits have accrued to evangelicals from the very agencies they oppose. A Fundamentalist chaplain recently remarked, for example, that the opportunity to proclaim the evangelical Gospel freely to servicemen had been safeguarded for him by the influence of the Federal Council of Churches with the national government. He did not mean that the Federal Council had interceded by any means for the historic evangelical message as differentiated from religious modernism, but rather that the whole chaplaincy plan from its inception was closely watched by the Council whereas the evangelicals more or less fell in with it.

Protestantism's embarrassing divorce is apparent. Whereas in previous eras of Occidental history no spiritual force so challenged the human scene as did Christianity with its

---

1. John C. Bennett's discussion of the "Four Christian Social Strategies" (i.e., Catholic strategy, the strategy of withdrawal, the identification of Christianity with particular social programs, and the double standard for personal and public life) is worth reading (*Christian Ethics and Social Policy*, pp. 32 ff). His proposed fifth strategy for relating Christian ethics to social policy falls short to the extent that, while breaking with many of the overoptimistic assumptions of the older Social Gospel, he nonetheless fails properly to relate Christian ethics to the apostolic insistence on individual regeneration through a saving union with the redemptive Christ.

superlife in the area of conduct, its supernatural world view in the area of philosophy, and its superhope in the area of societal remaking, the challenge of modern Fundamentalism to the present world mind is almost nonexistent on the great social issues. Through the Christian centuries, assuredly, the evangelical challenge came always in a specifically redemptive framework. But in modern times the challenge is hardly felt at all.[2] For Fundamentalism in the main fails to make relevant to the great moral problems in twentieth-century global living the implications of its redemptive message.

Hebrew-Christian thought, historically, has stood as a closely-knit world and life view. Metaphysics and ethics went everywhere together, in Biblical intent. The great doctrines implied a divinely related social order with intimations for all humanity. The ideal Hebrew or Christian society throbbed with challenge to the predominant culture of its generation, condemning with redemptive might the tolerated social evils, for the redemptive message was to light the world and salt the earth. No insistence on a doctrinal framework alone was sufficient; always this was coupled with the most vigorous assault against evils, so that the globe stood anticipatively at the judgment seat of Christ. Such, at any rate, was apostolic Christianity; such too was the spirit of the post-apostolic apologies. The emperors must come to terms with Jesus, if not in this life then in the next. If the kingdom of God was not realized on earth, the fault lay not with deity, nor with redemptive metaphysics, but with sinful man.

---

2. Many Roman Catholic writers suggest that the Protestant defection from the "universal (Roman) Catholic Church" is the cause of all Protestantism's difficulties. But the Reformation opened the door to a truly spiritual ecumenicity. True, religious modernism precluded an effective realization of that ideal. But it is still a possibility for evangelicalism.

This theologico-ethical emphasis runs through the Hebrew-Christian outlook. The ultimate values of Biblical supernaturalism are unchanging. New Testament ethics was no more entirely new than New Testament doctrine. The moral, as well as metaphysical, concepts had their Old Testament foregleams, simply because the Biblical view as a whole was rooted in the creative and revelational and regenerative God. In whatever sense the later Christian message did away with the law, it did not set aside any ultimate truths. Both in Old Testament and New Testament thought there is but one sure foundation for a lasting civilization, and its cornerstone is a vital knowledge of the redemptive God. In both eras it is wrong to worship false gods, to murder, to commit adultery, and for a reason more ultimate than that the prophet Moses said so. These deeds were wrong before Moses, yea even before Adam; they have been wrong always, and will be wrong always, because they are antagonistic to the character and will of the sovereign God of the universe. They are wrong for all creatures anywhere anytime. The universe is put together on moral lines; any attempt to build a civilization on other lines, whether before or after the coming of Jesus Christ into the world, foredooms itself. The ten commandments disclose the only secure foundation for a society without the seeds of dissolution; all cultures, cut loose from these principles, have in them the vitiating leaven of decay. And no culture can hope to fulfill such high prerequisites, minus a relationship with that God, holy and redemptive, who is the precondition for their very disclosure to man.

On Old Testament pages no less than New, then, the cardinal doctrines are not divorced from ethical implications. The social outreach of redemptional metaphysics begins for humanity at the very beginnings of the race; Adam implicates all humanity in his fall; the covenant singles out Abraham and his people to bless the world; the Mosaic writings constantly warn that national as well as individual faithfulness to the one true God determines the judgments or blessings of history. One stands with Moses at the close of the Penateuch, looking prophetically down the corridor of the nation Israel's history, to discover there a philosophy of events with the stamp of eternal validity upon it. The song of Moses, warning of God's judgment while extolling His mercy, is climaxed by counsel to observe "all the words of this law, for it is not a vain thing for you; because it is your life" (Deut. 32:46f). The major as well as minor prophets, lashing out with uncompromised vigor against social evils of the day, breathed the same social passion in a redemption context; the Hebrew world-life view could not look with indifference upon miscarriages of justice in the law courts, usury, plundering the needy, failure to feed and clothe the poor, and over-charging for merchandise.

The New Testament challenge to Greek-Roman culture was an inevitable outcome of the Hebrew-Christian spirit. John the Baptist stood with Moses, Isaiah and Amos in his social alertness. The very words of Isaiah were his rallying point in heralding the coming Redeemer: "The voice of one crying in the wilderness, Prepare ye the way of the Lord... all flesh shall see the salvation of God" (Luke 3:4-6). Assuredly, the message of redemption stood at the forefront of the Baptist's preaching. He identifies Jesus to the disciples as "the Lamb of God, which taketh away the sin of the world" (John 1:29), and not to them only, for Jesus' persecutors had "sent unto John, and he bare witness unto the truth" (John 5:33). But the Baptist's redemptive preaching was not on that account socially indifferent. He spoke to a "generation of vipers" (Matt. 3:7) and exhorted, "Repent ye; for the kingdom of heaven is at hand" (Matt. 3:2). He called for "fruits worthy of repentance" (Luke 3:8), declaring that "every tree which bringeth not forth good fruit is hewn down, and cast into the fire" (Luke 3:9). To the specific inquiry, "What shall we do then?" (Luke 3:10), he gives specific examples. Persons with two coats were to give to those without any. Those with abundant provisions were to share with the needy. Publicans were not to extort. Soldiers were not to commit violence nor accuse individuals falsely. They were to be content with their wages — which was probably not a pronouncement for preservation of the *status quo* in labor management relations, as some humanists insist upon misinterpreting it, but rather a warning against plundering innocent civilians. John's exhortations included "many other things" (Luke 3:18). In fact, his condemnation of adultery in the life of the King led to his own imprisonment and martyrdom: "For John had said unto Herod, It is not lawful for thee to have thy brother's wife" (Mark 6:18).

The social spirit of John's preaching was not contrary to Jesus' own message. Replying to the imprisoned forerunner's inquiry concerning the Christ, Jesus endorses a particular expectation about the Messiah which the Baptist had doubtless gleaned from the Old Testament: "Go and show John again those things which ye do hear and see: the blind receive their sight, and the lame walk, the lepers are cleansed, and the deaf hear, the dead are raised up, and the poor have the gospel preached to them" (Mt. 11:4-5; Lk. 7:22). In view of so central a passage, it is difficult to find room for a gospel cut loose entirely from non-spiritual needs. It is true that the New Testament repeatedly employs phrases like the blind seeing, the deaf hearing, and the dead receiving life, in the figurative sense of spiritual regeneration. But that cannot be said for the lame walking, nor for the lepers being cleansed; furthermore, Luke definitely prefixes Jesus' reply to John with the comment that "in the same hour he cured many of their infirmities and plagues, and of evil spirits; and unto many that were blind he gave sight" (7:21). There is no room here for a gospel that is indifferent to the needs of the total man nor of the global man.

Of course, Jesus does not declare that all effort must be bent for world peace; He shares the Biblical conviction that neither peace nor war is as deterministic of human felicity as redemption. Of course He does not declare that there must be a communistic distribution of world goods; He shares the Biblical conviction that redemption is the essential ingredient in the solution of economic problems. Of course He does not declare in formula how a western democracy and a Soviet communist state are to carry on international relations; He shares the Biblical conviction that there is a more relevant need in political science than the intercourse of secularized nations.

But He is not on that account disinterested in the nations and in the global man. One of the blind modern prejudices is our feeling that unless another mind attacks a problem in the way the contemporary mood does, he is not interested in it. The methodology of Jesus is a redemption methodology, and the modern formulas have been so different simply because of their presupposition that redemption is an alien concept for the contemporary world. But there is not a problem of global consequence but that, from the viewpoint of Jesus, redemption is a relevant formula. It is offered as the only adequate rest for world weariness, whether political, economic, academic, recreational. It stands in judgment upon all non-Christian solutions.

Paul's position likewise involves an ethical universalism, for he is concerned with more than individual morals. The gospel of Christ cuts across all human distinctions, and He is the lone Lord of humanity, with the only adequate relief for man's needs. The apostle to the Gentiles thus proclaims a social, as well as personal, Christianity. His missionary passion contradicts any view that he conceived of the believer's life as an exclusive privilege to be lived in monastic privacy; rather, he was spiritually aflame to bring the world to the feet of Jesus.

This early outlook, seeking to relate Christianity redemptively to the Graeco-Roman environment of the day, so characterized the apostolic witness that within three centuries the new religion had, in large measure, captured the then-known world. Whatever their view of the kingdom, the early Christians did not permit it to interfere with their world-changing zeal; they were not embarrassed that some opponents should suspect them of turning the world "upside down." This does not mean that early Christianity charted the course for social reform; rather, it furnished the basic principles and the moral dynamic for such reform, and concentrated on regeneration as the guarantee of bettered conditions.[3]

It is not denied, of course, that Roman Catholic imperialism soon substituted political aggrandizement for spiritual regeneration; the so-called Christian culture of the middle ages tended rather to be an outwardly ritualized form of Graeco-Roman culture, although the impact of the Christian witness could not be totally lost. In other spotty areas of church history, there appeared an emphasis on the other-worldliness of Christianity, as in the monastic movements. Thomas a Kempis' *The Imitation of Christ* may be a later

---

3. There is renewed appreciation today of the fact that a message which concentrates on individual regeneration may be on that very account socially relevant rather than socially irrelevant. The higher liberals learned many lessons from the war years 1914-46. Ernest F. Scott now reminds us that "Jesus' one remedy for social abuses is the renewal of the individual will. If men become different in their own hearts their actions will be different, and the outcome will be a new society, in which there will be right relations between man and man" (*Man and Society in the New Testament*, p. 197. New York: Charles Scribner's Sons, 1946).

expression of this mood, though he may be explicating not fundamental motives as much as personal morality.

Yet the early patriotic moralists attacked pagan ethical standards — idolatry, sensuous luxury, sexual looseness, theatrical obscenity, gladiatorial cruelties, infanticide and abortion, commercial deceit; everywhere they pitched the Christian message against social immoralities. Augustine's *City of God* insisted that the temporal and eternal cities exist concurrently in history, as against the view that the kingdom of God is to be identified with super-history alone. When Aquinas formulated in the thirteenth century the theological system which still is the frame of reference for Roman Catholic divinity, a detailed study of Christian ethics both social and personal was an essential part of his task.

Much of the blame for the early Renaissance interest in social theory must be attributed to the corruption within the Roman Catholic church, which led ultimately to the Reformational revolt. Martin Luther, the father of the Reformation, hurled his full weight against the medieval concept of a works-salvation, but the ethical implications of his Gospel message were not wrought out with complete satisfaction. Luther bemoaned the moral deterioration of his day, but he placed an underemphasis on sanctification in his teaching and example, and his conduct in the Peasants' War is not a happy chapter in the story of the Reformation. The Zwinglian Reformation in Switzerland, however, became more articulate about the civil and moral implications of regeneration, and the Calvinistic Reformation moved toward a truly catholic view of the Christian life. Calvin felt that the Hebrew-Christian tradition historically involved an articulate statement not only of dogmatics but of the social implications of redemption.

Today, Protestant Fundamentalism although heir-apparent to the supernaturalist gospel of the Biblical and Reformation minds, is a stranger, in its predominant spirit, to the vigorous social interest of its ideological forebears. Modern Fundamentalism does not explicitly sketch the social implications of its message for the non-Christian world; it does not challenge the injustices of the totalitarianisms, the secularisms of modern education, the evils of racial hatred, the wrongs of current labor-management relations, the inadequate bases of international dealings. It has ceased to challenge Caesar and Rome, as though in futile resignation and submission to the triumphant Renaissance mood. The apostolic Gospel stands divorced from a passion to right the world. The Christian social imperative is today in the hands of those who understand it in sub-Christian terms.

But evangelicalism is disturbed proportionately as it senses this contradiction of its own history. Fundamentalism is agitating today with two great convictions, the affirmation of which is necessary if Fundamentalism is to express the genius of the Christian tradition: (1) That Christianity opposes any and every evil, personal and social, and must never be represented as in any way tolerant of such evil; (2) That Christianity opposes to such evil, as the only sufficient formula for its resolution, the redemptive work of Jesus Christ and the regenerative work of the Holy Spirit. It rejects the charge that the Fundamentalist ideology logically involves an indifference to social evils, and presses the contention that the non-evangelical ideology involves an essential inability to right the world order. It is discerning anew that an assault on global evils is not only consistent with, but rather is demanded by, its proper world-life view.

Chapter IV.

THE APPREHENSION OVER KINGDOM PREACHING

IV.

The Apprehension Over Kingdom Preaching

THERE has been more millenial fanaticism in modern anti-supernaturalistic theories than in contemporary evangelicalism. One of the curiosities of church history is that the naturalistic world-view, so hostile to the Christian notion of the kingdom, finally embraced zealously the idea of an immanent millenium.[1]

The millenial enthusiasm or "carnal chiliasm" of Münzer and the Zwickau prophets and of Matthys and the Münster kingdom, is not representative of modern Fundamentalism. In non-dispensational Fundamentalism, amillenialists and premillenialists agree that the kingdom whether earthly or heavenly will be set up not by the flashed sword of Gideon but by the advent of Christ, though a real spiritual reign is insisted upon in Christ's present relationship to the church. In dispensational Fundamentalism, the keynote of the postponement theory is "no kingdom now, but rather a future kingdom." Therefore modern Fundamentalism has not shared the sentiment for an immediate and forced bringing in of the kingdom. That mood, rather, characterized modern liberalism, with its strategy for abolishing social inequities;

---

1. Herbert Spencer was an apostle of such optimism: "The inference that as advancement has been hitherto the rule, it will be the rule henceforth, may be called a plausible speculation. But when it is shown that this advancement is due to the working of a universal law; and that in virtue of that law it must continue until the state we call perfection is reached, then the belief in that state is removed out of the region of probability into that of certainty" (*Social Statistics*, p. 78. New York: D. Appleton and Co., 1883).

kingdom fanaticism had found, in recent times, a strange bedfellow indeed.

Nevertheless, Fundamentalism steadfastly proclaimed the future kingdom as a certainty, for the triumph of righteousness was inevitable in a moral universe. The post-millenial optimism that the kingdom was to be ushered in by the effort of believers prior to the return of Christ, was largely compromised by the first World War. Even previous to that time, however, cautious evangelicals like James Orr tempered their postmillenial optimism with the conviction that the final thrust in establishing the kingdom would require the advent of Christ.[2] In the aftermath of the second World War, evangelical postmillenialism almost wholly abandoned the field of kingdom preaching to premillenialism and amillenialism, united in the common conviction that the return of Christ is a prerequisite for the future golden age, but divided over whether it will involve an earthly millenium. Assured of the ultimate triumph of right, contemporary evangelicalism avoids a minimizing of earthly hostility to the gospel, as well as rejects the naturalistic optimism centering in evolutionary automatic progress. The bright hope of the immanent return of Christ is not minimized, and the kingdom hope is clearly distinguishable from the liberal confidence in a new social order of human making only.

Recent Fundamentalism increasingly reflects a marked hesitancy about kingdom preaching.

The tendency to identify the kingdom with any present earthly social order, however modified in a democratic or communistic direction, always has been resisted by evangelicals. As against secular humanism, Fundamentalism has consistently witnessed to the fact that any culture from which the redemptive element is absent is essentially distinct from the kingdom of God. It is this concept of supernatural

---

2. On this view, utopianism could be safeguarded against relapse only by the presence of the King.

redemption that furnishes the unique ingredient of the divine kingdom. Cultures which tend to be democratic rather than totalitarian may be preferential for many reasons, but they are not, therefore, to be equated with the kingdom. For this reason, Fundamentalism has resisted the *kingdom now* mood which characterized much liberal preaching.

On the other hand, Fundamentalism also discloses an apprehension over *kingdom then* preaching. This is partly due to prophetic extravangances which the second World War repudiated, though Fundamentalist excesses on this score hardly suffered as rudely as did the liberal optimism about the future. Nevertheless, the prophetic movement had numerous embarrassing elements. It was not only that dogmatic predictions, such as that concerning a revived Roman empire, sorely miscarried, though prophetic disillusionment was serious enough. For the tendency personally to identify an anti-Christ, the division of evangelicals not only over the millenial question but over such problems as the pre-tribulation, mid-tribulation or post-tribulation rapture, concentrated the emphasis on Fundamentalist differences rather than on the basic supernaturalistic ideology which they unitedly opposed to the prevailing empirical-naturalistic world-view. But even more serious was the fact that some Fundamentalist workers substituted a familiarity with the prophetic teaching of the Bible for an aggressive effort to proclaim Christ as the potent answer to the dissolution of world culture. As a consequence, they trained enlightened spectators, rather than empowered ambassadors. Prophetic conference, rather than pentecostal challenge, was their forte.

These factors have engendered a reaction involving the *kingdom then* message. Some responsible Fundamentalists have acknowledged unjustifiable inferences in their pre-war prophetic utterances. This does not involve, by any means, their error at all points. The humanists and modernists who are unmoved by fulfilled predictions such as a Palestine rejuvenated by the immigration of non-Christian Jews, must come to terms at all events with the fulfillment of Fundamentalist insistence that world events would wax worse rather than better. Nevertheless there has been sufficient basis for a frank confession of prophetic extravagance.

Furthermore, there is a noticeable shift in eschatological thinking. On the one hand, there appears a return to a more conservative type of pre-millenialism, such as that of Alford and Trench, with an accompanying tendency to discard dogmatism on details; if this continues, the eschatological preaching of next generation Fundamentalists will concentrate on the proclamation of the kingdom, the second coming, the bodily resurrection of the dead, and the future judgment, and will not concern itself too much with lesser events. On the other hand, some evangelicals revolting against the prophetic detail of dispensational premillenialism, are discarding premillenialism along with the detail, and shifting toward an amillenial position. It is not within the province of this study to set forth arguments for or against such a trend. The writer's own convictions are broadly premillenial, and he is not convinced that a discard of speculative accretions justifies an uncritical surrender of the whole premillenial structure; if the shift to amillenial grounds is made on firmer convictions, that is a different matter. But it is within the province of this volume to urge upon evangelicals the necessity for a deliberate restudy of the whole kingdom question, that the great evangelical agreements may be set effectively over against the modern mind, with the least dissipation of energy on secondary issues.

The writer was cautioned by a Fundamentalist spokesman, when this series of articles was projected, to "stay away from the kingdom." There is growing reluctance to explicate the kingdom idea in Fundamentalist preaching, because a *kingdom now* message is too easily confused with the liberal social gospel, and because a *kingdom then* message will identify Christianity further to the modern mind in terms of an escape mechanism.

Yet no subject was more frequently on the lips of Jesus Christ than the kingdom. He proclaimed kingdom truth with a constant, exuberant joy. It appears as the central theme of His preaching. To delete His kingdom references, parabolic and nonparabolic, would be to excise most of His words. The concept "kingdom of God" or "kingdom of heaven" is heard repeatedly from His lips, and it colors all of His works.

It is not purposed here to project any new kingdom theory; exegetical novelty so late in church history may well be suspect. Nor is it purposed to evaluate in detail the prevailing theories: that cannot be done competently in such brief compass. The writer's own convictions, while broadly premillenial, are not partial to the dispensational postponement theory of the kingdom; this is no necessary adjunct of the premillenial view. It appears more in accord with the Biblical philosophy of history to think of the church age in terms of divine continuity rather than of parenthesis, in terms of the amazing unity of the redemptive plan rather than in terms of an amazing interlude.[3] The writer feels

---

3. According to the postponement theory, Jesus was to set up the Davidic kingdom at His first coming but, due to His rejection, the "mystery form" of the kingdom was introduced. As a consequence, the divine plan during this church age is concerned, it is said, only with "calling out" believers. This theory has gained wide support in the north during the past two generations; many persons automatically identify if not only with all premillenialism, but with all Fundamentalism. Johannes Weiss, Albert Schweitzer and others of the so-called "consistent school of eschatology" contend that Jesus, viewed as a gifted human prophet merely, preached *only* a future eschatological kingdom—a view which has remote affinities to the postponement theory with its one-sided futurist emphasis, though of course there is here no thought of any offer of the kingdom to the Jews.

that the prophecies demand a future earthly kingdom, and are not fully exhausted by the idea of an eternal spiritual kingdom.[4] Nevertheless, the burden of these articles is not to press a personal kingdom viewpoint, but rather to promote an evangelical conviction that nothing is so essential among Fundamentalist essentials as a world-relevance for the Gospel. Whatever in our kingdom views undercuts that relevance destroys the essential character of Christianity as such.

No study of the kingdom teaching of Jesus is adequate unless it recognizes His implication both that the kingdom is here, and that it is not here.[5] This does not imply an ultimate paradox, but rather stresses that the kingdom exists in incomplete realization. The task of the Bible student is to discover (1) in what sense it is here; (2) in what sense it is to be further realized before the advent of Christ; and (3) in what sense it will be fully realized at the advent of Christ.

Matthew's Gospel, deliberately stressing the continuity between the Old Testament prophecies and their Messianic fulfillment in Jesus Christ, is the most Jewish of the Gospels. Here, if anywhere, one should find a clear indication of the meaning of the kingdom idea in the teaching of Jesus.

Jesus obviously did not usher in an earthly political kingdom at His coming. Further, He did not attempt to do so

---

4. James Orr expressed this sentiment in a delightful manner: "But this I would confess, that the idea of a latter day of glory on this earth of ours—a period of Sabbath rest and realization of righteousness—has a charm to my mind, and seems to me to have its roots in so much Old Testament prediction, that I cannot willingly forego it . . ." (*Sidelights on Christian Doctrine*, p. 174).

5. F. J. Foakes-Jackson and Kirsopp Lake insisted that the kingdom of God in the Gospels has a two-fold reference: it is a future kingdom, proclaimed as at hand; it is a present kingdom in the sovereignty of God. "All attempts . . . to explain these two meanings of the kingdom of God by eliminating one of them have failed'" (*The Beginnings of Christianity*, I, p. 280).

only to abandon the idea. The disciples did not go forth to overthrow the Roman empire by force of arms. Nor did Caesar come into necessary conflict with the kingdom idea; such conflict would ensue only when Caesar demanded what was God's due. The kingdom which Jesus introduced, it appears, was quite compatible with earthly government which did not interfere with the realization of the *summun bonam* in the lives of regenerate believers, but it could hardly be identified with any government in which the redemptive reference was not central. The main difference between the kingdom of God *now* and the kingdom of God *then* is that the future kingdom will center all of its activities in the redemptive King because all government and dominion will be subjected to Him. This difference overshadows the question, however important, whether the future kingdom involves an earthly reign or not.

The extent to which man centers his life and energy in the redemptive King *now* determines the extent of the divine kingdom in the present age. That kingdom is not to be totally identified with any earthly rule, though some have subserved and others have opposed the redemptive program. Human government need not conflict with divine government unless it so decrees and, if it does, the kingdom of God secures its ends primarily by spiritual rather than political revolution; eventually, however, because this is a moral universe and the inevitable wages of sin is death, the divine victory is won in both areas. Graeco-Roman culture fell before the medieval mind not because Jesus sought to pressure the Jewish government into line with His principles, nor because the disciples endeavored to destroy the Roman empire. Neither the fall of Herod's throne nor the overthrow of Caesar was an announced prerequisite for the *at handness* of the kingdom of God. That kingdom was a spiritual relationship of individuals to Jesus Christ as their redemptive King. It did not await the overthrow, or establishment, of any specified type of earthly political government; presumably it was compatible with any earthly rule that did no violence to the redemptive reference. A totalitarianism without such violence would be better than a democracy with it, and vice versa. But even then, a totalitarianism or a democracy with such a reference would not on that account be identified with the kingdom of God in its totality, for in the *then* kingdom all life and activity will have a redemptive center.

In the establishment of the *now* kingdom, the Gospel of Jesus does not ride rough shod in political power over the oppositions of men; in the establishment of the *then* kingdom, there will be evident a fiery and cataclysmic consummation. By true instinct the Christian church has prayed through the ages, after the Redeemer: "Thy kingdom come; Thy will be done on earth as it is in heaven." The Hebrew parallelism of this prayer declares how wide is the gap between the *new* kingdom and the *then* kingdom.

The apostolic view of the kingdom should likewise be definitive for contemporary evangelicalism. There does not seem much apostolic apprehension over kingdom preaching. We read that Philip preached "good news about the kingdom of God and the name of Jesus Christ" (Acts 8:12). Paul in the Ephesus synagogue boldly argued and pleaded "about the kingdom of God" (Acts 19:8), and identified the Ephesian elders in his farewell address as those "among whom I have gone about preaching the kingdom" (Acts 20:25). Arriving in Rome, Paul testified "to the kingdom of God, trying to convince them about Jesus both from the law of Moses and from the prophets" (Acts 28:23). For two years he lived in that city, "preaching the kingdom of God and teaching about the Lord Jesus Christ" (Acts 28:31).

The apostolic notion of the kingdom is characterized by the same *now* and *then* aspects discoverable in the teaching of Jesus.

The kingdom is not wholly future. Paul writes the Romans that the kingdom of God means "righteousness and peace and joy in the Holy Spirit" (Rom. 14:17). He writes the Corinthians that the kingdom of God "does not consist in talk but in power" (I Cor. 4:20). He writes the Colossians that the Father "has transferred us to the kingdom of his beloved Son, in whom we have redemption, the forgiveness of sins" (Col. 1:13). The author of the epistle to the Hebrews writes: "Let us be grateful for receiving a kingdom that cannot be shaken, and let us offer to God acceptable worship, with reverence and awe" (Heb. 12:28). The Apocalypst writes: "I John, your brother, who share with you in Jesus the tribulation and the kingdom and the patient endurance . . ." (Rev. 1:9). These passages, among others, argue clearly that the kingdom is a present spiritual reality in the lives of believers, being coextensive with the outworked redemptive and regenerative plan of God.

Yet the kingdom has a glorious future aspect. Paul writes the Corinthians that the coming of Christ and the resurrection of the righteous dead precedes the end-time "when Christ delivers the kingdom to God the Father after destroying every rule and every authority and power" (I Cor. 15:24). Quite clearly, the reign of Christ involves an era when all His enemies are not underfoot, and an era when they are. Again, Paul writes that "flesh and blood cannot inherit the kingdom of God" (I Cor. 15:50), explaining that perishable things cannot inherit the imperishable. He charges Timothy "in the presence of God and of Christ Jesus who is to judge the living and the dead, at his appearing and at his kingdom" (II Tim. 4:1), and adds, "The Lord will rescue me from every evil and save me for his heavenly kingdom" (II Tim. 4:18). Peter urges the brethren to "confirm your call and election . . . so there will be richly provided for you an entrance into the eternal kingdom of our Lord and Saviour Jesus Christ" (II Pet. 1:10-11). The Apocalypst looks ahead to the day when "the kingdom of the world has become the kingdom of our Lord and of his Christ, and he shall reign forever and ever" (Rev. 11:15), and to the day when "the salvation and the power and the kingdom of our God and the authority of His Christ have come" (Rev. 12:10). The disciples too, after the crucifixion and resurrection of Jesus, hear His instruction concerning the kingdom of God, and inquire when the kingdom will be restored to Israel (Acts 1:6). The present spiritual kingdom constituted by the reign of Christ in the hearts of believers clearly does not exhaust the declarations concerning a future kingdom, when every opposing or resisting power shall be subjected to Christ.

Contemporary evangelicalism needs (1) to reawaken to the relevance of its redemptive message to the global predicament; (2) to stress the great evangelical agreements in a common world front; (3) to discard elements of its message which cut the nerve of world compassion as contradictory to the inherent genius of Christianity; (4) to restudy eschatological convictions for a proper perspective which will not unnecessarily dissipate evangelical strength in controversy over secondary positions, in a day when the significance of the primary insistences is international.

Chapter V

THE FUNDAMENTALIST THIEF ON THE CROSS

V.

The Fundamentalist Thief on the Cross

THE two thieves between whom Jesus was crucified might, without too wild an imagination, bear the labels of humanism and Fundamentalism. The one on the left felt that Jesus had no momentous contribution to suffering humanity, while the one on the right was convinced of His saviourhood but wanted to be remembered in the indefinite future, when Jesus would come into His kingdom.

Contemporary Fundamentalism needs to meditate long hours on the Saviour's reply: *"Today* shalt thou be with me in paradise." The message for decadent modern civilization must ring with the present tense. We must confront the world *now* with an ethics to make it tremble, and with a dynamic to give it hope.

It is quite popular at the moment to crucify the Fundamentalist. That is not the object of this series of articles; there is no sympathy here for the distorted attack on Fundamentalism so often pressed by liberals and humanists. To conceal his own embarrassment, many a liberal today follows a planned strategy of thanking God he is not a Fundamentalist. A frequent pattern is to remark that of course the liberal repudiates the obscurantism of taking the whole Bible literally, or of thinking God dictated it without respecting the personalities of the writers, or of contending that God stopped working in human history 1900 years ago. What is not remarked is that no representative Fundamentalist thinks that either. But, by the device of differentiating liberalism from a position so extreme that only a mental incompetent would subscribe to it, the sting is supposedly removed from liberalism's death. The Fundamentalist is placed on the cross, while the liberal goes scot free in a forest of weasel words.

The intent of these articles, on the other hand, is to show that viewpoints identified with Fundamentalism have a right to that claim only as they share the historic doctrines and the historic superlife. Part of that superlife is a passion to bring men everywhere to a knowledge of Jesus Christ. A Fundamentalism from which such a passion is absent becomes an inessentialism. Here, if anywhere, the test of "negative pragmatism,"[1] appears appropriate indeed. If Fundamentalism ceases to "work," we have imported into it elements which violate the innermost essence of Christianity. The apostles were convinced not only that they possessed the one name under heaven whereby men must be saved, but also that they were the ambassadors for Christ whose faithful service measured the impact of redemptionism upon their generation. This volume covets for the whole evangelical movement a new life and vigor on the destitute world front.

The supernaturalist framework of historic Christianity is here espoused as the lone solution of modern dilemmas. That solution is not the renunciation of naturalism in the name of Platonic idealism, nor Kierkegaardian existentialism, but the reaffirmation of Hebrew-Christian redemptionism. When classic Fundamentalism is properly differentiated from other views, the stress does not fall on excesses or accretions unacceptable to the evangelical mind as a whole. The true differentia come into vital conflict with the

---

1. Pragmatism affirms that a thing is true because it works; Christianity rather that it works because it is true. Negative pragmatism—as Hocking set it forth—affirms merely that unless it works, it cannot be true.

controversial issues in modern thought. Fundamentalism insists upon a purposive and moral as over against a purely mathematical universe; it insists upon a personal God, as against impersonal ultimates whether of the space-time or *elan vital* variety; it insists upon a divine creation as over against a naturalistic evolution; it insists that man's uniqueness is a divine endowment rather than a human achievement; it insists that man's predicament is not an animal inheritance nor a necessity of his nature but rather a consequence of his voluntary revolt against God; it insists that salvation can be provided only by God, as against the view that man is competent to save himself; it insists that the Scriptures are a revelation lighting the way to the divine incarnation in Jesus Christ as the Redeemer of mankind, as against the view that they stand among many records of religious experience without a difference in kind; it insists that history is bound up with man's acceptance or rejection of the God-man, rather than that history is primarily what happens among nations; it insists that the future is not an open question, but that world events move toward an ultimate consummation in a future judgment of the race.

One needs to view Fundamentalism in this perspective before it is apparent how distorted is any identification in terms of eschatology only. There are, no doubt, Fundamentalists who do not express the true genius of Fundamentalism any more than some so-called Hegelians or Kantians are representative of the philosophers whose names they bear. There is no necessity for abandonment of the Fundamentalist fort, on such secondary grounds, nor for moving to an obscure neo-Fundamentalist position, or to so-called conservatism as differentiated from Fundamentalism; there is already too much terminological confusion, and one always runs the danger of being identified with liberal Fundamentalists who emphasize only the fundamentals of liberalism, and the further danger of encouraging a willingness to be misunderstood.

The revitalization of modern evangelicalism will not come by a discard of its doctrinal convictions and a movement in the direction of liberalism. For current history has decisively unmasked liberal unrealism. Precisely those non-evangelical ideologies which prevailed during the past generation have ended in frustration. They have not averted the most serious debacle in history, after displacing Christian supernaturalism on the questionable ground that it had not worked in earlier ages; the judgment of history, by clearer perspective than ours, will discern how directly such ideologies contributed to that debacle by undercutting supernatural sanctions.

The evangelical may often believe too much, but the sweep of his ideology at least includes the great essentials. The time has come now for Fundamentalism to speak with an ecumenical outlook and voice; if it speaks in terms of the historic Biblical tradition, rather than in the name of secondary accretions or of eschatological biases on which evangelicals divide, it can refashion the modern mind. But a double-minded Fundamentalism — which veers between essentials and inessentials — will receive little of the Lord, and not much of a hearing from the perishing multitudes.

The author's Reformed friends insist that Fundamentalism needs to incorporate into its doctrine a view of common grace, thus securing a vital philosophy of history. His amillenial friends insist that amillenialism is the neglected key; his premillenial friends terms this a shallow solution. Others suggest that the biggest evangelical need is a spiritual revival to sweep away what Dr. William Ward Ayer terms "pharisaical fundamentalism," applied to those — fortunately not numerous — who are doctrinally sound but ethically unsound. Dr. Ayer deplores the "pharisaical spirit of fundamentalism" and warns that "unless there is a resurgence of love, power and breadth of mind and spirit in our midst we shall more effectively deny the faith than the religiously-shallow modernists can ever do. Their following is limited; ours is large." Others hold that the basic need is for a common determination to concentrate on those great doctrines which can steer the modern mind aright at the points of severest tension.

The evangelical uneasiness is one of the most promising signs of the times, for it may issue in a formula providing a twentieth-century reformation within Protestantism and leading to a global renaissance within modern secularism. Evangelicalism already has the advantage of agreement on great doctrines, whereas no contemporary ideology can claim such great numbers who stand united on so wide a front. Liberalism is caught in transition, with little agreement. It swings indecisively between the notion of a personal God and a creative force for which the term "personal" may be a symbol; it swings inconsistently between acceptance of the tentativity of the scientific method and the claim that Jesus has an absolute meaning for history; it fluctuates uncertainly between its former view that man is essentially good and a view that man is somehow essentially bad, and when it adopts the latter it robs sin of its true character as sin. But Fundamentalism is agreed on the main doctrines of God, of creation, of anthropology, of soteriology, and of eschatology in its main peaks. It was great doctrine, centering in the Living Christ as Redeemer, that the early church proclaimed to the dying culture of its day.

To engage the time of the contemporary mind at secondary points is to miss our opportunity, for the main tenets of Biblical supernaturalism are most relevant to the modern tensions. The central affirmations of the Hebrew-Christian message need most to be heard. The hour now is so desperate that the Biblical view will strike upon modern indecision with a power directly proportionate to the immediacy or delay in its proclamation.

The evangelical answer is to be presented not primarily as a rejected opportunity, though it has been that through the centuries in differing measures, but as a present solution, if only men and nations will come to terms with Jesus. That they must come to terms with Him later is always a timely insistence, but not as timely right now as the emphasis that God works in history as well as in superhistory.

Perhaps this picture of Jesus standing at the tomb of our disintegrating renaissance culture can be emphasized by an allegory built on the raising of Lazarus. When death overtook Lazarus, and plunged his survivors into grief, Jesus came with assurance that "thy brother shall rise again." Martha replied, "I know that he shall rise again *in the resurrection at the last day*" (Jn. 11:24). Such Fundamentalism as reduces God's role in history largely to a preparation for future judgment may well pause at the tomb of Lazarus. There Jesus cried out, "I *am* the resurrection and the life . . . Lazarus, come forth!"

The problem of Fundamentalism then is basically not one of finding a valid message, but rather of giving the redemptive word a proper temporal focus. Christianity still affords the supreme dynamic, the supreme world-view, the supreme hope; wherever men tend to rest with a lesser dynamic, with a sub-Christian philosophy, and with a lesser hope, it is and always will be pertinent.

If Protestant orthodoxy holds itself aloof from the present world predicament it is doomed to a much reduced role; in the previous crises of culture, whether the challenge of the Graeco-Roman world in the apostolic age, or the challenge of a corrupt medieval Catholicism in the Reformation movement, orthodoxy led the battle for a new order, and was not content with a secondary or tertiary role. If the evangelical answer is in terms of religious escapism, then the salt has lost its savor.

Our obligation to speak is not lessened by our conviction of the immanent return of Christ. What if we rise tomorrow? — we are *here* today, and a global mission field is here with us.

Chapter VI

THE STRUGGLE FOR A NEW WORLD MIND

VI.

The Struggle for a New World Mind

IF HISTORIC Christianity is again to compete as a vital world ideology, evangelicalism must project a solution for the most pressing world problems. It must offer a formula for a new world mind with spiritual ends,[1] involving evangelical affirmations in political, economic, sociological, and educational realms, local and international. The redemptive message has implications for all of life; a truncated life results from a truncated message.

Evangelicalism may never succeed, on the missionary approach, in remaking the modern mind in such a way that the future world culture can be identified fully as a Christian civilization. In order to become globally vigorous, Fundamentalism need not share the dream, now being discarded by liberalism, of an immanent utopia; an adequate insight both into human nature and into New Testament truth furnishes good ground for doubt that the kingdom can be established without the advent of Christ.

But Fundamentalism does not share the recent tendency, found both in neo-supernaturalist and higher liberal circles, to view man as a sinner by an ultimate necessity of his nature, as though he were destined originally to contradiction and failure. The evangelical and non-evangelical views grow, at this point, out of differing attitudes toward primal anthropology. The Fundamentalist holds that primal man

---

1. See the author's *Remaking the Modern Mind* (Grand Rapids: Wm. B. Eerdmans Publ. Co., 1946).

was a divine creation, endowed with moral righteousness, so that man is not a sinner by a necessity of his original nature, but rather by voluntary choice; consequently, the hope for a better order is directly proportionate to the appropriation of redemptive grace in human society. The neo-supernaturalists and liberals adopt the evolutionary view of origins, and discard any notion of a fall from primal perfection involving man in original sin. Man's imperfection, on this approach, is identified with inherited brute instincts or the limitations of his nature as a man; the hope for a better order, on this view, is directly proportionate to his success in affirming a higher self as against his natural self, with a bias in the direction of failure. In the light of the two world wars, liberalism thus discards its faith in automatic progress which formerly characterized the social gospel; we are now told by Paul Tillich, for example, that "the authentic Christian message is never utopian."[2] Evangelicalism does not believe that man's progress is limited by man's nature as man, as much as by his refusal to appropriate divine regenerative grace.

Therefore evangelicalism can view the future with a sober optimism, grounded not only in the assurance of the ultimate triumph of righteousness, but also in the conviction that divine redemption can be a potent factor in any age. That evangelicalism may not create a fully Christian civilization does not argue against an effort to win as many areas as possible by the redemptive power of Christ; it can engender reformation here, and overthrow paganism there; it can win outlets for the redemption that is in Christ Jesus reminiscent of apostolic triumphs. If Christianity cannot bring new life to Russia, that is no argument for not bringing it to China; if it cannot bring reformation to Spain, that is no

---

[2] Van Dusen, Henry P. (Editor), *The Christian Answer*, p. 44. (New York: Charles Scribner's Sons, 1945).

reason for not bringing it to South America. A single voice that speaks for Jesus in our global conferences can be a determinative voice. The world has awakened suddenly to the astonishing potentiality of an individual veto. It is apparent how great nations are keyed to powerful leaders; a single statesman with the convictions of Paul would echo the great evangelical affirmations throughout world politics.

Evangelicalism will have to contend for a new order in education. The western concept of popular education has its legitimate rootage in the determination of the church to indoctrinate the masses in the major doctrinal essentials of the Christian world-life view. For the past three centuries, the state has steadily supplanted the church as the indoctrinating agency, and today secular education largely involves an open or subtle undermining of historic Christian theism.

Evangelicalism must contend, under such circumstances, for two great academic changes.

First, it must develop a competent literature in every field of study, on every level from the grade school through the university, which adequately presents each subject with its implications from the Christian as well as non-Christian points of view. The bias and prejudice to which modern secularism yielded, in the very name of a revolt against dogmatism and in the supposed interest of impartiality, is becoming increasingly obvious to anyone familiar with the modern mood. Evangelicalism must contend for a fair hearing for the Christian mind, among other minds, in secular education. Almost every philosophic viewpoint can be taught by men who hold those convictions — whether Platonism, Aristotelianism, Kantianism, Hegelianism, or whatever else — except that the universities seem studiously to avoid the competent presentation of the Hebrew-Christian view by those who hold it.

Secondly, evangelicalism must not let the fact that the state has now become an agent of indoctrination obscure the evangelical obligation to press the Christian world-life view upon the masses. The church and the publishing house are not fully adequate to fulfill this ministry; the importance of the evangelical school must be reaffirmed. The Protestant churches of America are planning postwar rebuilding and alterations in the amount of many millions of dollars; not all of this represents orthodox convictions, but a great bulk of it does. The program of home-front expenditure has been severely criticized, in view of the heightened missionary needs on foreign fields. Without purposing to minimize the foreign needs, it can be said that there is something unrealistic about this criticism. The distinction between home and foreign missions is a generation outmoded; Christianity again faces the apostolic task of seeking to transform an environment that is quite unilaterally hostile. Furthermore, since the churches have on their own account decided to apportion this money for reconstruction and expansion at home, a more realistic plan may be appropriate. From an investment standpoint, the average evangelical church building has many disadvantages.

The day has now come for evangelicalism to rethink its whole building program. By tremendous outlay of funds, most church communities provide a worship structure which usually stands idle except for two Sunday services and a mid-week prayer meeting, if the latter. No secular steward could long be happy about such a minimal use of facilities representing so disproportionate an investment. Out of the modern crisis may come a better stewardship. Perhaps the answer is the building of evangelical educational plants, with attractive auditoriums that will serve for worship purposes, providing a week-round program that out-educates the secular educators. The fact that Christian teachers are not over-numerous further attests the need for such a program. Beyond doubt the time is here for an all-out evangelical education movement, and alert churches will think through the wise investment of their funds. The maintenance of evangelical grade and high schools, and of evangelical colleges and universities, with the highest academic standards, promises most quickly to concentrate the thinking of youth upon the Christian world-life view as the only adequate spiritual ground for a surviving culture. A huge share of the gifts which made possible the present secular colleges and universities of America came in the first place from evangelicals with just such a vision; it remains for evangelicalism, despite the encrustations of modernism and humanism, to fulfill that vision. If it entails sacrifice, it will not on that account be displeasing to Jesus Christ.

Such education must not be only other-worldly, but must make its impact also upon all men and all nations with a contemporary evangel. It will not lose sight of the fact that the church's prime task is to challenge men and women individually in such numbers that the manifesto is global. As the world felt Hitler's threat at the borders of Czecho-Slovakia and Poland and England, and Mussolini's at the border of Greece, so too must it feel the promise of deliverance by Jesus at the fringe of our civilization, calling men to spiritual decision.

The Christian life must be lived out, among the regenerate, in every area of activity, until even the unregenerate are moved by Christian standards, acknowledging their force. The unregenerate are not, on that account, redeemed; nevertheless, they are more easily reached for Christ than those who have made a deliberate break with Christian standards, because they can be reminded that Christian ethics cannot be retained apart from Christian metaphysics. To the extent that any society is leavened with Christian conviction, it becomes a more hospitable environment for Christian expansion.

The evangelical mood must not withdraw from tomorrow's political scene. One can believe in separation of church and state, as do the Baptists, without sacrificing world statesmanship to men of godless convictions. The Roman Catholic church has trained its candidates for world diplomatic posts with singular vision; in today's world the ministry of world affairs is no less important than any other. Evangelicalism cannot remain silent, when society is being organized along the lines either of totalitarian absolutism or isolationist atomism; nor can it be content with a democratic way of life from which the redemptive element is abstracted. Always evangelicalism proclaims that the true center of a living community is God, known in His redemptive work through Jesus Christ; that kingships that ignore the true Lord of the universe are usurpative; that the value of human personality is guaranteed only in a redemptive context; that the liberties legitimately to be sought for man do not include a secularistic freedom from God; that without a transcendent spiritual ground in the living Redeemer no government can surmount the threat of disintegration.

Evangelicalism must not make the mistake, so common in our day, of regarding Communism or state Socialism as the adequate rectification of the errors of totalitarianism or the inadequacies of democracism. No political or economic system has utopian promise if the essential redemptive ingredient is missing from it. A redemptive totalitarianism is far preferable to an unredemptive democracy; a redemptive Communism far more advantageous than an unredemptive Capitalism, and vice versa. But the very element which is abstracted from currently proposed solutions is this redemptive element. The evangelical task will be to reproclaim it. No economic reorganization, however much it overcomes the antithesis of absolutism and individualism, is on that account to be identified with the kingdom of God and, further, only in a redemptive context can the antithesis be perfectly overcome. Communism may have more interest in individual rights than does Fascism, but it is no more to be identified with a Christian culture than is the democratic way of life. For it is the redemptive element that distinguishes Christianity, and it is the redemptive element that the jaded world culture so sorely needs.

Evangelicalism will be presumed not to have a mind on great world issues unless it speaks, but there is no justification for evangelical attempt at solution in non-redemptive frameworks. These have been tried and found wanting; let evangelicalism now speak the redemptive mind.

An efficient united nations organization may go a long way toward world peace, but it is not the best nor a permanent guarantee. Sharing the atom-bomb secret may go a long way toward removing international suspicions, but it is neither the best nor a lasting remover. Sacrificial distribution of food and clothing to the world's naked and starving multitudes may spare countless lives, but it does not provide a superlife which makes existence meaningful. Increasing the laborer's pay may remove some of the inequities of labor-management relations, but it makes no provision beyond the needs of the economic man.

What attitude then shall the evangelical take toward important modern attacks on deep-seated world problems when such efforts do not go deep enough to retain significance for the very improvements they seek to accomplish? This problem remains to be considered.

Of the necessity for a redemptive framework the evangelical has no doubt. But those who work for lesser reforms, and outside of that framework, will expect him to be on the side of right. What should be evangelicalism's attitude then?

Chapter VII

THE EVANGELICAL
"FORMULA OF PROTEST"

VII.

The Evangelical "Formula of Protest"

THE future kingdom in evangelical thought, it has already been insisted, does not displace an interim world program. That contemporary program in evangelicalism is (1) predicated upon an all-inclusive redemptive context for its assault upon global ills; (2) involves total opposition to all moral evils, whether societal or personal; (3) offers not only a higher ethical standard than any other system of thought, but provides also in Christ a dynamic to lift humanity to its highest level of moral achievement.

But the spearhead of the current attack on moral evils is not directed, as we have observed, by evangelical forces. Rather, the non-evangelical humanistic movements are heading up the agitation for a new and better world. The social program is, by and large, projected constructively today by non-evangelical groups.

Yet the non-evangelical camp has been plunged into considerable confusion, at the moment, by the collapse of its vision for an utopian world. The convictions of non-evangelicals are on the move; liberals are moving upward toward neo-supernaturalism or downward toward humanism, and some humanists are moving downward toward pessimism, while some others are impatiently marking time.

This creates the most favorable opportunity evangelicalism has had since its embarrassing divorce from a world social program, to recapture its rightful leadership in pressing for a new world order. Any conviction of foredoomed failure does not automatically cancel the missionary obligation. The futility of trying to win all does not mean that it is futile to try to win some areas of influence and life. An evangelical world program has its timeliest opportunity at the present hour.[1]

But a difficult problem is projected by the fact that evangelicals are found in fellowships which often seek elimination of social evils in a context which is not specifically redemptive, and often hostile to supernatural redemptionism. Since the evangelicals are convinced that a non-redemptive attack on any problem is sentenced to failure, what would be a consistent attitude in such circumstances? This is not an easy question to answer, and the writer does not pretend to offer more than preliminary reflection with regard to it. But it is a problem which confronted the apostolic church, and with the desupernaturalization of western culture it again looms large. The best evangelical thought may well occupy itself with the query in the immediate present. The spirit of the evangelical seminaries and colleges may largely determine the interpretation of social need which crystallizes during this post-war crisis period among Fundamentalist leaders. No framework is really relevant today unless it has an answer to the problem of sin and death in every area of human activity. Confronted by this problem, the evangelical mind will have to work out a satisfactory solution proportionate to its conviction of evangelical relevance.

The statement of a few pertinent considerations, however preliminary, may contribute to the ultimate solution, whether by action or reaction. Surely Christianity ought not to oppose any needed social reform. It ought, indeed, to be in the

---

1. The difficulty of relating the Christian social imperative to concrete decisions is acknowledged by spokesmen for higher liberalism also. John C. Bennett suggests some of the problems in *Christian Ethics and Social Policy*, chapter two. But difficulty is no excuse for indifference.

forefront of reformative attack. And it ought, if it has a historical consciousness, to press its attack on a redemption foundation, convinced that every other foundation for betterment, because of inherent weaknesses, cannot sustain itself.

While the evangelical will resist the non-evangelical formulas for solution, he assuredly ought not on that account to desist from battle against world evils. Just because his ideology is unalterably opposed to such evils, the evangelical should be counted upon not only to "go along" with all worthy reform movements, but to give them a proper leadership. He must give unlimited expression to his condemnation of all social evils, coupled with an insistence that a self-sustaining solution can be found only on a redemptive foundation. More vigorously than the humanists and religious modernists press their battle, the evangelical ought to be counted upon in the war against aggressive conflict, political naturalism, racial intolerance, the liquor traffic, labor-management inequities, and every wrong. And as vigorously as the evangelical presses his battle, he ought to be counted upon to point to the redemption that is in Christ Jesus as the only adequate solution. This appears to the writer to be the true evangelical methodology; to fill this form with content, in its application, is the difficult task which remains undone.

Evangelical action is not complicated within movements or organisms composed entirely of historic Christian theists, who, therefore, are united not only on the need for a social program, but also on the context within which such world renewal is a possibility. And yet only a minimal effort has been made in such circles, to articulate the Christian message in its social challenge. There are here and there conservative denominational groups, like the Reformed movements and the great Southern Baptist Convention, which have maintained or are beginning to reflect a vigorous social interest. But to capture for the church all of the social zeal through redemptive categories, would involve even here a considerable change.

But the problem of social reform is more complicated when projected in great assemblies, often religious in nature, in which the membership is composed on inclusive lines, so that evangelicals, liberals, and humanists must act together. The evangelical voice in such a group cannot maintain silence when evils are condemned by others. But neither can it yield to a non-evangelical framework. Therefore, the path of evangelical action seems to be an eagerness to condemn all social evils, no less vigorously than any other group, and a determination (1) when evangelicals are in the majority, to couple such condemnation with the redemptive Christian message as the only true solution; (2) when evangelicals are in the minority, to express their opposition to evils in a "formula of protest," concurring heartily in the assault on social wrongs, but insisting upon the regenerative context as alone able to secure a permanent rectification of such wrongs. Thus evangelicals will take their stand against evil, and against it in the name of Jesus Christ the deliverer, both within their own groups and within other groups. To do this, is to recapture the evangelical spirit. Just how to express such protest in a positive rather than negative way, beyond a minority committee report, remains to be studied. Every provision of democratic parliamentary procedure must be graciouly employed, rather than to misrepresent evangelical conviction at this point. Fundamentalists, uneasy about ecclesiastical bondage, are usually more alert to what they oppose, than to what they propose.

There are Fundamentalists who will insist immediately that no evangelical has a right to unite with non-evangelicals in any reform. It is not the task of this volume to evaluate the possibility or impossibility of evangelical loyalty to Christ within large modern denominations, each differing somewhat in organization and condition. Assuredly, no demand for loyalty can be recognized by the evangelical as higher than that by Christ Jesus, and each evangelical must settle, to the satisfaction of his own conscience, whether such loyalty is best served, or is impeded by loyalty within his denomination. But unrestricted loyalty to Christ cannot be interpreted as consistent with a tacit condonement of great world evils.

Apart from denominational problems, it remains true that the evangelical, in the very proportion that the culture in which he lives is not actually Christian, must unite with non-evangelicals for social betterment if it is to be achieved at all, simply because the evangelical forces do not predominate. To say that evangelicalism should not voice its convictions in a non-evangelical environment is simply to rob evangelicalism of its missionary vision.

It will be impossible for the evangelical to cooperate for social betterment with any group only when that group clearly rules out a redemptive reference as a live option for the achievement of good ends. If evangelicals in such groups are not accorded the democratic parliamentary right of minority action, there remains no recourse but that of independent action. Action there must be if evangelicalism is to recapture the spirit of its evangel. In non-evangelical groups, the evangelical must have opportunity to witness to the redemptive power of Jesus. Because of his convictions, he ought never to vote for something lower than his position except with an accompanying protest. This is a far truer road of expression for his convictions than to decline to support an attack on admittted evils — because the latter course tacitly withdraws his opposition to that which the Redeemer would unhesitatingly condemn.

In point of fact, those movements for a "pure evangelicalism," which have come out of larger denominational groups, have not infrequently done so with a sacrifice of social vision and a concentration on redemptive rescue of individuals from an environment conceded to be increasingly hostile. The point here is not that they needed to become socially indifferent as a consequence of a rupture with denominationalism, but rather that such movements so frequently sacrifice an evangelical ecumenicity, and replace a world view with a fragmentary isolationism that "breaks through" its adverse environment with atomistic missionary effort, at home and abroad, with whatever heroic and genuine sacrifices.

It cannot be held then that the social indifference of evangelicals is attributable to organic denominational associations with liberalism. For Fundamentalist churches in no liberal association whatever are often as socially inactive as others. Curiously, some Fundamentalist churches in liberal associations have had more ecumenical awareness by far than many churches in purely evangelical environments.

And yet it remains true that evangelical convictions need a united voice; the force of the redemptive message will not break with apostolic power upon the modern scene unless the American Council of Churches and the National Association of Evangelicals meet at some modern Antioch, and Peter and Paul are face to face in a spirit of mutual love and compassion. If, as is often remarked, the Federal Council of Churches is the voice of Protestant liberalism in America, Protestant evangelicalism too needs a single voice. When such a unity comes, the present competitive spirit of evangelical groups shall be overruled to the glory of God, and the furtherance of the Gospel witness. If this does not come, groups most responsible will inevitably wither.

Chapter VIII

THE DAWN OF A NEW REFORMATION

VIII.

The Dawn of a New Reformation

THE need for a vital evangelicalism is proportionate to the world need. The days are as hectic as Nero's Rome, and they demand attention as immediate as Luke's Macedonia.

The cries of suffering humanity today are many. No evangelicalism which ignores the totality of man's condition dares respond in the name of Christianity. Though the modern crisis is not basically political, economic or social — fundamentally it is religious — yet evangelicalism must be armed to declare the implications of its proposed religious solution for the politico-economic and sociological context for modern life.

However marred, the world vessel of clay is not without some of the influence of the Master Molder. God has not left Himself entirely without witness in the global calamity; He discloses Himself in the tragedies as well as the triumphs of history. He works in history as well as above history. There is a universal confrontation of men and women by the divine Spirit, invading all cultures and all individual lives. There is a constructive work of God in history, even where the redemptive Gospel does not do a recreating work. The evangelical missionary message cannot be measured for success by the number of converts only. The Christian message has a salting effect upon the earth. It aims at a re-created society; where it is resisted, it often encourages the displacement of a low ideology by one relatively higher.

Democratic humanitarianism furnishes a better context for human existence than political naturalism, except as it degenerates to the latter.

Modern evangelicalism need not substitute as its primary aim the building of "relatively higher civilizations." To do that is to fall into the error of yesterday's liberalism. Its supreme aim is the proclamation of redeeming grace to sinful humanity; there is no need for Fundamentalism to embrace liberalism's defunct social gospel. The divine order involves a supernatural principle, a creative force that enters society from outside its natural sources of uplift, and regenerates humanity. In that divine reversal of the self-defeating sinfulness of man is the only real answer to our problems — of whatever political, economic, or sociological nature. Is there political unrest? Seek first, not a Republican victory, or a labor victory, but the kingdom of God and His righteousness. Then there will be added — not necessarily a Republican or labor victory, but — political rest. Is there economic unrest? Seek first, not an increase of labor wages coupled with shorter hours, with its probable dog-eat-dog resultant of increased commodity cost, but the divine righteousness; this latter norm will involve fairness for both labor and management. But there will be added not only the solution of the problems of the economic man, but also those of the spiritual man. There is no satisfying rest for modern civilization if it is found in a context of spiritual unrest. This is but another way of declaring that the Gospel of redemption is the most pertinent message for our modern weariness, and that many of our other so-called solutions are quite impertinent, to say the least.

But that does not mean that we cannot cooperate in securing relatively higher goods, when this is the loftiest commitment we can evoke from humanity, providing we do so with appropriate warning of the inadequacy and instability of such solutions. The supernatural regenerative grace of God, proferred to the regenerate, does not prevent His natural grace to all men, regenerate and unregenerate alike. Because He brings rivers of living water to the redeemed, He does not on that account withhold the rain from the unjust and just alike. The realm of special grace does not preclude the realm of common grace. Just so, without minimizing the redemptive message, the church ministers by its message to those who stop short of commitment, as well as to regenerate believers.

The implications of this for evangelicalism seem clear. The battle against evil in all its forms must be pressed unsparingly; we must pursue the enemy, in politics, in economics, in science, in ethics — everywhere, in every field, we must pursue relentlessly. But when we have singled out the enemy — when we have disentangled him from those whose company he has kept and whom he has misled — we must meet the foe head-on, girt in the Gospel armor. Others may resist him with inadequate weapons; they do not understand aright the nature of the foe, nor the requirements for victory. We join with them in battle, seeking all the while more clearly to delineate the enemy, and more precisely to state the redemptive formula.

These sub-Christian environments which result from an intermingling of Christian and non-Christian elements, however much they fail to satisfy the absolute demand of God, are for the arena of life more satisfactory than an atmosphere almost entirely devoid of its redemptive aspects. It is far easier, in an idealistic context, to proclaim the essential Christian message, than it is in a thoroughly naturalistic context. Life means more in a context of idealism, because true meaning evaporates in a context of naturalism; for that reason, the preaching of a more abundant life finds a more favorable climate in the former. Though neither is to be identified with the kingdom of God, Anglo-Saxon democracy is a relatively better atmosphere by far than German totalitarianism was, and what made it better is the trace of Hebrew-Christian ideology that lingers in it.

While it is not the Christian's task to correct social, moral and political conditions as his primary effort apart from a redemptive setting, simply because of his opposition to evils he ought to lend his endorsement to remedial efforts in any context not specifically anti-redemptive, while at the same time decrying the lack of a redemptive solution. In our American environment, the influences of Christian theism are still abroad with enough vigor that the usual solutions are non-redemptive, rather than anti-redemptive, in character. Such cooperation, coupled with the Gospel emphasis, might provide the needed pattern of action for condemning aggressive warfare in concert with the United Nations Organization, while at the same time disputing the frame of reference by which the attempt is made to outlaw such warfare; for condemning racial hatred and intolerance, while at the same time protesting the superficial view of man which overlooks the need of individual regeneration; for condemning the liquor traffic, while insisting that it is impossible by legislation actually to correct the heart of man; for seeking justice for both labor and management in business and industrial problems, while protesting the fallacy that man's deepest need is economic. This is to link the positive Christian message with a redemptive challenge to the world on its bitterest fronts. Christian ethics will always resist any reduction of the good of the community to something divorced from theism and revelation; its conviction that non-evangelical humanism cannot achieve any lasting moral improvements in the world as a whole, because of the lack of an adequate dynamic, will engender the vigorous affirmation of a Christian solution.

Not that evangelical action stops here; this is hardly the beginning of it. One of the fallacies of modern thought, with which non-evangelical groups have been so much taken up in recent years, is that the mere "passing of a resolution" or the "writing of a book" in which the proposed method was set forth, automatically constitutes a long step on the road to deliverance. But too often the action stopped with the resolution or the book. Western culture was flooded with solutions for deliverance, from every sort of idealism and humanism, during the very years that it walked most rapidly to its doom. The same danger attends any evangelical revival.

The evangelical task primarily is the preaching of the Gospel, in the interest of individual regeneration by the supernatural grace of God, in such a way that divine redemption can be recognized as the best solution of our probems, individual and social. This produces within history, through the regenerative work of the Holy Spirit, a divine society that transcends national and international lines. The corporate testimony of believers, in their purity of life, should provide for the world an example of the divine dynamic to overcome evils in every realm. The social problems of our day are much more complex than in apostolic times, but they do not on that account differ in principle. When the twentieth century church begins to "outlive" its environment as the first century church outreached its pagan neighbors, the modern mind, too, will stop casting about for other solutions. The great contemporary problems are moral and spiritual. They demand more than a formula. The evangelicals have a conviction of absoluteness concerning their message, and not to proclaim it, in the assault on social evils, is sheer inconsistency. But the modern mood is far more likely to react first on the level of Christianity as a life view, than at the level of Christianity

TITLES IN THIS SERIES

The Evangelical Matrix
1875-1900

■ 1. William R. Moody
D. L. Moody,
New York, 1930

■ 2. Joel A. Carpenter, ed.
The Premillennial Second Coming:
Two Early Champions
New York, 1988

■ 3. - 6. Donald W. Dayton, ed.
The Prophecy Conference Movement
New York, 1988

■ 7. Delavan Leonard Pierson
Arthur T. Pierson
New York, 1912

■ 8. Helen Cadbury Alexander Dixon
A. C. Dixon, A Romance of Preaching
New York, 1931

■ 9. Amzi C. Dixon
The Person and Ministry of the Holy Spirit
Baltimore, 1890

■ 10. Arthur T. Pierson, ed.
The Inspired Word: A Series of Papers and Addresses Delivered at the Bible Inspiration Conference, Philadelphia, 1887
London, 1888

■ 11. Moody Bible Institute Correspondence Dept. *First Course — Bible Doctrines, Instructor— R. A. Torrey; Eight Sections with Questions,*
Chicago, 1901

The Formation of A Fundamentalist Agenda 1900-1920

■ 12. Amzi C. Dixon,
Evangelism Old and New,
New York, 1905

■ 13. William Bell Riley
The Finality of the Higher Criticism; or, The Theory of Evolution and False Theology
Minneapolis, 1909

■ 14.-17 George M. Marsden, ed.
The Fundamentals: A Testimony to the Truth
New York, 1988

■ 18. Joel A. Carpenter, ed.
*The Bible in Faith and Life,
as Taught by James M. Gray*
New York, 1988

■ 19. Mark A. Noll, ed.
*The Princeton Defense
of Plenary Verbal Inspiration*
New York, 1988

■ 20. *The Victorious Life:
Messages from the Summer Conferences*
Philadelphia, 1918

■ 21. Joel A. Carpenter, ed.
Conservative Call to Arms
New York, 1988

■ 22. *God Hath Spoken: Twenty-five Addresses
Delivered at the World Conference on
Christian Fundamentals, May 25- June 1, 1919*
Philadelphia, 1919

Fundamentalism Versus Modernism 1920-1935

■ 23. Joel A. Carpenter, ed.
*The Fundamentalist -Modernist Conflict:
Opposing Views on Three Major Issues*
New York, 1988

■ 24. Joel A. Carpentar, ed.
*Modernism and Foreign Missions:
Two Fundamentalist Protests*
New York, 1988

■ 25. John Horsch
*Modern Religious Liberalism: The Destructiveness
and Irrationality of Modernist Theology*
Scottsdale, Pa., 1921

■ 26. Joel A. Carpenter, ed.
*Fundamentalist vesus Modernist
The Debates Between
John Roach Stratton and Charles Francis Potter*
New York, 1988

■ 27. Joel A. Carpenter, ed.
*William Jennings Bryan on
Orthodoxy, Modernism, and Evolution*
New York, 1988

■ 28. Edwin H. Rian
The Presbyterian Conflict
Grand Rapids, 1940

Sectarian Fundamentalism
1930-1950

■ 29. Arno C. Gaebelein
Half a Century: The Autobiography of a Servant
New York, 1930

■ 30. Charles G. Trumball
Prophecy's Light on Today
New York, 1937

■ 31. Joel A. Carpenter, ed.
*Biblical Prophecy in an Apocalyptic Age:
Selected Writings of Louis S. Bauman*
New York, 1988

■ 32. Joel A. Carpenter, ed.
*Fighting Fundamentalism:
Polemical Thrusts of the 1930s and 1940s*
New York, 1988

■ 33. *Inside History of First Baptist Church, Fort
Worth, and Temple Baptist Church, Detroit:
Life Story of Dr. J. Frank Norris*
Fort Worth, 1938

■ 34. John R. Rice
*The Home — Courtship, Marriage, and Children: A
Biblical Manual of Twenty-Two Chapters
on the Christian Home.*
Wheaton, 1945

■ 35. Joel A. Carpenter, ed.
*Good Books and the Good Book: Reading Lists by
Wilbur M. Smith, Fundamentalist Bibliophile*
New York, 1988

■ 36. H. A. Ironside
Random Reminiscences from Fifty Years of Ministry
New York, 1939

■ 37 Joel A. Carpenter, ed.
*Sacrificial Lives: Young Martyrs
and Fundamentalist Idealism*
New York, 1988.

Rebuilding, Regrouping, & Revival
1930-1950

■ 38. J. Elwin Wright
*The Old Fashioned Revival Hour
and the Broadcasters*
Boston, 1940

■ 39. Joel A. Carpenter, ed.
*Enterprising Fundamentalism:
Two Second-Generation Leaders*
New York, 1988

■ 40. Joel A. Carpenter, ed.
Missionary Innovation and Expansion
New York, 1988

■ 41. Joel A. Carpenter, ed.
*A New Evangelical Coalition: Early Documents
of the National Association of Evangelicals*
New York, 1988

■ 42. Carl McIntire
Twentieth Century Reformation
Collingswood, N. J., 1944

■ 43. Joel A. Carpenter, ed.
The Youth for Christ Movement and Its Pioneers
New York, 1988

■ 44. Joel A. Carpenter, ed.
*The Early Billy Graham:
Sermons and Revival Accounts*
New York, 1988

■ 45. Joel A. Carpenter, ed.
*Two Reformers of Fundamentalism:
Harold John Ockenga and Carl F. H. Henry*
New York, 1988